Market Research in Health and Social Care

This text provides a comprehensive and rigorous introduction to the relevance, planning and management of market research in the areas of health and social care which have developed in Britain and most industrialized countries. There is a growing need for market research to support the global trends in the health and social care policies which place increasing emphasis on the views of service users and the public at large. Coupled with this is the pressure to target resources, achieve value for money and evaluate the effectiveness of services. Market research has a major contribution to make to these needs.

Market Research in Health and Social Care draws on the practical experience gained from more than a decade of developing and applying innovative techniques. It is intended for managers and professionals, planners and purchasers, and students of public services management and marketing, and contains instruction on research methods with a selection of real case studies.

Key features include:

- an explanation of how managed markets provide the context for market research
- a comprehensive guide to choosing the appropriate survey method
- recommendations for commissioning, monitoring and implementing results
- practical advice on undertaking successful projects including post-graduate MSc and MBA projects
- a comparative international perspective

Mike Luck is a part-time Teaching Fellow at Aston Business School and a member of the Public Services Management Research Centre. **Rob Pocock** is Chief Executive of M.E.L. Research at Aston Science Park. **Mike Tricker** is Senior Lecturer at Aston Business School and a member of the Public Services Management Research Centre.

Market Research in Health and Social Care

Edited by Mike Luck, Rob Pocock and Mike Tricker

London and New York

First published 2000
by Routledge
11 New Fetter Lane, London EC4P 4EE

Simultaneously published in the USA and Canada
by Routledge
29 West 35th Street, New York, NY 10001

Routledge is an imprint of the Taylor & Francis Group

Typeset in Baskerville by RefineCatch Limited, Bungay, Suffolk
Printed and bound in Great Britain by TJ International Ltd,
Padstow, Cornwall

British Library Cataloguing in Publication Data
A catalogue record for this book is available from the British Library

Library of Congress Cataloging in Publication Data
Market research in health and social care / edited by Mike Luck,
Rob Pocock, and Mike Tricker.
　　　p.　cm.
　　'Published simultaneously in Canada.'
　　1. Medical care – Marketing – Research. 2. Human services –
Marketing – Research. 3. Medical care – Great Britain – Marketing –
Research. 4. Human services – Great Britain – Marketing – Research.
I. Luck, Mike. II. Pocock, Rob. III. Tricker, Mike.
RA410.56 .M363　2000
362.1′068′8 – dc21　　　　　　　　　　　　　　99–087923

ISBN 0–415–20754–1 (hbk)
ISBN 0–415–20755–X (pbk)

Contents

7   Data preparation   116

ROB TINSLEY AND JULIE GREEN

8   Processing personal data: the legal framework   129

GRAHAM PEARCE

**17 Patient and staff views of a new appointment system in a
South African health centre**   **257**

MAX BACHMANN AND HASSAN MOHAMED

**18 Market research in the emerging market of forensic
mental health**   **265**

DAVID SALLAH

Part 4
Prospects for market research   277

19   The prospects for market research in health and social care   279
MIKE LUCK AND ROB POCOCK

Figures

Tables

Contributors

Max Bachmann is Senior Scientist, Medical Research Council Health Service Collaboration, in the Department of Social Medicine, University of Bristol. He is a specialist public health physician and has an MSc in Public Health. He is starting a programme of research on chronic disease management in primary care, with particular emphasis on diabetes. Primary care services can improve population health through control of risk factors and early detection of complications, but only if patients and professionals are motivated and services are accessible, acceptable and well organized. This entails eliciting and understanding patients' and professionals' views using epidemiological and qualitative research methods.

Günther Botschen is a Senior Lecturer in Marketing at Aston University. He took his first degree (Magister) and his Doctorate in Business Administration at the University of Innsbruck, Austria. He has worked as a lecturer and researcher in the field of marketing since 1986 at the University of Innsbruck in the Department of Marketing and Retailing. In 1993 he spent six months as visiting professor at Tulane University, New Orleans, USA. His main areas of research include the development and implementation of positioning strategies, benefit segmentation, aesthetic atmospherics, innovation and branding in services. He has published in many journals including the *European Journal of Marketing*, *Journal of Business Research* and *Zeitschrift fur Marketing*.

Martina Botschen is a Lecturer in Marketing at Aston University. She obtained her first degree (Magister) in Business Administration and completed her PhD at the University of Innsbruck, Austria. She has worked as a lecturer in the field of marketing since 1990 at the University of Innsbruck. In 1993 she spent six months as visiting lecturer at Tulane University, New Orleans, USA. Her research interests are in marketing orientation and its measurement. She has published in the *International Journal of Research in Marketing*, the *Service Industries Journal* and in several marketing books.

During their work for this book **Martina and Günther** have realized that little research has been done about interactive effects of user integrating methods. An interesting field of research for the future will be studying the impact of different user integrating methods on public service employees, for example how the form of collaboration with users influences the motivation and commitment of the employees.

Graham Flynn is the Project Manager for the Centre for Excellence in Telematics in the School of Computer Science, University of Birmingham. Its role is to provide technology transfer, training and consultancy to enterprises with the West Midlands. He has an MSc in Computer Science from Birmingham University and an MBA from Aston University. His MBA dissertation forms the basis for Chapter 16 and he is intending to apply SERVQUAL to assess the service of the Centre.

Julie Green is the survey manager for the Public Services Management Research Centre at Aston Business School and also Quality Co-ordinator for Aston Business School. Recent research projects include managing the survey elements of two studies on the income and expenditure of charitable organizations for the Central Statistical Office (now the Office for National Statistics). She has also worked recently on two projects for the Local Government Management Board – 'Managing within limited resources' and 'Evaluation of local government services'. She was responsible for the survey elements of the 1991 *Survey of Local Councils in England* carried out on behalf of the Department of the Environment. Researching into material for use in this book has prompted her to experiment with the new technology that is becoming available in the field of survey work.

James J. H. Harrison is a Principal with the Business Development Consultancy which is an 'arms length' NHS management consultancy organization based in Birmingham. He is also a Visiting Fellow at Aston Business School. He has an MSc in Public Sector Management and a PhD, both from Aston University. His doctoral research was concerned with governance in health care settings. He sees market research as an increasingly important medium for shaping services, involving, and in some measure accounting to, stakeholders. The challenge which market research faces is to move beyond being simply a technique to becoming an organizational orientation.

Jill Jesson is a behavioural scientist. She was awarded a PhD by Aston University in 1988. Since then she has been employed as Principal Consultant in Health and Social Care with M.E.L. Research, Aston Science Park. She is also a part-time Research Fellow at Aston University. She teaches research methods to postgraduate students and the sociology of health and illness to undergraduate students. Her main research interests are pharmacy practice research, which covers the interface between pharmacy and the consumer, the new professional roles in advising GPs on prescribing and exploring the potential impact of new roles for pharmacists in public health. Her current work with M.E.L. Research focuses on applied qualitative and developmental research projects which support and inform community health development. A recent successful project achieved the introduction of a 'zero tolerance' campaign against domestic violence in a regeneration housing estate.

Jackie Kimberley recently moved to become a Quality Assurance Manager for Sandwell Social Services Department. Before that she worked for Birmingham Social Services Department as a Quality Adviser and also as a Performance and Quality Review Manager for the Housing Department. She studied for an MBA as a distance learner at Aston University. Her MBA dissertation forms the basis of Chapter 14. She sees that the survey approach has relevance for the government's Best Value initiative which emphasizes the importance of obtaining the views of service users. Their views are essential but one has to remember that they form only one part of a very complex picture. The survey also helped her to understand the complexity of social interaction and enhanced her sensitivity towards her fellow human beings.

Mike Luck is a part-time Teaching Fellow in the Public Services Management Group in the Aston Business School. Before coming to Aston University he worked for the World

Health Organization (WHO) in Indonesia and carried out consultancy for the WHO in Pakistan and Africa. His research interests cover market research in health and social care and men's health. He is co-author of *Men's Health: perspectives, diversity and paradox* published by Blackwell Science in 1999.

Hassan Mohamed is Epidemiologist for the City of Cape Town Municipality, South Africa. He has the postgraduate qualification of MMed (community health), University of Cape Town. He intends to take forward the research described in Chapter 17 through conducting and encouraging similar research initiatives and advocating the use of the results of such research to health service managers.

Mary Parkes is currently Head of Health Policy and Strategy, Mental Health with Coventry Health Authority. She has twenty years experience in the NHS in a number of organizations. Having developed an appreciation of the value of market research she is currently working to ensure that the views of users and carers influence the planning and delivery of mental health services – a theme endorsed by the National Service Framework for Mental Health. She believes one of the main issues in the NHS today is that of making decision making more explicit and evidence-based, and getting public support and involvement, particularly into Primary Care Groups, who will be responsible for the majority of commissioning in the future.

Graham Pearce is Jean Monnet Lecturer in European Integration at Aston Business School. He has undertaken research for the European Commission on the economic impact of the EU Data Protection Directive and the current global challenges to the European model of data protection. He is presently examining issues relating to EU initiatives in the field of electronic commerce.

Rob Pocock is Chief Executive of M.E.L. Research, of which he was co-founder, in the Aston Science Park. He has an Honours degree in Physics and a PhD from Aston University. He has directed a considerable range of research contracts for government departments including the Department of Health, and commissions from many local and health authorities. The collaboration between M.E.L. Research and the Pharmacy Practice Research Group at Aston University has won Department of Health research awards to study customer views of community pharmaceutical services using a multidisciplinary approach.

David Sallah was until recently Director of Clinical Services, Priory Healthcare. He has an MSc in Public Sector Management and a PhD ('Developing outcome measures for forensic mental health'), both from Aston University. He considers that a major challenge for forensic mental health services arises from the NHS White Paper (*The New NHS, Modern and Dependable*) which provides the basis for canvassing the views of users. Services will have to develop innovative approaches for tapping into users' views.

Jill Schofield is Lecturer in Health Services Management and Organizational Behaviour, Aston Business School. Before coming to Aston she has worked as a manager in the NHS and for BUPA. She has a BA in Geography, University of Manchester, and a PhD ('The implementation of public policy: capital investment decision making in the British National Health Service') from Aston University. Her recent research projects have concerned the development of Calman/Hine oncology centres, the health of prisoners and the strategic staffing challenges for primary care.

Rob Tinsley is currently working as a web development consultant with emphasis on the implementation of web-based communication in public organizations, market research and the design of appropriate user interfaces. Recent projects include flagship economic information and investment sites for the City of Birmingham. His education includes a BSc (Hons.) in Management Science from the University of Warwick where a final year introduction to research methods was his first contact with serious research in the social sciences. Later an ESRC studentship enabled him to gain his doctorate at Aston University with a controversial investigation into the effectiveness of marketing mix variables in small shops using data obtained mainly by observational techniques. He has found that preparation of material for this book has focused his attention on the considerable gulf that exists between practice and theory in research design. He intends to explore this theme further in his teaching and writing.

Mike Tricker is a Senior Lecturer in the Public Services Management Group of the Aston Business School. He helped establish the Public Sector Management Research Centre which has earned a reputation as one of the leading centres for the evaluation of public policies and programmes. He graduated from Birmingham University with a First Class Honours degree in Geography. His research and teaching has focused on applications of market research techniques for evaluating public policies and for guiding their future development.

Acknowledgements

The editors wish to thank:
Jane Winder who succeeded in turning the chapters submitted in various formats and software from the authors into a consistent clear text; also Debbie Evans and Jean Elkington who produced the figures and tables; and Angela Nicholls and Barbara Jagger who carried out the interviewing for the Home Care example in Chapter 4.

Part I

Markets and market research

The three chapters in Part 1 describe the social and political context of the markets in health and social care and how this provides opportunities for market research. There is a comparative international perspective and an overview of recent developments.

Chapter 1 explains the purpose of the book and its structure and shows how different readers can make best use of it. The chapter also explains why market research is becoming more relevant for health and social care. It includes the essential definitions of health and social care and of market research.

Chapter 2 starts by describing the structures of welfare states and the main transitions which have led to planned markets in health and social care. The role of market research is explained in some detail and recent applications in the British public sector are described. Alternative definitions of 'need' are debated and the relevance of market research is discussed. How market research relates to social research is explained. Finally, the most recent developments in British health and social care markets brought about by the Labour government elected in 1997 are described.

Chapter 3 moves in from the international and national perspectives of the previous chapters to show how health and social care organizations in Britain have been affected by public sector reforms, in particular becoming market oriented. The way in which marketing is used for strategic and tactical applications is explained. This leads into suggestions as to how managers and professionals should commission market research and supervise its implementation in order to inform and evaluate their marketing plans.

Chapter 1

The relevance of market research for health and social care

Mike Luck

In this chapter the reader will gain an understanding of:

- the purpose of the book
- the structure of the book
- who the book is intended for and how they may make best use of it
- why market research is becoming more relevant for health and social care
- definitions of health and social care
- definitions of market research.

1.1 Purpose

The book will show the relevance of market research in health and social care within the rapidly changing political and social context and give a comprehensive and rigorous introduction to research methods and how they should be used in planning and management of research projects.

In England, the Secretary of State for Health has recently announced the introduction of a national survey of patients and users which will be repeated annually. He said:

> It is quite extraordinary that the National Health Service has been in existence for half a century, without patients and users having an automatic right to a voice at the heart of the service . . . For the first time the NHS will have systematic evidence to enable the health service to measure itself against the aspirations and experience of the people who use it. The new NHS will listen and learn from what patients say . . . It will mean that local NHS managers and health professionals can take direct account of patients' views and opinions when deciding how best to deliver better services.
>
> (Department of Health, 1998b)

Many countries are considering major strategic revisions to health and welfare structures. In Britain, for example, changes are taking place from the previous government's reliance on market mechanisms, principally in financial terms, to the present government's emerging proposals for a more complex purchaser–provider split balancing health needs, equity, quality and cost.

In Europe there is a growing sharing of ideas between health services and between professionals and academics (see OECD (1995) and Ham (1997)). Many countries in the Asia Pacific region look to the UK for models of effective public service management.

The book will be based on a wider range of practical experience, teaching at postgraduate and undergraduate levels, and field testing. The examples used in the book are all based on practical experience and can be used as examples of good practice by health and social care students in Britain and other countries.

1.2 Who the book is for

The evolution of national economies from the previous industrial base towards a service base means that teaching in business schools and in departments of public administration are taking on a stronger orientation towards developing, managing and marketing services. Boundaries between private and public sector courses are much less rigid than they used to be.

At the *undergraduate* student level, market research is widely taught in business courses either as part of obligatory marketing modules or in specialist options. The majority of these modules now link private and public sector applications and students are aware of the opportunities for project work and future employment.

Postgraduate business MBAs include a heavy concentration on marketing including awareness of and application of market research. Public Service MBA and MSc courses include modules on quality and customer care which cover market research. Almost all postgraduate courses require a module on research methods prior to a research project which forms the basis of the dissertation. Three of the chapters in this book, by Parkes, Kimberley and Flynn, are based on MBA dissertations.

There are an increasing number of tailored (continuing professional education) courses for *health and social service employees* involving accreditation: managers, public health professionals, nurses, general practitioners and practice managers.

We believe that there are an increasing number of *managers and professionals* who are keen to expand their knowledge and skills to cope with their ever-changing world of work and who aspire to a public service ethic of excellent service. Whether or not they attend formal courses we believe that this book can be useful to them.

1.3 Defining health and social care

We need a starting definition in order to provide focus but do not want to be restricted by arbitrary boundaries based on out-of-date configurations.

What is meant by health has concentrated people's minds for some considerable time. There are some widely agreed international definitions:

> The extent to which an individual or group is able, on the one hand, to realize aspirations and satisfy needs and on the other hand, to change or cope with the environment. Health is therefore seen as a resource for every day life, not the objective of living: it is a positive concept emphasizing social and personal resources as well as physical capacities.
>
> (WHO, 1985, p. 36)

The WHO Regional Office for Europe published Targets for Health for All (WHO, 1985), arising out of the Alma Ata Conference and Health for All by the Year 2000. The European targets reflect the industrial base of the member countries and have three main foci: the promotion of lifestyles conducive to health, the reduction of preventable conditions, and the provision of care which is adequate, accessible and acceptable to all.

The *dimensions of health* proposed by Ewles and Simnett (1992) are:

Physical Health: concerned with the mechanistic functioning of the body.

Mental Health: the ability to think clearly and coherently – distinguished from emotional and social health, although there is a close association between the three.

Emotional (Affective) Health: the ability to recognize emotions such as fear, joy, grief and anger and to express such emotions appropriately – also means of coping with stress, tension, depression and anxiety.

Social Health: the ability to make and maintain relationships with other people.

Spiritual Health: connected to religious beliefs and practices for some people; for others it is to do with personal creeds, principles of behaviour and ways of achieving peace of mind.

Societal Health: personal health is inextricably related to everything surrounding that person and it is impossible to be healthy in a sick society.

The *social model* proposed by Dahlgren and Whitehead (1991) relates behavioural and social influences on health and is being widely used. It emphasizes interactions between these different levels, for example, the way in which individual lifestyles are embedded in social and community networks and in living and working conditions, which are themselves related to the broader social, cultural and economic environment.

The Birmingham Public Health Report (Birmingham HA, 1995) uses the Dahlgren and Whitehead model to explain the different policy levels at which action can be taken to improve health and explores the role of the Health Authority at these levels. For example:

Level 1. Advocacy of broader health policies.
Level 2. Commitment to local health strategy in partnership with other agencies.
Level 3. Developing the capability of local communities and individuals.
Level 4. Screening for preventable risk factors.

As well as the frameworks proposed by professionals and researchers it is important to understand what lay people mean when they talk of 'health' and how this influences their behaviour. Lay concepts of health have been researched (Blaxter, 1990). The main findings are that concepts of health have three main dimensions:

- health as absence of disease
- health as the ability to cope with daily living and physical and mental stress
- health as a positive state of well-being.

But people cannot be expected to be completely consistent. A person may have contradictory views on their health at the same time.

1.3.1 Markets and customers

The definition of market research given below by McQuarrie (1996) refers to 'markets and customers'. In the case of health and social care there are a profusion of terms to refer to which need to be clarified and related:

- customer – implies someone who has financial resources to make their own decision whether or not to purchase a good or service
- client – in Britain used by social services to indicate a person for whom a service is being provided. The decision to start to provide and when to discontinue the service is usually taken by the social service professional who is employed by local government
- patient – indicates a person in receipt of medical or nursing care. The decision to start to provide and when to discontinue the service is usually taken by the health service professional, in Britain employed by a National Health Service (NHS) trust
- consumer – a person who receives a service
- citizen – a person, usually an adult, with the democratic right to vote who may, in some countries, have a constitutional right to receive some health or social care services

In health and social care we need to think of markets which are stratified in relevant ways such as by age, sex, ethnicity, class; in health care by primary, secondary and tertiary needs; in social care by residential and domiciliary needs. We shall find substantial differences between, for example, markets for mental illness, acute surgery, learning difficulties, child care.

1.3.2 Regions and countries

We attempt to make this book relevant internationally. Although our basis is in our British experience and in applying market research in British health and social care we try wherever possible to draw comparisons with situations in other countries. We set up structures for description and analysis which are relevant to different countries and give a number of comparisons and discussions of relevance to other countries. We want to develop and use concepts which are *not country specific* such as the actual and feasible forms of national welfare state, and also to show how applications of market research do have to be tailored to be *country specific*.

1.4 Defining market research

In this section we provide a preliminary definition which will evolve throughout the book. As with defining health and social care in the previous section, we need a starting definition in order to provide focus but do not want to be restricted by arbitrary boundaries based on current or even out-of-date configurations.

Market research is defined by the British Market Research Society as:

> The means used by those who provide goods and services to keep themselves in touch with the needs and wants of those who buy and use those goods and services.
>
> (Chisnall, 1986, p. 6)

In the case of health and social care the definition needs to be expanded beyond 'those who provide' to include those who commission and purchase. One of the features of public service is that needs may be identified which (potential) users do not perceive or are not able to articulate such as people with dementia, infants, people with learning difficulties. There may be differences of opinion about needs between the views of the client, a lay carer, health and social care professionals. Market research will not be able to resolve these differences but must be aware of who the 'stakeholders' are and how to represent their views.

A more recent definition by McQuarrie is:

> Market research refers to any effort to gain information about markets or customers . . . whenever markets grow or change complexion, economic conditions fluctuate, competition intensifies, or technology evolves rapidly, the payoff from doing effective market research can be substantial.
>
> (McQuarrie, 1996, p. ix)

For health and social care in most countries McQuarrie's conditions apply: markets have been changed by government intervention and increased interest of the private and independent sectors, world economic conditions fluctuate, for example the recent decline in Asian economies, in some subsectors completion intensifies, and technology is an ever-present driving factor in the health sector. This book is, of course, aimed at helping market research to be effective and we want to emphasize that ineffective market research, however enthusiastically applied, can be damaging to its reputation.

The key questions which need to be asked at the beginning of a potential market research project are:

- WHY is the information needed?
- WHAT information is to be collected?
- HOW will the information be used?
- WHO will use the information?
- WHEN is the information needed?

Market research methods can be divided into primary and secondary data collection. Primary data collection refers to data collected for the first time, such as through interview or questionnaire surveys, whereas secondary data are taken from other sources that have already carried out primary data collection. There is often enthusiasm to start primary data collection before an assessment has been made as to whether suitable secondary data exist which may be used more quickly and cheaply to answer the research questions. Given the great wealth of data that is collected in health care, secondary data should not be overlooked.

Kotler and Clarke (1987) made few concessions to the unique features of health care and asserted that the standard marketing model (and hence market research) can be applied relatively easily to the health sector (in the USA). Sheaff (1991), however, emphasized the need for special adaptation of marketing concepts in the (UK) health context for reasons such as:

- the ethical separation of health promotion from health care provision
- multiple stakeholders, especially the power of consultants to act independently of business managers
- patients are not discriminating consumers
- choice of provider is limited in many areas.

Sheaff has developed his ideas into the 'hybrid model' which was published in 1991 in the very early days of the internal market.

The concepts of 'relationship marketing' have been applied in the UK NHS by McNulty *et al.* (1994) who emphasize:

- the small number of purchasers
- the high degree of regulation from the centre by Department of Health and NHS Executive
- the high discrimination of general practitioner (GP) purchasers.

1.5 Outline of the book

The book is organized in four parts. Part 1 starts with this introductory Chapter 1, then proceeds in Chapter 2 to explain why market research is relevant from an historical and an international perspective. Chapter 3 does the same for the British context with particular emphasis on the organizational features of commissioning and managing market research to achieve marketing objectives. Part 2 describes the variety of methods which are available for conducting market research. Emphasis is put on how to make choices between the methods in order to achieve project objectives within the inevitable financial and time constraints. Part 3 provides a selection of case studies of the application of market research for health and social care objectives. Some of these were carried out as MBA projects, others by professional research consultants. Attention is paid to the practical details of setting up and managing projects, and then disseminating results. Part 4 contains a single chapter which reviews the emerging potential for market research and summarizes the themes from the previous chapters.

Each part starts with an outline which gives more detailed information on the chapters which it contains.

1.6 How to use the book

Managers and professionals may want to start with Chapter 3 which discusses the key reasons why market research is relevant for health and social care organizations and how market research can be set up, commissioned and managed. They may then wish to read one or more of the case studies in Part 3 which are nearest to their own situation in order to get a feel for the reality of market research. They should then read Chapter 19 which looks ahead to a broader role for marketing and market research in the future. If they are considering commissioning or taking part in market research, they will find it useful to read Chapter 4 where the respective roles of commissioner and contractor are explained within the framework of a market research project.

Students may want to start with the more theoretical and international perspectives explained in Chapter 2 to give them a basic framework. They should read one or more of the case studies in Part 3, particularly those carried out by MBA students, Chapters 14, 15 and 16, to give them a feel for the reality of doing market research. They are then likely to want to read about the methods in Part 2 to help them make the appropriate choices. Chapter 3 should be read in order to get to grips with the organizational settings in which they are going to carry out their project.

There are some common features of each chapter intended to help the reader draw links between theory and practice. Chapters start with a set of *learning objectives*. Having read a chapter it is sensible for the reader to check whether these objectives have been met. There are numerous summaries of *key points* throughout chapters. All chapters in Parts 1 and 2 except this chapter contain *examples* of applications of market research in addition to links to the case study chapters in Part 3. Each chapter ends with a selection for *further reading* and with *discussion topics* which can be reviewed by the individual reader or, better, discussed in a group.

Further reading

McQuarrie, E. (1996) *The Market Research Toolbox*, London: Sage.

McNulty, T., Whittington, R., Whipp, R. and Kitchener, M. (1994) 'Implementing marketing in NHS hospitals', *Public Money & Management* 14 (3): 51–57.

Chapter 2

Markets and market research

Mike Luck and Rob Pocock

In this chapter the reader will gain an understanding of:

- the main categories of welfare states from an international perspective
- recent transitions in the welfare state in different countries and how this has affected health and social care markets
- recent developments in health and social care markets in Britain since the change of power to the Labour Government in 1997
- definitions of 'need' for health and social care and how this affects the demand for market research
- how social research and market research are related
- how market research has been applied throughout the public sector in Britain.

2.1 Introduction

This chapter provides a description of how ideas of markets have developed in health and social care and how the use of market research has developed as a consequence. We take a broadly chronological approach and start by describing how health and social care systems were organized in the context of the post-World War II consensus on the role of the welfare state before market ideas were put into practice in Britain and other European countries. The transition to the market is described: first in terms of the new political ideology in Britain; then the changes in European welfare states, and the growth of market research in the UK public sector is described. In Section 2.4 we discuss how the impact of the market has introduced the contract culture and how this has produced a need for information from market research. Finally, in Section 2.5 we begin to speculate on the developments arising from the change of government in the UK which raise fundamental new challenges for health and social care systems and consequently for market research. This chapter forms an overview at the conceptual and national level which is taken down to the organisational level in Chapter 3.

2.2 Before the market

2.2.1 The lack of market research

In his comprehensive textbook on marketing Chisnall (1986) had only a short section on marketing for the public sector. Although considerable resources had been put into national level surveys, he detected 'a distinct reluctance to adopt a research-oriented approach to policy decisions at regional and local levels' (Chisnall, 1986, p. 287). A review of the market research literature about that time, 1985, showed that the majority of health care applications had been in the USA (Kotler and Clarke, 1987).

A comprehensive review of health surveys in Britain by Cartwright (1983) demonstrated that the majority of these surveys had been for research purposes commissioned from outside the National Health Service (NHS). There had been a number of patient satisfaction surveys, but there was no indication that the results had been incorporated into a market strategy. She classified the purposes of surveys to contribute to the identification or description and measurement or analysis of:

1   health and illness
2   the nature of disease
3   needs for different sorts of care
4   factors associated with the use of services
5   the effects of care
6   acceptability of care, and
7   the organization of care.

(Cartwright, 1983, p. 1)

Nevertheless, as the following Example shows, there were NHS staff who saw the need for market research before the market reforms were introduced.

Example: Market research before the market

When we (Aston University Public Sector Management Research Centre) started the market research project for South Birmingham Health Authority in 1985, the Authority had been developing a proactive public relations strategy, including the circulation of a community health newspaper to every household in the District four times a year. Senior managers, with backing from members, had begun to develop an organizational setting where health care programmes were established for each of the major client groups under programme directors. The market research project was set up:

> as an important vehicle for gaining insight into the behaviour of programme populations and ascertaining customer response to the service within programmes.

(Luck et al., 1988, p. xii)

The three-year study had been jointly commissioned by South Birmingham Health Authority and the West Midlands Regional Health Authority's Research Advisory Group on Health Promotion. The terms of reference were:

1   To provide the Authority with basic data on health attitudes and behaviour of its population;

2   To explore the differences in health attitudes and behaviour between differ-
    ent population groups ... and the practical implications of these differences
    for the policies and priorities of the South Birmingham Health Authority;

3   To monitor and evaluate the effectiveness of health promotion and preven-
    tion programmes ...;

4   To assess the benefits and costs of a market research facility for the three-
    year period so as to lead to an informed decision as to whether and how it
    should be continued.

(Luck *et al.*, 1988, p. 13)

The research methods which were used in this project will be described and
discussed in detail in Part 2. In summary they included:

- a large-scale postal questionnaire in which many of the questions were
  related to coronary heart disease risk factors
- an associated smaller-scale personal interview survey
- surveys of client groups including the elderly, people with learning difficulties
  ('mental handicap' at the time), and women. These surveys concentrated on
  clients' assessments of current services as well as preferences for new or
  modified services.

One of the important features of this project, relatively unique at that time, was
the attention given to setting up an organizational structure for the research
which involved managers and professionals in order to ensure the maximum likelihood that the results would be used. Stuart Dickens, the South Birmingham
Health Authority's District General Manager, made his commitment clear at the
time:

> It is that degree of integration with the heart of the business that confirms my
> belief in market research as one of the key diagnostic tools for determining
> need and relevance. I am sure that we will see a strategic response over time as
> the results are assimilated into our service planning, and they must be assimi-
> lated if we are to see any return on our investment, and more pertinently if the
> views of the customer are to mean anything at all.
>
> (Luck *et al.*, 1988, p. xiii)

This careful organizational design and the attention given to ongoing communications was intended to overcome the poor level of implementation mentioned by
Cartwright (1983) in the previous section. The general requirements for success
are described in Chapter 3 and set out in programme form in Chapter 4.

2.2.2 Health and social research

Since the criticisms of health service research by Cartwright (1983) about the fragmented and unfocused nature of health and health services research, the field has expanded considerably. But it is only recently that an authoritative integrated framework has been provided (Bowling, 1997). We shall discuss key features of her framework which are relevant to market research (not listed as a topic in the index). We shall expand from her concentration on health to our focus on health and social care. She distinguishes between:

- health research, which studies the state of physical and mental health of individuals and groups
- health services research, which includes identification of health needs and the provision of health services to meet those needs
- health systems research, which takes a wider view of the structural and environmental influences on health including housing, education and pollution.

Our definition and use of market research has relevance and overlap with each of these three categories of research, although there has been more emphasis on health (and social) services research than health (and social) care and health (and social) systems.

She defines the scope of research (*with our emphasis added*) to cover:

- evaluating health services (*our overlap is with quality of care*)
- social research on health (*our overlap is with lay definitions of health and social status, lifestyle and patient, client, user and carer satisfaction*)
- assessing health needs through demography and epidemiology (*our overlap is with secondary sources such as census data and large-scale national surveys*)
- costing health services (*our overlap is in designing market research that is co-ordinated or integrated with health economics for cost-effectiveness and cost–benefit studies*).

2.2.3 Analysing welfare states

Before proceeding to describe how markets in health and social care have developed, it is necessary to consider the wider context of welfare state regimes, how the desire for change developed, and what are the contextual factors in different countries which have mediated the implementation of a market.

Esping-Andersen (1990) has classified the welfare regimes in the industrialized countries into three categories:

- 'liberal' regimes such as the USA, Canada and Australia, where benefits are extremely limited
- 'corporatist' regimes such as Austria, France, Germany and Italy where welfare was introduced as a citizen's right during the consolidation of the state at the end of the nineteenth century but benefits were limited and there is strong reliance on the family to provide basic care
- 'social democratic' regimes in the Scandinavian countries, which was intended to provide benefits of the highest quality, not at the minimum level as in the other regimes.

Much of the analysis of welfare states has assumed that the post-World War II situation was relatively stable. Recently, however, Esping-Andersen (1996) has shown that this period of stability was coincidental and that the globalization of the world economy with the emergence of the Asian countries as well as the liberalization of central and eastern European countries requires new forms of analysis.

In many countries, including Britain, a major factor in consideration of the structural reforms in the direction of markets was the wish to control health service costs. The three main methods of financing health services have been:

- from central government taxation – UK, New Zealand, the Scandinavian countries, and more recently Italy and Spain
- from compulsory insurance, the Bismarck approach – mainly in the continental European countries such as Germany, Italy and France
- from voluntary insurance – USA.

Compulsory insurance has two main versions: public contracts between insurance companies and hospitals and doctors as in Germany, thus providing a public market; reimbursement where the individual purchases services from the hospital or doctor and is reimbursed by the insurance company, which provides a private market. With voluntary insurance there may be a measure of public subsidy such as Medicare in the USA.

It is worth remembering that in the UK the Thatcher government, having assessed other systems, decided against a major structural reform of NHS financing. However, major changes took place in the boundaries between health and social care with the 'Care in the Community' initiative which was published in 1981, well before the market was introduced. This encouraged the shift of long-term care from institutions towards remaining at home as long as possible with domiciliary services coming into the home. It was envisaged that small local voluntary organisations would play a major part. Thus contracting was introduced in the 1980s before competition in the 1990s.

One conclusion which is important for market research is that there is not a single uniform market for health and social care. Thus long-term social care and short-term health care produce very different forms of need and provision and hence produce very different forms of competitive markets. We shall find that the relevance of and demand for market research varies between different types of market (Wistow *et al.*, 1996).

2.3 The transition to the market

In this section we describe the transition to health and social care markets which took place in Britain in the early 1990s, we use this description to draw out some of the key features of planned markets (Hudson, 1994) and, finally, make some comparisons with health and social care markets in other countries. We show how market research has developed in the British public services and we emphasize that these relatively recent developments should not be seen as an end point or stable state.

2.3.1 The ideology in Britain

Two major ideological thrusts of the Thatcher government in Britain, which was elected in 1979, was to liberalize the economy making it more competitive in international markets and to introduce competition into the public sector. Competition in housing and secondary education were introduced in the mid-1980s and this was followed by direct services in health and social care, which were seen to be politically more contentious, in the early 1990s. Contracting local authority services such as construction and maintenance, refuse collection and schools catering was introduced in the early 1980s. Competition for indirect services in the NHS such as laundry and catering was introduced in the late 1980s.

Among the key features of the ideology were liberalization of state control and increase in public choice. It was assumed that reduction of state control would lead to an emphasis on efficiency and value for money rather than formalization of bureaucracy and defence of the *status quo*. The introduction of markets would stimulate innovation of services and increase the number of providers which would increase choice.

In the UK, the liberalization retained public funding: in health care through the centrally funded NHS; and in social care a mixture of central government and local government funding. The resulting market structure was called a 'quasi-market' by Le Grand (1990), although many continental European writers refer to 'planned market'. Key features of the British quasi-markets are: separation of the purchaser and provider roles; contracts for the provision of services on an annual basis; stimulation of a wider range of providers and new services, particularly in social care, including state, 'independent' (voluntary and private) services.

Le Grand (1993) considers that the criteria for judging the effectiveness of planned markets are:

- efficiency, leading either to the same quality service for less cost, or a better quality service for the same cost
- choice, the user has a range of services to choose from, and these services are responsive to the user's needs
- equity, the availability and use of a service is primarily determined by need, and not by ability to pay or by forms of stratification such as class, sex, age or ethnicity.

A key feature of the debate about planned markets is whether it is possible to achieve all three criteria or, if not, what should be the trade-offs between them. *Market research has a part to play in assessing the realities of choice and of equity.*

It is not necessary in this book to describe in detail the ways in which different countries move towards or away from markets. Nevertheless, an outline of the introduction in Britain will display some general options which may be compared later between countries and some distinction drawn between essential and contingent features of change. In Britain, the legislation for both health and social care, set out in the NHS and Community Care Act (1990), was preceded by two White Papers, *Working for Patients* for health care (Department of Health, 1989a) and *Caring for People* for social care (Department of Health, 1989b).

For health care, funding was allocated on a population basis to health authorities which have distinct geographical boundaries and to General Practitioner Fundholders (GPFH). The health authorities are government agencies responsible to the National Health Service Executive governed by a Board of appointed non-executive directors and employed executive directors. Health authorities are required to assess the needs of their population and then purchase services which maximize the health gain for their population. This raises the potential for major conflict with the criterion of consumer choice.

For social care the government, somewhat reluctantly, took the decision that the purchasers should be elected local authorities whose remit was to develop a mixed economy of care consisting of a (limited) range of direct provision, and increases in provision by the independent sector, and the private sector. In many cases this has required local authorities to enable the development of providers where they did not exist or which only existed in an informal state not yet capable of drawing up, implementing and monitoring service contracts. Emphasis was put on the role of the local authority in contracting for quality and not just for cost. This has raised major questions about how to measure quality and whose measures should be included, because different stakeholders may put different weights on components of quality. *Market research has a part to play, especially in assessing the views of users and carers.*

2.3.2 Market research in the UK public sector

Bovaird and Tricker (1997) have reviewed the role of market research in assessing service quality in the UK public sector. They show that local authorities have been using market research since well before the market reforms of the 1980s, mainly in assessing public opinion and surveys of residents about housing provision. Cleveland County Council started carrying out public opinion panels three times yearly from the mid-1970s, and the Department of the Environment developed a 'Housing Survey Kit'. These are examples of the two main uses of market research: surveys of residents about a broad range of services and surveys of users of particular services. Market research methods (which will be described in Part 2) have included: questionnaire surveys by post, by face-to-face interview, by telephone interview, by comment card after service use, and by residents panels; focus groups; exit polls at elections; citizens juries; scrutiny panels. The Audit Commission (1995a) has played an important part in legitimating the role of market research in local government.

The Sandwell Residents Survey was carried out in 1996. It was intended to track progress made since previous surveys in 1989 and 1995. Questions were therefore repeated which, although not ideal in themselves, made comparisons valid with the earlier surveys. Some questions were included which conformed with the Audit Commission national guidelines so that comparisons could be made with other local authorities. The survey attempted to investigate issues of prioritization between services in which local politicians had expressed interest. This example illustrates three features of market research:

* tracking trends over time by using the same questions in successive surveys
* using standard questions so that comparisons can be made between different agencies, authorities, areas
* choices between descriptive behavioural questions and evaluative attitudinal questions.

Example

A Birmingham hospital outpatient department survey was used to assess user satisfaction with services. In order of importance to users the factors were reliability, responsiveness and empathy of staff, reassurance, with tangibles such as furniture being least important. One finding was that users' expectations were lower than expected. *Market research can be involved in setting of standards and expectations not just measuring them.*

There have been complaints that market research, although seen to be useful, is too expensive and takes money away from direct service provision. Major problems at this stage is the carrying out of poorly designed market research studies and the misleading interpretation or manipulation of results. Bovaird and Tricker (1997) recommend that there should be:

> a collaborative approach, on a much larger scale, between local authorities, health agencies and other national bodies. However . . . it is only likely if the lead is taken by an external body with regulatory powers, such as the Audit Commission.
>
> (Bovaird and Tricker, 1997, p. 19)

2.3.3 Welfare states in transition

In this section we review health and social care from the perspective that they are components of the welfare state. When examining national welfare states it is important to recognize the long-term evolution and potential for future change. There is the danger of assuming that there was an archetypal stable 'golden age' after World War II and that the recent changes towards the market described above for Britain can either be reversed or some new stable welfare regime can be reached in the near future. A review of welfare states in all continents except Africa (Esping-Andersen, 1996) shows that the apparent stability of welfare states in Western Europe was the result of a contingent combination of forces in capitalism which provided economic growth and full employment allied to post-war political consensus in support of the role of the state and for equality. The economic and political factors have changed: there is the move towards deregulated global capitalism with the associated break-up of a relatively homogeneous industrial working class dependent on a male wage earner; many countries have decreased fertility and increased life expectancy so that the number of older people is increasing and the dependency ratio is increasing rapidly. The OECD (1988) projections are that ageing alone will double or triple health expenditure and have a similar effect on pensions unless services and benefits are altered drastically.

The increasing heterogeneity of the life course with more female employment, few if any jobs for life, single parent families and increased consumer expectations make it necessary that welfare states are able to provide a variety of responsive services. *Market research should have an important part to play in accessing expectations and monitoring satisfaction.*

Scandinavian countries have often been described as the 'ideal' welfare state. Expansion of social services and employment for women went hand-in-hand: public day care for children and maternity and paternity leave led to very high levels of employment for women. However, this was achieved with a high degree of gender segregation: women concentrated in public sector jobs, mainly low skilled, and males in the private sector. Thus any cut-backs in the public sector affect women disproportionately.

The *neo-liberal countries* such as the USA, Britain and New Zealand have emphasized deregulation in private and public sectors. The changes have been more radical for Britain and New Zealand which were among the pioneer welfare states. Nevertheless, despite the rhetoric of radical dismantling of the welfare state by politicians, change has been achieved by gradual erosion of benefits and greater selectivity. Some politicians have assumed that the private market for health and social care finance through employment insurance schemes will replace state provision. Whatever the benefits for average levels of employment, it is clear that there have been increases in the numbers of people trapped in poverty through ill health and low skills and unable to afford adequate insurance.

The *Bismarck model* countries such as Germany, France and Italy have attempted to retain the features of a well-paid male workforce by encouraging early retirement. There is the underlying assumption that married women provide basic social services. For example, public child care coverage in Germany, the Netherlands and Italy is below 5 per cent compared with 50 per cent in Denmark and Sweden (Esping-Andersen, 1996, pp. 11, 18).

Ham (1997) compares the process of reform of health care systems in different countries. In the UK, a central plan in outline only was implemented with a 'big bang' political reform. Competition was between providers within fixed budgets allocated to purchasers from central government. In the Netherlands, in contrast, a very detailed plan was intended to be implemented incrementally over a long period of time but, because of the difficulty of achieving a lasting political consensus, many of the proposals have not yet been implemented. Competition is between the purchasers (insurers) who are under pressure to reduce costs and premiums. The process in Sweden has been described as 'bottom up reform' where the decentralized system has allowed local government politicians to produce a variety of local developments.

Two major changes in the market situation are highlighted in our case study chapters. In Chapter 17, we see market research being applied in the post-apartheid situation in South Africa where huge changes are taking place in the distribution of health resources. In Chapter 18, David Sallah shows how market research is highly relevant as forensic mental health services are being moved from the bureaucratic control of the Home Office into the NHS planned market.

It is important to recognize that health and social care systems contain a variety of markets with different characteristics and, as we shall see in later chapters, with differing needs for market research. Flynn *et al.* (1996) have carried out a series of case studies of community health services. Here health and social care overlap. They show how the high degree of devolvement of decision making to the front-line operators, principally community nurses, and the inappropriateness of separating technical nursing procedures from social support make the specification of contracts difficult. The introduction of a competitive market with an adversarial approach between purchasers and providers is likely to fracture the important trust and collaboration needed to provide quality and efficiency in this sector.

2.4 Impact of the market

It has been a trend through the last decades of the twentieth century, throughout Europe, to introduce 'market forces' into the planning and provision of public services. Within the UK, no force has influenced the health and social care services more than the policies and measures associated with this trend. The politics of this trend are interesting in themselves for health service managers analysing the social and political climate in which they work. For the purposes of this book, however, our focus is on the way in which this process has influenced the changing needs for market and consumer research in health and social care.

Since our previous book (Luck *et al.*, 1988), the key changes that have impacted on the need for market research are:

•   the creation of a purchaser–provider split in the organization of services
•   the formalization of contracts and purchasing plans as devices to implement this change

- the prioritization of targeted health promotion and disease prevention activity around the key targets in the Health of the Nation document
- consumer rights initiatives including the 'Patients' Charter'
- the move towards a patient-centred and primary care-led NHS.

More recently, following the change of UK government in 1997, there have been further important developments:

- the creation of Primary Care Groups run by a board of clinicians (the principle of 'clinical governance')
- new systems for accessing health advice such as the telephone-based 'NHS Direct' service
- new systems for health care planning based on the Health Improvement Plan (HImP) involving multi-agency approaches and in particular the close involvement of health authorities and local authorities
- the higher profile given to the 'public health' model of health and illness, throwing much more emphasis on the need to improve physical, environmental and social conditions as a way of tackling the root causes of ill health and health inequalities.

2.4.1 Defining need

These more recent developments are examined in more detail in Section 2.5. Each of these factors has, in its own way, affected the market for health and social care and the related need for consumer and market research. For example, the creation of a purchaser–provider split in the NHS, as described in the previous section of this chapter, has effected a culture shift in the organization. This is often referred to as the 'contract culture' – in itself a controversial aspect of management. The change of ethos opens the way for various new roles for market research, built around the nature of a contractual relationship.

The first angle on this relationship is that of contract specification. What aspects of service should be built into a contract? The purchasing body has the task of developing contract specification, and the patient-centred philosophy of health care planning suggests that patient need should be at the centre of this process. But this raises a further and very fundamental issue for market research – what is 'need' – and who defines need? In a seminal work, Bradshaw (1972) identifies four different dimensions or definitions of need:

- self-perceived or felt need
- expressed need (revealed in actual demand)
- comparative need (usually based on relativistic factors such as inequality)
- normative need, as defined by professionals or others who define norms.

Western health care planning is traditionally based on normative perceptions of need as identified by clinicians. The clinician decides what services are needed to provide appropriate therapeutic care for patients. Within the contract culture, this dimension may be reinforced if the clinicians drive the contract specification process. On the other hand, the prospect is opened up for a greater recognition of the other dimensions of need. For example, the culture of the health and social care services is sensitive to inequality and the ethical desire to overcome it (the inverse care law). Political factors have mitigated against this in the UK during the 1980s, to the extent that the Health of the Nation papers on the issue have been entitled 'variations in health' because of the political difficulty with the term inequality (Department of Health, 1995). There is a strong dynamic tension within the NHS establishment over this, but the introduction of contracting is a mechanism that offers potential to formalize the provision of services specifically to tackle inequality.

Self-perceived need is similarly a source of internal tension. Clinical perspectives on need have traditionally left the patient little room to self-define need. The 'sick role' behaviour of many patients serves to reinforce this view that the clinician is the only one competent to judge the patient's condition and to determine what care is 'needed'. Pulling against this, however, is the increasing resistance of people to the power of the clinician and the so-called 'medicalization' of health care. This resistance has been expressed through various means, such as the search for alternative therapies, or the consumer rights angle that has led to many claims for compensation for failure to diagnose or provide appropriate care. Bond and Bywaters (1998) have spoken for many women in their analysis of the medicalization of the menopause, which has moved from being seen as a natural process of bodily development to a 'condition' amenable to pharmaco-therapy, psychotherapy and all kinds of other 'treatment':

> Women's decisions to give up HRT [hormone replacement therapy] represent the creation of individual frames of reference but their physicians appeared disinterested in the knowledge thus generated.
>
> (Bond and Bywaters, 1998, p. 75)

Women's changing self-perception of the menopause is interesting because it reflects the attitudinal ambiguity embodied in the earlier comments. For example, do women see HRT as a means of liberation from the perceived adverse effects of bodily development, or is it yet another product of Western medical tradition and the power it ascribes to the clinician to influence women's bodies?

As a conceptual framework therefore for exploring the role and position of market research in health and social care, we believe Bradshaw's analysis of need is helpful. Just one illustration shows its comprehensive capacity to break down complex problems into categories each of which might benefit from the information gained through market research. Prostate cancer has become a key health issue for men and the potential merits of prostate cancer screening has generated considerable 'political' debate.

Example: Prostate cancer and the 'need' for a national screening programme

Self-perceived need

Michael Korda, editor-in-chief at the US publishing company Simon & Schuster, has had radical treatment and written a book about it (Korda, 1997). He says that men have fears:

> that treatment entails a risk of the two dreaded 'I' words, incontinence and

impotence, and that scares them so much they don't want to think about the disease.

(The Guardian, 26 November 1996)

Expressed need

It is likely that Korda's publicity in the USA and the efforts of The Prostate Research Campaign in the UK, together with the private sector offering the PSA test, will increase the felt need of men and their partners who often take the health initiatives in a family, and, hence, increase the expressed need by demanding tests and biopsies.

Normative need

The scientific assessment of prostate screening and treatment is damping down the enthusiasm of doctors to develop prostate screening and treatment services. The NHS Centre for Reviews and Dissemination has published a review which summarizes research evidence and comes up with extremely cautious conclusions (NHS CRD, 1997). This should decrease the normative need.

Comparative need

Unlike breast cancer screening, which has been shown to reduce mortality, prostate cancer screening has not yet been evaluated and there are several reasons why it may be less effective. The most sensitive screening tests for prostate cancer cannot predict reliably whether a man has a cancer that will progress to cause ill health or death. There have been no reliable evaluations of the effect of treatments for early prostate cancer on mortality. Active treatments can result in major complications such as incontinence and impotence.

Overall it is not known whether screening for prostate cancer does more good than harm.

The introduction of a contracting culture opens up the prospects for patient aspirations to be more formally recognized in the care specified in the contract. An excellent example of this is to be found in the introduction of *Changing Childbirth* – a radical departure in maternity services provision (Department of Health, 1993). This model both increases the role of women in determining the model of care they choose, and secondly reflects a strategic shift in care management, away from the consultant and towards the primary care professional, in particular the midwife. Maternity services contracts are increasingly reflecting this shift in care management, and there are examples of consumer research (quoted as case studies later in this book) that illustrate this.

So what can we conclude about the impact of the market-based model of health care planning and delivery that has set the direction of the health and social care services since our last book (Luck *et al.*, 1988). Has it strengthened or weakened the value of market research?

It may be axiomatic that a stronger focus on market forces and social marketing carries with it an integral need for more market research. But what is evident from the experience of health care development over this period is less straightforward. It is certainly the case that market research has been extensively used by both purchasers and providers over this period. But it is equally evident that the 'market' for market research is becoming increasingly diverse and there is increasing demand for a variety of different tools and techniques that can serve different kinds of need for market research information. Thus we now have:

- census-based 'market needs analyses' in which computerized population data are used on a small area basis by public health clinicians and service planners to identify locality-based service needs, and Geographic Information Systems (GIS) used to assess service accessibility in relation to need
- consumer or user satisfaction surveys (postal or user-based self-completion surveys, personal interviews) are used to rate the quality of service provision
- professional consultation techniques (self-completion sheets, telephone interviews, group discussions) are used to identify the needs for service development by practitioners
- public consultation techniques (personal interviews and focus groups) are used to identify public perceptions of need and the adequacy of provision
- user involvement techniques such as panels, citizens juries and focus groups are used to develop ideas for service development and address image issues that can affect service uptake and the overall perception of service quality
- population surveys are undertaken to monitor progress towards targets such as Health of the Nation key area targets.

These examples are given to illustrate the wide variety of techniques currently used and the different needs they serve. Later in the book we look at these options in more detail and highlight the range of service providers that has developed, from national and local market research companies to universities and individual consultants who specialize in particular areas. Marketing analysts will argue that this is a classic example of market development, where the increasing sophistication of the market leads to product diversification and segmentation of buyers and suppliers into categories with particular specialisms or niches.

This shows graphically why we have felt it necessary to produce a new book that reflects this strategic growth in the need for market research in health and social care, and the changing means by which these needs are met.

2.5 Recent developments

In the previous section we have touched on the changing context over the past decade since our previous publication, and the impacts these changes have had on market research. In this section of the report we take the above discussion a stage further by looking ahead and anticipating the prospective developments that follow from the change of government in the UK in 1997.

The new government's policy towards health care is evolving steadily over a period of years. However, we have to take seriously the Prime Minister's stated declaration to make fundamental and far-reaching changes in the system intended to 're-position' the service for the twenty-first century. We are not in a period of minor service adaptation. There will, we suspect, be equally substantial developments in the role that market research will play in this period of change. One of the fundamental key merits of market research is as an instrument to assist the management of change, and it would be surprising indeed if market research in health care were not even more crucial over the next decade than it has been in the previous one.

In the key policy White Paper *The New NHS: Modern – Dependable* (Department of Health, 1997), and *Saving Lives: Our Healthier Nation* (Department of Health, 1999), a core agenda for health care development over the coming decade is set out. For the purposes of our consideration of the role of market research, we have focused our discussion on to five fundamental themes within this agenda:

- primary care development and the creation of Primary Care Groups as the fundamental basic unit for planning and delivering primary health and social care, covering populations of around 100,000
- a mainstream commitment to a 'public health' approach to health and illness – with actions to tackle poverty and physical, social and economic deprivation lying at the heart of the measures needed to improve the nation's ill health
- a recognition that health and social care management requires a genuinely inter-agency approach, with no one agency able to act effectively on its own (see Chapter 11 for a market research application in this setting)
- measures to address health inequalities being the primary mechanism for improving the overall level of public health (meaning therefore that the health of the least healthy has to rise faster than the healthier), expressed in the Health Improvement Programme
- the creation of a number of tools and techniques to deliver the strategy, such as Healthy Living Centres (see Chapter 12 for a market research application in this setting); the focusing of activities in key settings (schools for children, workplaces for adults and neighbourhoods particularly for the elderly); and the use of the 'Best Value' concept as a basis for determining contracted services.

These five themes within the new government agenda each in their own way sets a certain need for market research. It is important also to note that while the strategy is new and different from that of the previous administration, there are fragmented 'embryonic' examples of the way market research has been used over the previous decade in contexts which now come together in the new government's strategy. In the course of this book we shall present a number of examples of this pedigree. One particularly good example is the study of community health development in the Bentilee Single Regeneration Budget (SRB) project in Stoke, an excellent example of integrated multi-agency working, with a fundamental public health model geared to tackling unemployment and poor housing as well as constructing a 'Healthy Living Arcade'.

The evolving nature of health care models and the changing nature of the associated market research requirement is also well illustrated in the development of the 'Healthy Living Centre' concept. This can be traced back to the 'Peckham' health centre of the 1930s, a somewhat idealized paternalist model that in itself reflects the model of human co-operation of the Owenite movement of the early industrial revolution. In our own work we saw an attempt in the early 1990s for a 'new Peckham' health centre to be created in the Castle Vale area of Birmingham as part of the Housing Action Trust (HAT) redevelopment of that large outer city municipal estate. The market research we undertook for that project was very firmly driven by a 'user needs' concept, and the influence of the contract culture of that period is evident in the form of market research undertaken. By 1997, the Stoke SRB study and the resulting 'Healthy Living Arcade' was more firmly community-led with residents taking a strong part in the survey design, agenda setting, the interviewing itself and interpreting the implications of the results. The felt need of residents was paramount. In the future Healthy Living Centre (HLC), it might be expected that a stronger inter-agency service planning approach will be needed than in any of the earlier models, and this may create new needs for multi-client market research commissioning. The 'Best Value' approach to service contracting is likely to create a need for continuing community monitoring of service development and delivery – possibly through the kinds of Citizens Panels that have grown up as part of the 'Modernising Local Government' agenda. This evolutionary timeline is illustrated in Figure 2.1.

HLCs have become an important and attractive 'setting' bringing together a number of the elements of the new health and social care paradigm in the UK. HLC initiatives are not, of course, necessarily based around the physical nucleus of a building. Quite a number of the more innovative models are 'virtual' centres or networks and could be said to reflect communities of interest rather than geographical centres.

The £700 million available for funding HLCs under the New Opportunities Fund (a derivative from the National Lottery) has been an important investment but the concept of the HLC has developed a momentum of its own aside of the particular scheme receiving New Opportunities Fund support. This is a good indicator of an idea that has more to it than the simple availability of extra resources. A very fundamental characteristic of the HLC concept is that it is needs led and community centred and by virtue of this fact, appropriate forms of market research are integral to the design process. Moreover, this is market research to reflect the community agenda, and its function is key in ensuring the whole HLC initiative is not simply the health professionals packaging their services in a novel way.

To conclude, we can anticipate a further growth in demand for market research amongst those who plan, develop and implement health care services, as we move into the next

Timeline	Health Centre Concept	Health Care Concept
1930s	Peckham	paternalist
1992	Castle Vale	user surveys
1997	Stoke SRB	community involvement
2000	Healthy Living Centres	multi-agency Best Value service

Figure 2.1 How health centre concepts have changed.

millennium. This demand will be multi-agency and cross-disciplinary, and will have a strong lay involvement at the key stages of design and interpretation. The technical and professional skills of the market researchers themselves are likely to be stretched as never before. We hope some of the material in this book will help those who are looking to develop and strengthen their own capability to meet these new and demanding needs.

Further reading

Bowling, A. (1997) *Research Methods in Health. Investigating Health and Health Services*, Buckingham: Open University Press.

Hantrais, L. (1995) *Social Policy in the European Union*, Basingstoke: Macmillan.

Le Grand, J., Mays, N. and Mulligan, J. (1998) *Learning from the NHS Internal Market*, London: Kings Fund.

Saltman, R., Figueras, J. and Sakellarides, C. (1998) *Critical Challenges for Health Care Reform in Europe*, Buckingham: Open University Press.

Saltman, R. and von Otter, C. (1995) *Implementing Planned Markets in Health Care*, Buckingham: Open University Press.

Chapter 3

Strategy, marketing and market research in health and social care organizations

James J. H. Harrison

In this chapter the reader will develop an understanding of:

- the context in which health and social care organizations operate and in particular the impact upon them of public policy reform
- the emergence and definition of marketing and its application in strategic and tactical settings
- the commissioning and management of market research.

3.1 The context

The nature of both health and social care services has changed, as has the boundary between them, and their relationship with a wider and continuously changing environment. This is both as a consequence of, and the need to respond to, substantial public policy reform.

The introduction of market-like mechanisms by the Conservative government in the 1980s (Kavanagh and Seldon, 1991; Hutton, 1996), the emergence of a new public management (Hood, 1991), indeed of managerialism (Pollitt, 1990), marked a tangible movement away from a largely stable and planned approach to health and social care services in favour of the adoption of private sector patterns of management. Public sector reform on this scale was not, however, unique to the UK (see e.g. Hurst, 1991), with most Western democracies revising their thinking largely as a consequence of escalating health and social care costs and changing demographic profiles. Central planning was in decline, quasi markets were in the ascendant (Thompson, 1991). In the NHS, for example, reform along these lines resulted in:

- the separation of purchasers from providers
- the introduction of contractual relationships to regulate the exchange of resources for services, within the framework of an 'internal' market, together with
- the creation of NHS Trusts, and
- GP fundholding practices (Department of Health, 1989a).

Such changes had both intended and unintended consequences for health and social care organizations. These included:

- the emergence of competition for work and thus resources between providers *within* the health care system, together with

- competition amongst providers *between* the health and social care sectors e.g. Age Concern expanded its direct service capability and thus offered a challenge to conventional NHS providers in the provision of some services (Thornton, 1988).

Contestability, at least in theory, therefore extended market testing beyond Compulsory Competitive Tendering (CCT) initiatives for support services (see e.g. Flynn and Walsh, 1988) on the margins of health and social care services to, in some cases, the services themselves. Whilst this competition for resources was more apparent than real (Accounts Commission, 1997; Paton *et al.*, 1997), the threat it implied did act as a spur to improve efficiency.

Change of this type does not take place in a vacuum. The post-war 'baby boomers' were emerging as an increasingly vocal, economically and politically active group who sought from health and social care services the range, quality and choice they experience on holiday or in the purchase of a car. This mood gave birth to both consumer legislation and to the Charter movement (see e.g. Department of Health, 1996b; Cabinet Office, 1998b). Citizens, however, whilst increasing the value and reliance they placed upon such services, were not inclined to protect them from the 'discipline' of the internal market nor to accept higher levels of taxation.

The election in May 1997 of a *New* Labour government has done little to change the fundamental circumstances in which health and social care organizations find themselves. This has arisen because costs continue to increase and demography to shift alarmingly; in particular a declining birth rate and the survival into late age of an increasing number of the population. These demographic factors alone will have a profound impact upon the need for health and social care services, employment and working patterns and thus upon the economy necessary to support and sustain such services. In addition, *New* Labour has made a number of political and economic choices that include:

- the adoption (initially) of the outgoing Conservative government's public spending plans
- a desire to distance themselves from a 'tax and spend' image in order to secure the middle ground of politics
- a commitment to prudence
- a need to manage down public spending (and public expectations).

Indeed the recent White Paper *The New NHS: Modern – Dependable* (Department of Health, 1997), whilst claiming to have swept away the internal market, has retained separate NHS Trusts and will regulate the exchange of resources via 'agreements' rather than contracts. GP fundholding is to be replaced by GPs becoming involved in a new organizational form, the Primary Care Group. The White Paper therefore foresees a future that will retain many of the artefacts if not all the values of the market place. There are, however, ambiguities. Talk of collaboration, partnership and openness are at odds with some measure of contestability over resources and the requirement, currently in Local Government, to demonstrate 'best value' and, more widely, to achieve *Better Quality Services* (Cabinet Office, 1998a). We now turn to discuss how health and social care organizations can reconcile vestiges of the market with these new – and not so new – values and, in particular, to consider strategic analysis and organizational orientation.

3.2 The impact of reform on strategic management

Although the process of reform described above was driven by a variable mixture of political ideology and economic reality it also represented an attempt to rectify a number of difficulties or weaknesses associated with public services. In terms of Local Government, for example, Walsh (1989) characterized this as a difference between a traditional and a new management approach to the delivery of services (see Figure 3.1).

However, the principal difficulties associated with health and social care organizations were rather more fundamental and included:

- the absence of a profit incentive
- funding being divorced from a market, and
- the existence of monopoly power.

Health Service reform, in particular, sought to introduce measures which required providers to 'win' income competitively and to do so within given quantitative and qualitative service parameters (NHS Management Executive, 1990). This occurred alongside other initiatives that were calculated to stimulate a mixed economy of health care provision (Willets and Goldsmith, 1988). The removal of guaranteed funding in favour of competition and the opening up of the potential of service provision to a wider range of producers has had a profound effect upon health and, in due course, social care organizations. Health care, once safe behind its entry barriers, found itself challenged both from within and from without (see Figure 3.2).

The old order and its certainties were fast disappearing. Provider dominance was being

Traditional Approach	'New Management' Approach
• Large and centralized	• Responsive
• Self-sufficient	• Small and decentralized
• Professionally dominated	• Consumer controlled
• Concerned with structure	• Concerned with process

Figure 3.1 Public service orientation in local government.

Source: Adapted from Walsh (1989)

From	To
• Centralized control	• Decentralized decision making
• Concern for procedures	• Concerns for outputs
• Preoccupation with operations	• Concerns for customers
• Functional specialism	• Cross-functional working
• Rules	• Values
• Cost literacy	• Cost awareness

Figure 3.2 The impact of reform upon the NHS.

Source: Townsend *et al.* (1991)

broken with the power of the professions being subjugated to management (Griffiths, 1983). Government initially became less directly involved (Department of Health, 1989a) but later both more assertive and much more controlling (Department of Health, 1997). Consumers also found a voice and began to assert demands in terms of quality, access, choice and participative control (Walsh, 1989). The net effect of both the process and impact of these reforms was to alter irrevocably the nature of health and social care services and, more importantly, how they were perceived by those who provided and used them (see Figure 3.3).

Faced with change, uncertainty and instability on such a scale it was necessary for managers to find new paradigms to explain and to map the unfamiliar terrain in which they now found themselves. Marketing was an obvious and ready solution. In addition to the provision of a set of tools, marketing provided an orientation, a way of doing business and of delivering services. Furthermore, it was consistent with an evidence-based approach to management (Stewart, 1998), itself modelled upon an evidence-based approach to medicine (see e.g. Muir Gray, 1998).

3.3 The application of marketing

3.3.1 Marketing defined

Marketing can be defined in a number of different ways, indeed in a review of more than fifty definitions Crosier (1975) classified them into three groups:

- marketing as a *process* 'enacted via the marketing channel connecting the producing company and its market'
- marketing as a *concept* or philosophy of business i.e. 'the idea that marketing is a social exchange process involving willing consumers and producers'
- marketing as an *orientation* 'present to some degree in both consumers and producers: the phenomenon that makes the concept and the process possible'.

One definition which reflects something of all of these dimensions and is consistent with marketing in health and social care settings is 'the effective management by an organization of the exchange relations with its various publics' (Kotler and Clarke, 1987). Also appropriate – and salutary – is:

> The marketing concept states that a business is most likely to achieve its goals when it organizes itself to meet the current and potential needs of customers more effectively than its competitors.

> (Doyle, 1994)

From	To
● Growth	● Survival
● Allocation	● Income
● Self-directed	● Customer focused
● Fixed structural form	● Variable geometry

Figure 3.3 Critical perceptual changes following health and social care reform.

The purpose of health and social care organizations is to serve, i.e. to optimize the health and/or welfare status of consumers through the provision of work, accommodations or ministrations. Such organizations deal with 'natural' needs/markets based on the organization's origins, patterns of usage, core technologies and key competences. Things, of course, can and do fluctuate due to e.g. political, environmental, social or technical change. It is at times such as these that health and social care organizations need to reassess and revise their mission, conduct a marketing audit and ensure the existence of an appropriate marketing strategy and accompanying objectives.

Before turning our attention to such activities, it is also important to consider the influence of the primary orientation or mindset of an organization upon the way it conducts itself, defines and pursues its objectives. In the past this was often characterized as a production bias, i.e. orientated towards meeting the needs of the professions or providers (itself an important driver of public sector reform). More recently, however, this has become a financial bias, i.e. meeting obligations to organizational or stakeholder interests and to government. In part, such biases are themselves a product of the changing environment and the demands faced by organizations and in part a reflection of the values and interests of the dominant coalition or leadership cadre within these organizations. One might expect, for example, very different biases if a health or social care organization was to find itself under direct political, managerial, clinical or lay control. It makes sense therefore for such organizations to *always* maintain a clear focus upon customers and their needs, for as Doyle (1994) reminds us, 'a market is defined by a need, not a product'. Whilst financial strength may avoid failure, it is service quality – and an unequivocal customer orientation – which will ensure success.

3.3.2 Marketing: a strategic perspective

The distinctions between strategic and tactical dimensions of marketing in health and social care organizations are, in practice, less obvious at first sight than one might imagine. In a NHS Trust, for example, while the Trust headquarters may have primacy in respect of strategic thinking and marketing, in reality, it must do so in *very* close association with its operating divisions or clinical directorates, who both inform and operationalize many of the outcomes. This is all the more important in circumstances where divisions or directorates provide a diverse array of services – in effect, are almost separate 'businesses' – than in those Trusts who provide a more homogeneous range. Such an interactive approach is shown schematically (see Figure 3.4).

An obvious starting point must be the definition by the organization of its *mission or purpose statement* which typically sets out the organization's *raison d'être* and frequently contains some reference to supra-ordinate objectives and also, perhaps, something about the manner in which these are to be achieved (Young, 1991). This is a prime responsibility of the corporate entity and is therefore crucially dependent upon the quality of both leadership and corporate governance (Harrison, 1998). Nonetheless there is much to be gained by involving divisions, directorates or field centres in the process since they will certainly inform and may contribute to the debate. As a consequence, they will be better placed to locate their own portfolio of activities within, to generate a sense of ownership and commit themselves to, the resultant statement. The configuration of the organization may also (effectively) structure the market, but, where this is not the case, the organization and/or its components must look to the characteristics of care group, specialty, life cycle, geography, demography

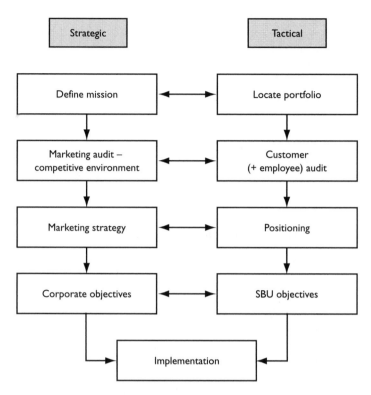

Figure 3.4 Strategic–tactical dimensions of marketing in a health and social care environment.
SBU, Subordinate business unit.

or psychographic factors as a basis of market segmentation (Kotler and Clarke, 1987; Sheaff, 1991).

Next, the organization must conduct a *marketing audit* through which it seeks to understand the competitive environment (which is usually undertaken centrally), customer – and increasingly – employee's attitudes and views (often undertaken by subordinate business units). This is not an inevitable but rather a helpful distinction, which allows the Trust board, Social Services committee, or Charity trustees to understand the 'big' political, economic, social and technical picture. The need to understand customer, consumer and employee (Harrison, 1996b; Hartley, 1997) attitudes and views may be better addressed by divisions, directorates or field centres who are physically and perceptually closer to them. Such organizations frequently commission market research in support of their marketing audit (see e.g. Luck *et al.*, 1988; Sheaff, 1991).

Building upon the understanding to be derived from the marketing audit, health and social care organizations must next construct a *marketing strategy*, which will give shape and form to the organization's marketing activities. Here again there is much to be gained from some differentiation between the organization's headquarters and its divisions, directorates or field centres. The former developing a 'basket' of target markets with which the organization is strategically concerned whilst subordinate business entities influence both their absolute and relative positioning in terms of e.g. price, quality and other service or organizational characteristics. Such attributes could, where appropriate, be fashioned into welfare 'brands' that are both the heritage of the organization and provide confidence in terms of customer decision making. Examples of welfare branding might include some of the better known charities, e.g. Age Concern, or prominent London Teaching Hospitals, e.g. The Great Ormond Street Hospital for Sick Children.

The final strategic dimension is to formulate and act upon an appropriate range of *marketing objectives* to derive from the marketing strategy. A number of these will be corporate and thought of as truly strategic whilst others, perhaps the majority, are more grounded in the activities and pursuits of subordinate business units. Clearly there is a need for some degree of accommodation between these organizational elements in an effort to ensure that the resultant objectives are robust and internally consistent. Marketing objectives may be concerned with 'social profitability' (Hayward, 1996), service or market innovation, market share or resource performance.

Example: Birmingham Dental Hospital

This study was undertaken to address the uncertainties associated with the NHS internal market. The position of the Birmingham Dental Hospital (BDH) was, however, very different from a typical NHS provider in the sense that a Dental Hospital exists to fulfil educational purposes, with the provision of clinical services being an important, but secondary, consideration. Funding in these circumstances derives from a Special Increment for Teaching and Research (SIFTR) allocation in respect of the former and from a subscription contract in terms of the latter. It follows therefore that any change to the allocation or reduction in referrals would seriously damage both the role of the institution as an educational establishment and the economy of the hospital.

BDH's market is coterminous with the NHS West Midlands region and is populated by some 1399 General Dental Practitioners (GDPs) who are independent contractors, and by 155 Community Dental Officers (CDPs) who are salaried dentists employed by the health authorities. Both groups make clinical decisions that influence the nature and number of referrals made to BDH. Given their importance it was decided to conduct a postal survey in order to:

- analyse the characteristics of referral agents
- identify and quantify market segments
- isolate critical factors in the use of services, and
- elicit the views and attitudes likely to influence market development.

A survey of a representative sample was rejected in favour of a census of all those concerned, i.e. the entire population. A bespoke questionnaire was developed for the purpose and adopted having been piloted via an expert panel. The survey itself was conducted during the latter half of 1994 and a response rate of 74.5 per cent was achieved by means of careful design, scrupulous survey administration and one written reminder.

A full account of the study's findings can be found in Harrison *et al.* (1997). In general terms, however, the data did provide a comprehensive response to the questions posed above. More importantly, the findings enabled the management team to:

- *be more effective in negotiating and managing service contracts* – a much improved knowledge base led to more effective negotiations with the purchasing health authority and an improved approach to the management of waiting lists
- *focus upon service quality and thus maintain market share* – by having detailed knowledge of high and low referral densities BDH was able to differentiate its approach between sustaining those who do and identifying and encouraging those who do not
- *manage service change* – the data also provided the impetus for internal change, e.g. performance differences between specialties. In addition, it prompted one specialty to develop a satellite treatment centre, thus responding both to apparent demand and the inhibiting effects of physical distance.

3.3.3 Marketing: a dynamic process

Marketing, however, is not a linear but a dynamic process that is informed by both the parameters of the organization's strategy and by events (see Figure 3.5). In this model there are two planes: potential service – actual service, and service design – service evaluation. The four resultant fields, each located at the conjunction of two of these planes (when read clockwise), represent differing stages in the 'cycle of provision' which require differing marketing responses. In the *thinking field*, the organization is in analytical and decision-making orientation, undertaking detailed epidemiological analysis and classical market research to identify lifestyle or need (Luck *et al.*, 1988). This analysis will inform purchasing decisions in a health authority (NHS Management Executive, 1992) or campaigning strategies for a major charity.

In the second or *acting field*, the organization now takes *informed* action. This may take the form of Citizen's Juries (which seek much more active and focused participation), or processes which consult (seeking validation of proposed action), or inform (which makes intentions known to) legitimate constituencies (see e.g. McFadyen and Farrington, 1997; Khan, 1998). Such mechanisms variously allow for or encourage respectively 'campaigning, veto or involvement' (Morris and Lindow, 1993) and can also be seen as processes which exercise some degree of both control and accountability (Glyn and Perkins, 1997). In this phase, the organization might also choose to be more forceful than tentative and thus seek to either create a climate of need or expectation to which it can respond, or, to actively promote either the organization (Lloyd, 1998) or its specific programme or service offerings.

In the penultimate or *listening and reflecting field*, the organization either reacts to the community's response to being involved, consulted or informed, or, having chosen to proceed with a particular programme or service offering, will seek to assess service delivery via audit mechanisms or to evaluate user experience. The former has grown steadily over the years (Mann, 1996) but has been given added impetus in health care settings with the emergence

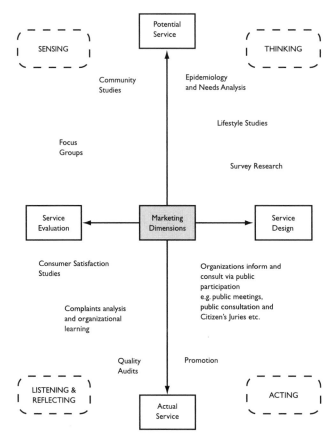

Figure 3.5 Mapping marketing and market research in health and social care organizations.

of clinical governance (Department of Health, 1998a). User experience is an equally common feature on the health and social care landscape, with consumer satisfaction studies being a feature of health care contract/agreement standards (Batchelor *et al.*, 1994) and by being normatively reinforced via e.g. the Charter movement (Citizen's Charter Unit, 1996).

In the final or *sensing field*, health and social care organizations 'engage' with their (wider) community or constituencies in order to establish a dialogue with them about the nature and range of the services provided. This is in contrast to a narrower concern with the individuals' experience of a specific service. This can take place on a modest scale through the medium of the focus groups (Fleming *et al.*, 1993) or on a substantial scale via e.g. the proposed annual survey in the NHS (Department of Health, 1998b). The cycle is thus complete, but only to the point at which the organization re-enters phase one on a continuous cyclical journey.

3.3.4 Marketing: a tactical tool

In health and social care organizations the marketing analysis and strategic processes described above define both the orientation of and to the organization, together with the broad direction in which services will evolve and be delivered. This is in some contrast to marketing management, which tends to concern itself more with the means by which strategic marketing objectives can be both shaped and transformed into action. This might almost be thought of as 'marketing up' and as 'marketing down', respectively. Examples of the former might include influencing the identification of target markets and perhaps proposing or conducting market research but, more obviously, with product development, framing an appropriate marketing mix and monitoring progress.

Those who deliver and therefore thoroughly understand the service concerned influence *product development* most potently. Important influences here include the effects of new technology, new means of distribution, market or segment redefinition, new legislation or environmental shock (Doyle, 1994). It is the ability to identify, understand and respond appropriately to these factors – whilst keeping the customer and *their* needs at the forefront of their mind – that distinguishes the effective health or social care organization from the rest. Ultimately, however, the product of strategic analysis and careful positioning has to be reconciled within the framework of the *marketing mix*, i.e. the unique blend of product, price, place and promotion (McCarthy, 1978) which defines and thus characterizes the service offering. Health and social care organizations tend to disproportionally favour the element promotion, wrongly believing that this *is* marketing, and/or that the remaining elements are largely immutable. The growth in new technology and the effect this has upon service range and sophistication and, increasingly, the emphasis upon place and the manner of service delivery ensure a lively debate concerning the marketing mix for some time to come.

The embodiment of marketing management is, however, the *marketing plan*. This sets out – within a defined business-planning context (Edwards *et al.*, 1993) – the analysis and action relevant to an organizational component. Such a plan would, typically, contain:

- an executive summary
- a situational analysis – local context and strengths, weakness, opportunities and threats (SWOT) analysis
- broad marketing objectives
- marketing strategy – identifying target markets and differential advantage
- marketing mix
- resource and budgetary considerations, and
- a timed and costed action plan.

3.4 Commissioning market research

The need for market research in health and social care organizations may be prompted by one of two conditions:

- the need to demonstrate a commitment to an outward-looking customer focus or
- the need to find the answer to a particular (marketing) question.

This distinction is an important one for, in the former, the act of commissioning market research can – in effect – become the goal, whilst in the latter there is a genuine desire to obtain and to act upon the answer to the question or questions concerned. If an organization has the capability and the confidence it may undertake the work itself but, more frequently, a brief is developed and tenders invited via a press advertisement, from a closed list of potential contractors or from an existing collaborator. Potential external providers include management consultants and academics.

Consideration will need to be given to the preparation of *the brief* (see e.g. Hope, 1992) which should concentrate on:

- setting out the organizational and market context
- defining the questions to which answers are sought
- explaining the purposes to which the answers to the questions are to be put, together with
- any technical, temporal or other constraints, and include
- any associated documentation potential contractors are required to complete and return.

Organizations should avoid too much detail in their brief in favour of encouraging contractors to be innovative in their thinking and approach. This may require the client to subsequently revise their original thinking or negotiate to a mutually satisfactory conclusion.

Organizations will also need to consider *the manner and framework within which the selection decision is to be taken* (see e.g. Gray, 1989; Hope, 1992). These will vary between health and social care organizations, however, critical considerations will include determining:

- the detail of the tendering process in the context of the organization's standing financial instructions (SFIs)
- the criteria against which tenders will be judged
- who within the organization is to make the selection decision, and isolating and dealing with any actual or potential conflicts of interest
- whether and if so, how, contractors make any presentations or are interviewed as part of the decision-making process and, finally
- the time-scale of the selection process and the manner in which the decision is to be conveyed to prospective providers.

3.5 Managing a market research project

The management of a market research project begins during the commissioning and tendering process with each of the parties seeking to establish rapport and the basis of a comfortable, effective and business-like relationship. This will be influenced by the strategies of the commissioning organization and the contractor, i.e. whether the parties see the particular commission as an isolated interaction or as one within a longer-term commercial relationship. The growing importance of this latter dimension has seen the steady emergence of relationship marketing (see Figure 3.6).

Whatever view is taken, the quality of the relationship has to be founded upon a clear and shared understanding of the *roles individuals will play* and the rights and responsibilities which accompany them. These roles include:

- *the project sponsor* who is a (usually senior) manager within a health or social care organization who defines the question or questions to which answers are sought or who identifies the opportunity to conduct market research

Transactional Marketing	Relationship Marketing
A focus on a single, here and now, transaction	Building stable, long-term customer relations
An emphasis upon the product or service at the centre of the transaction	An emphasis upon the product or service benefits and their relevance and value to the customer
Little concern with initial or after-sales services	An emphasis upon higher levels of initial service and quality and subsequent satisfaction
Low levels of vendor and customer commitment	High levels of vendor and customer commitment
Vendor and customer have limited contact and pursue almost completely separate interests	Vendor and customer have high levels of contact and enjoy an inter-related and mutually beneficial relationship

Figure 3.6 Transaction versus relationship marketing.

Source: Adapted from Payne and Ballantyne (1993)

- *the client* is the individual in the health or social care organization who commissions the market research, awards the contract and leads the project on behalf of the sponsor
- *the liaison officer* is a (perhaps less senior) manager within the health and social care organization who acts as the day-to-day contact point, is a provider of information and project facilitator
- *the managing consultant* is the individual leading the project on behalf of the contractor organization and may vary between a partner of a commercial consultancy to an expert academic or industry marketer.

A sensible initial step in a market research project is to establish a project *steering group*. This group becomes the focus for regular, structured and formal contact between the active actors, i.e. the client, liaison officer, managing consultant and other interested parties, some of whom may join or leave the process throughout the duration of the project. The project sponsor does not normally become involved in meetings of the steering group, frequently choosing to distance themselves from the detail, or seeking to exert influence upon events via the project's client. This can lead to difficulties in some circumstances when the consultants are required to deal with a project client who does not have the final authority to agree priorities, action or resource allocation without reference to an 'absent' sponsor. Whatever the nuances of the steering group dynamics, the provider should assume an early responsibility for the development of a project purpose statement and a project timetable. Whilst these will almost certainly have been included in the project brief in rudimentary form, they need to be developed from the hypothetical to the actual, from the general to the specific.

The *purpose statement* is an explicit, shared and written declaration of the purposes, focus and principal deliverables, i.e. project-specific outcomes (see Figure 3.7). Such a document helps to shape the behaviour and thinking of all of those involved and is the basis and legitimacy for all that follows. The purpose statement can, of course, be renegotiated, but this too should be an explicit process with all parties clearly understanding and accepting the consequences of any such decision.

The *project timetable* builds upon the purpose statement and both sets out a sequence of timed events to be pursued and reflects any temporal needs or constraints on the part of the client organization (see Figure 3.8). The timetable should set out the phases of the projects, their overlap/interaction and include provision for slippage and final reporting. Although the contractor is likely to play a more active part in its development, the project timetable should also be explicitly and mutually agreed.

Managing market research projects can give rise to difficulties. In terms of the *difficulties associated with commissioning organizations*, some clients may have little inclination to become actively involved, preferring to leave 'the details' to the contractor, or they may wish instant results and thus become impatient with a sometimes lengthy process. Neither view is neces-

---

The purpose of the exercise is to undertake:

- a comprehensive survey of staff opinion across all sites
- involving all major employment groups, to
- identify their views, attitudes and expectations towards the working environment and
- to explore the potential of a range of HR intiatives, and thus,
- inform decisions and choices concerning future human resource policy.

Figure 3.7 Example of an internal market research purpose statement.

Source: Harrison (1996b)

PROJECT ELEMENTS	Feb	Mar	Apr	May	Jun	Jul	Aug	Sep	Oct	Nov	Dec	Jan	Feb	Mar	Apr
Develop purpose s/ment	▨	▨													
Agree methodology	▨	▨													
Develop question themes		▨	▨	▨											
Develop questionnaire				▨	▨										
Expert panel piloting						▨									
Finalize questionnaire						▨	▨								
Develop covering letter/s								▨							
Survey admin – prep								▨							
Configure software									▨						
First mailing									▨						
Second mailing										▨					
Data entry										▨					
Analysis and reporting											▨	▨			
Presentation													▨		
KEY MILESTONES						▲		▲		▲			▲		

Figure 3.8 Market research project plan.

Source: Harrison (1996a)

sarily realistic but they may contain the seeds of serious future difficulty if not sensitively managed in the project group and, in particular, the discussion and agreement of a purpose statement and project timetable. Other dangers include clients who want the research to provide confirmation of what they *know* to be the truth, or occasions when client organizations request (or direct) providers to rewrite what they regard as unexpected or unacceptable findings. Such circumstances raise serious ethical issues and test the integrity of the provider. Problems such as these are best prevented. This can be addressed during the course of the initial discussions prior to formal tendering at which time:

- providers need to assess the culture and ethical climate within the client organization, and
- the organization concerned assesses the 'terms of business' and ethical credentials of the potential market research providers.

Should such problems still arise, they will need to be discussed to a mutually acceptable conclusion or the premature termination of the project.

In terms of the *difficulties associated with providers of market research*, perhaps the commonest difficulty is the inability of the provider to understand the political and other nuances associated with, and the value base of, the health or social care organization concerned. This may take the form of an overtly 'product' or 'commercially' orientated approach that some public or personal service organizations would find deeply offensive. Whilst providers may possess the technical ability to undertake market research, they may lack a sensitive understanding of the context in which the work is to be undertaken. Other problems may be associated with the provider seeing the project simply as income or as an opportunity to pursue *their* interests and objectives and thus they may pay insufficient attention to the organization's priorities or timetable. Such difficulties are best prevented. This can be addressed during tendering:

- when the client organization needs to judge the suitability and not just the technical capacity of potential providers, and
- via robust project management, where client organizations hold providers to account in a steering/project group arena.

Complete failure to deliver the sought for outcome is rare but can happen. Should this seem a possibility, payments can be suspended pending further discussion or, in extreme circumstances, steps taken to recover any payments.

Given the sensitivities which surround fees and payments and what (on either side) can go wrong, careful thought needs to be given to the use of public and donor monies. It is prudent for contracts to be agreed in writing. Payments should also be phased. One approach might involve an initial payment to the provider of around a quarter of the full contract price, for a further quarter to be paid in instalments throughout the duration of the project and for the balance to be paid on satisfactory completion of the work. Such an approach has the virtue that it recognizes, accepts and shares the potential risks. The initial payment reassures the provider that the client is serious and committed to the project, the phased payments acknowledge the need to maintain the provider's revenue stream and the final payment provides the client organization with both reassurance and the leverage to ensure a satisfactory outcome.

3.6 Conclusions

This chapter has sought to outline the environmental context in which health and social care organizations find themselves and to draw attention to the impact of public policy reform upon their role and function. Both have required these organizations to be more outward looking and customer sensitive – factors that have influenced their adoption of marketing – to both explain and shape new relationships and patterns of service. Marketing has been defined against this backdrop and a distinction drawn between its application in strategic and operational environments. The former focused upon corporate responsibilities and collaborative patterns, the latter upon framing and taking forward management's marketing agenda. The chapter concludes with a step-by-step consideration of the issues and processes associated with the commissioning and management of market research. Methodological considerations and detailed applications will be the subject of subsequent chapters.

Discussion topics

- To what extent does the policy climate influence the need for and approach to market-ing and market research?
- How might our definition or interpretation of marketing influence our approach to its application?
- Who should most influence the development of a marketing strategy – the corporate entity concerned, its operating units, customers or consumers?
- To what extent does an organization's business plan and its marketing strategy need to be reconciled and how might this be achieved?
- How might you approach the development of a market research brief and what elem-ents should it contain?
- What differences might exist between commercial consultants and academics as poten-tial market research providers?

Further reading

Department of Health (1997) *The New NHS: Modern – Dependable*, London: HMSO.
   The basis of the current wave of reforms including Primary Care Groups and Health Improvement Programmes which influence the structure of the health care 'market' and hence opportunities for market research.
Doyle, P. (1994) *Marketing Management and Strategy*, London: Prentice Hall.
   Private sector view on marketing and market research.
Glyn, J.J. and Perkins, D. (1997) 'Control and accountability in the NHS market: proposition or logical impossibility?', *International Journal of Public Sector Management* 10(1/2): 62–75.

Part 2

Market research methods

The chapters in Part 2 explain, with numerous examples, how to design and implement market research including the choice of survey methods and data preparation and analysis.

Chapter 4 sets out a framework for the activities in a market research project which is divided into five stages. The framework shows how the market research commissioner and contractor interact during the project. Chapter 5 explains why and how the qualitative methods of ethnographic observation, focus group and narrative are applied in market research. Chapter 6 compares the strengths and weaknesses of alternative research designs, and then reviews the practical skills required in managing questionnaire and interview surveys. Chapters 7, 8 and 9 show how to handle the data preparation, the legal framework for data processing, and the analysis of data in the market research project framework. Chapter 10 describes three recent developments in methods which involve the user participating in interactive service design. Each method is illustrated with an application in public services in Austria.

Chapter 4

Design and management of market research

Mike Luck

In this chapter the reader will gain an understanding of:

- the three types of activities which take place in a market research project
- how these activities take place in a sequence and how they are related
- the relationship between the market research methods which are explained in the following chapters in Part 2
- the application of the methods in the case studies described in Part 3.

4.1 Introduction

In this chapter we show how to design and manage market research projects and this provides the framework for the following chapters in Part 2.

In Chapter 3 we have described the context which generates the demand for market research. This may come from the general need to demonstrate an outward-looking customer focus, or from the need to find the answer to a particular marketing question. We will illustrate how these different needs have occurred in a number of case studies and how the context should be taken into account in the project design.

4.1.1 Perspectives and stages

The project design and management framework described in this chapter is based on a classification of activities which will describe the *perspectives* of the research commissioners and of the research contractor. The latter is then divided into project management and data management. Differences in roles and responsibilities between commissioner and contractor have been pointed out in Chapter 3. The contractor's perspective has been divided into two columns, project management and data management. This is to emphasize the importance of project management which is often under-emphasized or even ignored in textbooks, and because some or all of the activities in data management may be subcontracted.

Figure 4.1–A shows these activities taking place in five *stages*. *Before the project* there has to be recognition of the need for market research by the commissioner and the search for proposals and development work by the contractor. The first phase of the project proper is *setting up* and getting organized. Then there is the main *data gathering* stage. This is followed by *dissemination* of the findings and report writing. Finally, there is follow-up work *after the project*.

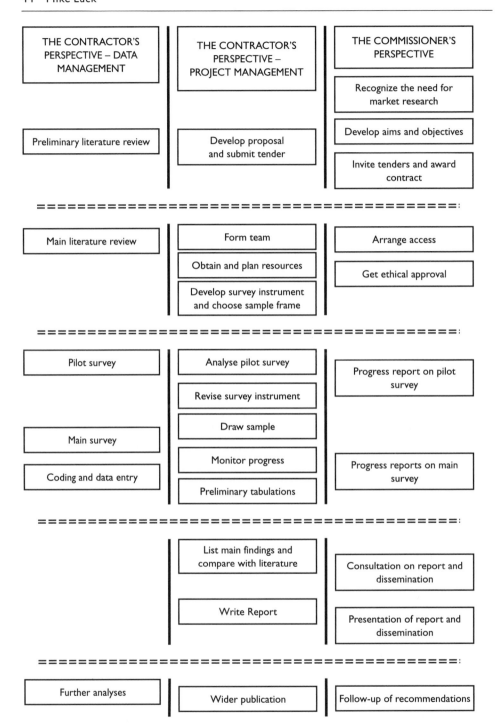

Figure 4.1–A Activities in a market research project.

Most texts on research methods concentrate on how to generate and analyse information. But in our experience communication and project management are equally important. These activities proceed as linked processes, and we use the three-columns in Figure 4.1 to show how this takes place. To be successful a project requires that all three columns of activities proceed in a co-ordinated fashion which meet both the externally defined needs and maintain internal rigour and coherence. Methods such as GANTT charts and Critical Path Analysis (CPA) can be used for detailed planning and scheduling. We shall illustrate how these processes were carried out in the case studies.

Case studies from health and social care market research in the chapters in Part 3 illustrate these activities and show some of the choices that have to be made at different stages of the project. We now give a brief description of the one particular difficult case study which is presented in six sections throughout this chapter to illustrate some of these difficulties in project management and in the relations between commissioner and contractor. The case studies in Chapters 14, 15 and 16 show how MBA projects were carried out.

Example: Home Care (1)

The social services department of a city council wanted to be able to measure the quality of life and satisfaction with services of older adults receiving home care services. The purpose of the research was defined as:

> to develop and test a cost effective model for measuring quality of life and service user satisfaction among older adults receiving home care services each year.

The proposal was put out to tender and was awarded to Public Services Management Research Centre (PSMRC). A key feature of this project was that the time-scale for carrying out the research was very short. As discussed later, this had a profound effect on all aspects of the project.

4.2 Before the project (Figure 4.1–B1)

4.2.1 The policy context

The broad policy context needs to be understood because it will influence the degree of generality or specificity of the perceived need for market research. As suggested in Chapter 3 the sponsoring organization may be wanting to demonstrate to stakeholders, including its own staff, that it does have a customer focus or there may be a particular marketing question for which it is seeking an answer. In health care the pressure on health authorities, health trusts and primary care groups to develop a customer focus may be 'top–down' coming from the NHS Executive or Department of Health. In this case we would expect a degree of uniformity to be specified, however the choice of topic and population group for the market research would be left to a local decision given the increased awareness that locally designed strategies are more successful. The aim would be to develop a *learning project* with considerable participation from staff in the sponsoring organization. Alternatively, the need to demonstrate the commitment to a customer focus may arise at the local level, for

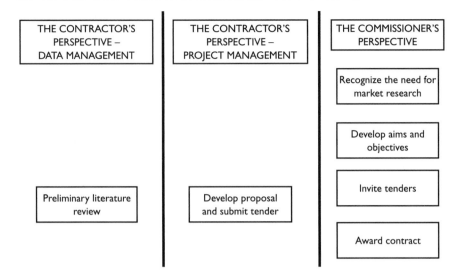

Figure 4.1–B1 Activities in a market research project – before the project.

example due to the appointment of a new Board member or in response to a local pressure group.

In the case that the original impetus is to *answer a particular marketing question*, the setting up of the project is likely to be self-contained with an external agency, and the pressure will be on getting quick results. This will be more important than building a long-term learning process.

Communicating with project sponsors

In Chapter 3 we identified three roles in the sponsoring organization: the project sponsor, the client and the liaison officer. In larger projects these three roles are likely to be separate as in the South Birmingham Market Research (SBMR) programme, see below. In a smaller project, however, two or even all three of these roles could be combined in one person, such as in Chapter 15. In other projects, such as Chapter 11, there is a combination of agencies including local authority and voluntary and community organizations. In Chapter 12 we see that the health authority and local authority sponsored the project. This can mean much more time is needed for both formal and informal communications, and there is the ever-present danger that sponsors' perception of the aims and objectives will drift apart.

Problems will arise through the confusion of terms. In some contexts 'client' will be used to refer to recipients of the service such as patients in hospital or older people receiving home care; in other contexts 'client' will be used for the organization or its representative manager who will make use of the information from the market research.

Good communication is important and is required at a number of levels. Ideally, mutual understanding needs to be built up between the project sponsors and the market research team. The project sponsors need to understand the capabilities and limitations of market research in order that they do not overestimate what can be achieved nor underestimate the types of questions that can be explored. For example, it may be that small-scale qualitative methods are more appropriate than large-scale quantitative methods to answer some types of question. From the research team's perspective they need to have some understanding of the policy context and when and in what form answers will be needed. This sort of understanding may be built up through educational workshops which encourage semi-structured discussions. A degree of trust needs to be built up without losing the proper conventions of client–contractor relations. Building up a shared understanding can be among the most important processes early in a project.

Formal project management requires proper monitoring which feeds into regular meetings and written reports. Internal research group meetings, at least once a month, will chart progress. A short report will be sent to the client and face-to-face meetings held to review the report supported by informal communications.

Finally, there will be different forms of dissemination of results. The commissioner is likely to want not only to receive the specific answers to their questions, but to provide wider dissemination to interested parties such as community health council, voluntary organizations and local media. Often this will be done most effectively by commissioner and contractor together.

Project or programme?

A key aspect of setting up market research is the intended length of the relationship. Is it going to be a long-term relationship with a broad aim such as developing a customer focus throughout the whole organization or a short-term relationship with the specific objective of answering a particular marketing question? We would tend to call the former a market research 'programme' and the latter a market research 'project'. The SBMR was clearly a programme, whereas several of the MBA/MSc case studies were clearly projects. Of course there are going to be market research activities which fall in between the two extremes. What is important is that the sponsors and the researchers are in agreement about this issue, so that misunderstandings do not emerge later.

We consider that a project will normally proceed through three stages: setting-up the project, including arranging the research team, conducting the literature search and carrying out pilot surveys; secondary and primary data gathering and analysis; and dissemination, which includes preparing the findings, writing the report and disseminating the results.

Before the project starts, however, there will be preparation of contract by the commissioner, preparation and submission of tenders by potential contractors, and selection and award of tender by the contractor. A commercial market research consultancy may be submitting five tenders for every one awarded. A university group may be able to be more selective because staff costs are covered by other activities such as teaching and funded research. This advantage means that it will only need to tender for projects where it has particular expertise and reputation and therefore have a higher proportion of successful tenders. Postgraduate projects for PhD and MBA/MSc will not normally be put out to tender, nevertheless there will usually be a preliminary stage of negotiations in order to define a project which is suitable from the point of view of academic standards and where there is a guarantee of access for data collection.

4.2.2 Aims and objectives

In the 'before' stage the commissioner may carry out all of the preparation of the project brief internally and then invite potential contractors to submit tenders, so that this is a one-way communication. The potential contractors then have to make their own assessment of the brief including selection of methods and costing, and submit the tender. There is rarely room for negotiation. The Home Care project is an example where the contract was put out by the Social Services Department at very short notice with no possibility for negotiation.

Twenty years ago when contracting was much less formalized, in the case of the SBMR project the client only had a preliminary idea that it wanted to develop a customer focus and that market research would be a part of a long-term learning process. It therefore asked the Aston University Public Services Management group, known to have some expertise, to join in discussion about the potential for market research. The discussion led to setting up an MBA project by two postgraduates in order to carry out a feasibility study of the potential for market research. In this case, therefore, the Before stage consisted of a dialogue over several months in which both parties learnt about the other's needs and capabilities. This led to the definition of the proposal and award of the contract. This curious, but ultimately successful, process pre-dated the current insistence on competitive tendering which is not always the best way to undertake innovative research.

A third situation is where it is the market research organization which has the idea for research, perhaps stemming from an earlier project, and seeks a sponsor. In the case of Childhood Accidents, M.E.L. Research had completed a number of successful projects on accidents using secondary data from police records and Accident & Emergency departments. It now felt that there was the need for more fundamental primary research into children's perceptions of risk. To do this they had to look for an intermediary, the Child Accident Prevention Trust, who helped to find a potential sponsor, Texaco. We can see this as a form of research entrepreneurship: the research contractor does not remain passive, waiting for requests for tenders, but actively promotes ideas and seeks intermediate supporters and funders.

Setting aims

The setting of clear aims and objectives for the research project is important in providing focus for market research and for minimizing the risk of dispute at later stages in the project. The overall aim may be set quite broadly in the case of the 'learning' project (SBMR) or very specific in the 'problem-solving' project (Home Care). In both cases there should be precise objectives which are operational and feasible derived from the aim. The only exception to this rule could be for fundamental PhD research although, even here, there are dangers from starting without some degree of precision. The objectives should specify the types of information to be collected, the purpose for which it will be used and how it will be reported.

The three MBA projects reported in Chapters 14, 15 and 16 show different types of aim. Mary Parkes' aim (see Chapter 15) was *to find out why* there had been low take-up of family planning services in Coventry. Jackie Kimberley's aim (see Chapter 14) was *to develop a method* for quality measurement in residential and nursing homes. Graham Flynn's aim (see Chapter 16) was *to measure customers' valuation of services* provided by the laboratory in order to develop the marketing plan.

Invite tenders

The commissioning organization will often have prepared a list of approved contractors. It may invite proposals by open tender or from a short-list of three research organizations. In a few special situations, it may select a single contractor with particular expertise for development work.

4.2.3 Preliminary literature review, develop proposal and submit tender

The purposes of the key literature review are:

1   To provide understanding and justification for the choice of research methods to include in the proposal.
2   To find out whether there have been any market research studies carried out on the topic.
3   To identify ways in which key concepts have been operationalized by others.

This will clarify whether the study has to be innovative and developmental or can repeat or adapt methods already used and tested or challenge common knowledge.

Most consultancy organizations will be keeping a regular watch on academic and professional journals using electronic databases, but the 'grey literature' (internal reports) is more difficult to keep under scrutiny. Quite a lot of this scanning will be carried out during the 'investment' period – see M.E.L. Research's Farming Calendar below.

On the other hand, the research organization will not want to commit too much effort to literature searching for a competitive tender which it may not win and clients are often reluctant to pay for it.

It has proved difficult to find published reports of market research in health and social care. What has been done seems to remain in internal reports, the 'grey literature', which is not only difficult to find, but when found is often written in a way which is extremely condensed and meaningful only to the contractor who has been involved throughout the project. The only publicly available comprehensive description of market research in health and social care is in our earlier book (Luck *et al.*, 1988). Quite a lot of the ideas from that book are included here as the South Birmingham Market Research case study. We believe that Luck *et al.* (1988) is still worth reading for someone who intends to develop expertise in market research. The book was then followed by the request from the West Midlands Regional Health Authority's Research Advisory Group for Health Promotion to produce *A Manual of Market Research for Health Promotion* (Luck, 1991). Most of the ideas in the manual are updated and extended here. The manual may still be worth consulting by someone who is intending to specialize in market research for health promotion. We are not aware of any publication which has superseded it.

Trade-offs

In every project there has to be a trade-off between the scope of the objectives and the size of the budget and the duration of the project. This trade-off may be carried out for better or worse by the commissioner in the 'predetermined' project where the budget and time-scale will have been specified in the contract document. If the contractor has experience of commissioning market research then this balance may be appropriate and feasible. Contractors quite often find, however, that they are set an unreasonable task. This is common in the 'end-of-the-year' contract where a public sector organization finds that it is likely to be underspent by the end of the financial year and looks around for ways of spending at short notice. It may then pull down an old proposal and put this out to contract at very short notice with a budget that would be suitable except that the time-scale is too compressed. The potential contractor then has the options of either not tendering or tendering knowing that the objectives are not really feasible except by cutting corners with the risk of dispute later on.

In a 'learning' project there may be negotiation before the contract is awarded to balance objectives with budget and time-scale, or agreement that there will be some negotiation during the project. Both of these options require a degree of trust between contractor and commissioner.

How to set the budget and time-scale which is important for both commissioner and contractor to understand although in different levels of detail, is explained below.

Proposal

Perhaps because of commercial secrecy, it is very difficult to obtain information about the costs of market research projects. In her comprehensive review of health surveys, Cartwright (1983) was unable to obtain reliable information on the costs of surveys which she had reviewed. She recommended that researchers should give information, funding bodies should demand it and publishers should request it. Therefore, we provided the fixed and variable costs of three surveys (Luck *et al.*, 1988, Table 12.2) and the magnitude of the surveys in terms of the number of responses and the number of questions. Since then we have been unable to find published costs of other surveys. Although this level of detail is normally provided with bids the clients do not want to make this information public.

In most surveys, the costs of set-up and dissemination are largely independent of the size of the survey, but the cost of gathering the data is quite closely related to the size of the survey. For a postal self-completion questionnaire, the cost of printing, mailing with a Freepost envelope, coding and data entry are linear with the size of the survey. Similarly, the costs of an interview survey, printing the interview schedule, payment of interviewers, travel costs, coding and data entry are linear with the size of the survey.

The second major element of costs is that of the salaries of the staff who manage the project and supervise the interviewers and data processors. For a commercial organization they would have to be costed to include salaries and a proportion to represent their time spent on activities not directly paid by clients such as marketing the organization and preparing tenders, etc. If a health or social care organization is doing the market research with its own staff then it may decide not to charge their salaries which are already paid from revenue. There is however an opportunity cost of the work that they would otherwise do. For an academic organization, senior staff time may not be charged if the work is done as part of the time paid by the university's routine budget. This would be more likely to be the case where the project is seen to be adding to knowledge and be contributing to research rather than consultancy. Research fellows and research assistants are employed on fixed-term non-renewable contracts. Commercial organizations need longer-term relationships with their staff otherwise the expertise will be taken elsewhere when they move on.

The third main feature to consider in costing a market research project is whether it is a new development in which there has to be a large learning component for staff which needs to be costed. Thus there could be extensive consultation with the staff in the contractor organization about the detailed content of the survey instrument and then there would have to be testing through a 'pre-pilot' and pilot. If, on the other hand, the application is routine and the survey instrument can therefore be taken 'off-the-shelf' then the fixed costs can be much smaller. Nevertheless, even in the latter case, we would insist that the survey instrument is piloted properly.

Table 4.1 shows the staff days required for a survey using street interviews to find out about young people's knowledge of and attitudes to HIV/AIDS. In this case the commissioner was quite closely involved in the design and in the dissemination. This has the advantage that the agreement is genuine on both sides, although it meant that senior contractor staff did spend more days in discussion with the sponsor/liaison officer than if the project had been 'hands-off' from the contractor's side.

4.2.4 Award contract

The commissioning organization may be bound to accept the lowest tender, but in many cases it can reserve the right to balance quality against cost. This is becoming more acceptable with 'Best Buy'.

Table 4.1 Costs of street interview survey – young people and AIDS

	Research officer (days)	Research assistant (days)	Non-staff costs (£)
Agree topics	2		
Literature review	3	2	
Consultation	2		
Team development	3	2	
Pilot	1	4	
Revision	1		
Printing			300
Training	1	5	
Room hire			500
Interviewing	2	58	
Coding	1	8	
Loading	1	8	
Checking	1	2	
Basic analysis	1	2	
Computer overhead			1,250
Analyses	5	5	
Report writing	6	5	
Meetings	2		
Total days	32	101	
Daily rate £	200	125	
Column totals £	6,400	12,625	2,050
Total			21,075

The Market Research Farming Calendar

The annual financial spending cycle of many public service organizations in the UK, including the NHS, has become a major issue of public debate. For example, NHS Trusts running short on their revenue budgets have received adverse comment for delaying surgery until the next financial year.

On the other hand, consumable spending decisions (purchases of non-recurring items) are frequently left to the last moment in the annual spending cycle, when the overall year's finances are clear. As financial management has become more tightly regulated, this pattern has become more intense. Externally commissioned market research has to compete in this context, leading to a pattern of procurement reflecting the annual spending cycle, peaking in the months from December to March when surveys often get commissioned at short notice with unreasonably tight time-scales (see the Home Care case study).

For the suppliers of market research, whether university or independent consultancies, this pattern presents significant practical problems. Research staff have to work like beavers in the 'harvest' quarter but then run short of work during the rest of the year.

January–March   HARVEST
  All staff busy deployed on client contracts.
April–June   INVEST   'sowing seeds'
  Focus is on buying new equipment, learning new software, staff training, examining trends and competition, developing new initiatives.
July–September   PROMOTE   'feeding and watering'
  Emphasis is on general publicity, promotional events, publishing articles, attending conferences, visiting collaborators and established clients, promoting new initiatives.
October–December   MARKET   'tending to growth'
  Preparing for the spending period through Direct Marketing mailings, following up leads and expressions of interest, negotiating and securing new commissions.
January–March   HARVEST again

Example: Home Care (2)

This project is a prime example of 'client dithering' and extreme time pressure. The policy context had been discussed between the social services department (SSD) and PSMRC during 1998 but the research could not be pursued because of lack of funding. The main emphasis had been upon quality of life and user satisfaction in residential and nursing homes, and home care was only added at a later stage. This gap between the first discussion and the subsequent contract with additional objectives meant that the earlier literature review was not fully appropriate and there was not enough time to extend it properly.

The proposal had been resuscitated close to the end of the financial year because of an unexpected availability of funding (similar to the Southwark project described in Chapter 11). This put immense pressure on PSMRC to carry out the research in a short time-scale. Although a verbal assurance was given that the contract has been awarded there was a further delay in getting written confirmation of the contract which further reduced the time-scale. The Contracts Section in SSD who had commissioned the research were also very busy and, subsequently, were not able to provide much support in arranging access.

Looking back on this project the question is: 'Should PSMRC have undertaken the project given these poor pre-conditions?'

4.3 Setting up the project (Figure 4.1–B2)

4.3.1 Form team

Select staff

It is important to pay attention to building an effective research team. A large market research consultancy may have a wide range of skilled people to select from but, even in this situation, care is needed in order to ensure that they work together as a team. In other situations the selection of staff and getting them to work together is more complex. This would be the situation in smaller consultancy organizations with few staff, or where the research is carried out by freelance researchers, in university groups, or where the research is going to be conducted in-house by the health or social care

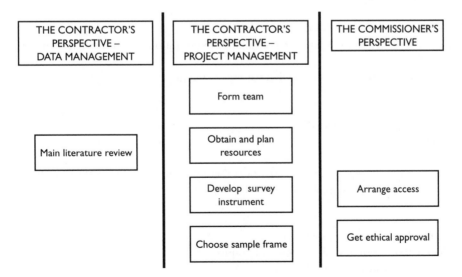

Figure 4.1–B2 Activities in a market research project – setting up the project.

organization. In all these latter situations the work is going to be carried out by people who are working part-time on the project, many of whom do not have loyalty to the contractor organization.

Of course the structure of a market research team can vary, but a prototype might consist of the following roles:

Project director
- senior member of the contractor organization who has ultimate responsibility for the project
- not involved in the day-to-day activities, but retains an overview of progress
- likely to be responsible for a number of projects at any one time
- considerable part of their time is spent seeking new projects and preparing proposals.

Project manager
- responsible for the day-to-day activities of the project
- managing the staff
- liaison with the commissioning organization
- likely to be managing more than one project unless it is a very large one.

Consultant
- specialist knowledge of the sector
- experience in liaison with clients.

Fieldwork supervisor
- responsible for supervising the interviewers including quality control.

Data processing supervisor
- responsible for planning and supervising coding and data entry
- preliminary analysis.

Interviewers
- a large commercial market research consultancy organization may have their own full-time staff
- other contractors will recruit through a variety of channels.

Data processors
- carrying out coding and data entry
- preliminary tabulations.

These specialists may have to be 'borrowed' from other organizations, or other tasks, or from a list of freelance specialists kept by the contractor organization.

Analysts
- reviewing the preliminary tabulations
- producing more complex tabulations and graphs
- carrying out statistical tests of the data.

In a large consultancy organization the above roles may be filled by different people whereas in a small organization many of the roles may be filled by the same person.

It is likely, then, that a market research team will consist of a variety of people with different expertise, many of whom will have not worked together and for whom this project is only a part of their work. In order to get good results the project director and project manager need to allocate time for induction so that the staff understand the importance of the project and their roles and develop some commitment to it. This is going to pay off in a good standard of work, and in staff offering suggestions as to how to improve the work from their own experience. They will not do this if they are just treated as 'dogsbodies'.

The alternative to taking on freelance staff is to subcontract work out to another organization. Particularly in large-scale projects, areas of work such as interviews or data processing can be subcontracted. There is, however, the risk of losing quality control and, without very clear specification, of tasks being non-optimal. Subcontracting is going to be most successful when the work is being repeated regularly, such as for patient and client satisfaction surveys which are repeated at regular intervals.

There are a range of options for how the market research is shared between the contractor and commissioning organizations. The commissioning organization may want to save money by doing some of the work itself, saving direct costs but incurring opportunity costs, or it may want to build up its own expertise so that it can do the work itself in the future. In the SBMR project, the health authority wanted to develop its skills in survey methods and did carry out a repeat of the postal questionnaire lifestyle survey at a later date. It is probably easier to do this with a postal questionnaire survey using a previously designed questionnaire. The main tasks of selecting the sample, mailing questionnaires, recording returns, coding and data entry can be defined in precise steps. However, an interview survey which requires using experienced interviewers is more difficult to manage.

What is more practicable and probably more useful is for one or more members of the commissioning organization to be involved in aspects of the project so that they gain understanding of the opportunities and limitations of market research. This will put them in a stronger position to make good use of the findings, and to commission relevant and feasible projects in the future.

4.3.2 Main literature review

When the organization has been awarded a contract, this follows on from and develops the Preliminary Literature Review. The purposes of the review are:

1   To provide a comprehensive review of possible research methods, including recent developments.
2   To find out whether there have been applications of market research and social surveys in the topic area which could be used for comparison of findings
3   To collect examples of questionnaires and survey instruments which could be used or adapted.

The stages in the literature search are:

Manual search

Manual search of journals on library shelves, follow up references in relevant books and journals, and obtaining conference proceedings.

Electronic search

1   Set focus and boundaries in terms of key words, years to be searched, countries and languages.
2   Use electronic databases such as MEDLINE and BIDS to find titles and abstracts that are relevant.
3   Extend search to manual catalogues.
4   Consult experts.
5   Contact or visit key information centres such as National Centre for Voluntary Organisations, Kings Fund, National Council for Reviews and Dissemination.

Filter and assess

1   Sift through titles and abstracts for relevant material.
2   Obtain original texts through purchase, visits, Inter Library Loan, and other forms of borrowing.

Read critically

1   Skim read the whole article to make sure that it is relevant.
2   Decide whether there is a clear statement of the problem and its context.
3   Decide whether there is a clear statement of the methods used.
4   Decide whether there is a clear statement of what happened to the findings.
5   Where appropriate, follow up with the authors to get further information such as obtaining questionnaires and identify problems such as access to respondents.

Review search

1   Decide whether you have obtained enough, too much or too little information.
2   Hence decide to terminate, expand or restrict the search.

Write up the literature review

1   Prepare a draft review which will be updated later and used in the final report.

4.3.3 Arrange access, get ethical approval

Communications between commissioner and contractor need to proceed at both formal and informal levels. As suggested in Chapter 3, there needs to be a regular meeting where the formal progress review is carried out. This will regularly include the liaison officer and, where necessary, the project sponsor. The purpose is to monitor the progress of the market research and to assist with any difficulties such as access; there should be interim targets or milestones set at the beginning of the project and progress can be judged against these. There are dangers that large steering groups pull the researchers in different directions and result in lack of focus in the research.

From the perspective of the commissioning organization, the meeting will also provide the opportunity to consider how the dissemination will be handled. For example, if there are changes of staff who will be expected to make use of the findings, they can be brought into the meetings or briefed outside of the meetings. In the SBMR project two members of the contractor (M.L. and R.P.) remained throughout whereas no member of the commissioner organization remained through the entire three years of the programme.

In some cases interim findings may be used as they occur. For example, in SBMR, the finding from the lifestyle survey that the *Health Journal* was not being distributed properly was used immediately to make changes in the distributor and to increase monitoring.

From the point of view of the contractor, it is important that there is proper recording of the minutes of the steering group. The contractor will have to hold internal meetings to review progress with data collection. In cases where research is subcontracted, progress with subcontractors must be monitored closely.

The steering group will also be the place to review how access is being carried out. 'Getting in, getting on, getting out and getting back again' needs to be monitored.

Approval of the ethics committee should be a task for the commissioning organization. We have found, however, that clients who are inexperienced in commissioning market research may expect the contractor to do this. Ensuring confidentiality will also be in the remit. This will be particularly important where there is a small-scale qualitative survey included in the project so that it will be difficult to disguise comments from individual respondents.

Ethical considerations occur throughout the health and social care market research project (Jesson, 1997; see also the British Sociological Association's *Statement of Ethical Practice*, 1996):

1   Deciding whether to do the survey is unethical if the method is not able to answer the research question or the team is not competent to do so. This can be a particular problem if the sponsor expects answers with an inadequate budget or too short a time-scale.
2   During the sampling where confidential records are needed (see the discussion below about getting Local Research Ethics Committee approval).
3   Fieldwork requires explaining clearly to the respondent who you are, why the study is being carried out, how the person was chosen, what will be done with the information. It is unethical to start an interview without doing this and unethical to obtain information under false pretences.
4   Content of the questionnaire. Certain subjects may be particularly sensitive such as information from people who are terminally ill, prostitutes, marginal groups, sexual activity. This sensitivity may also affect the interviewers (see the Home Care Example).
5   Data processing. Ensure that computer data cannot be linked to individuals or leaked by data processing staff (see Chapters 7, 8 and 9). Data must be stored so that it can be reviewed for malpractice, as the example in Figure 4.2 shows.
6   Presentation of results. Especially in small-scale qualitative surveys it may be difficult to camouflage particular places, organizations or respondents. Sponsors may want to suppress information in reports or even whole reports which may potentially embarrass them.

Survey research involving NHS patients will require approval from the Local Research Ethics Committee (LREC). These committees exist principally to ensure research interventions do not undermine the rights of patients to receive treatment appropriate to their

'Evidence of unmet need in the care of physically disabled adults'

The BMJ is retracting the above paper by MH Williams and C Bowie (*BMJ* 1993; 306:95-8) at the request of Dr Bowie. The General Medical Council found Dr Williams guilty of professional misconduct in February 1998 on charges which included research fraud. Dr Williams was responsible for the data collection of the original interview and examination survey in 1989 and the follow up telephone survey in 1990. Dr Bowie has been unable to verify that the data collection was carried out in an honest way. He did not scrutinize the data sheets at the time of the surveys; the data sheets of both surveys have been destroyed; and none of the 18 people still alive in Somerset and contacted by telephone six years later could remember the telephone interview.

Figure 4.2 Evidence of professional misconduct.
Source: BMJ (6 June 1998), 316

condition, and the context in which they are of prime importance is in clinical trials of new therapies based on the Randomized Control Trial (RCT).

LRECs are, however, becoming increasingly involved in assessing consumer research which is community-based or in a 'naturalistic' (uncontrolled) setting. A good example is the consumer research into maternity services in Coventry, where M.E.L. Research interviewed 450 mothers who had given birth within the past 12 months. They were asked about various aspects of the care they had received before, during and after the birth. The study required access to health authority data on the identity of mothers who had given birth over this time period, and such data could not be released until LREC approval had been obtained.

There has been much debate on whether LRECs are empowered or competent to comment on the adequacy of social research. It is axiomatic that social research does not operate with the RCT paradigm and many of the 'rules' in RCT methodology are impracticable within the naturalistic setting and inconsistent with the semi-structured nature of much social research.

A further problem has arisen within large area studies where the approval of many LRECs is required. For example, M.E.L. Research and Aston University were commissioned in 1996 to carry out a review of GP out-of-hours services in the West Midlands by the former West Midlands Regional Health Authority. In total fourteen LRECs had to be approached. Submissions had to be made on forms which varied considerably between the LRECs, thus adding to the cost of the project and postponing the start date until all LRECs had replied. Comments varied from 'no ethical concerns therefore may proceed' to 'the study will not produce valid results'. Two of the LRECs refused approval. This caused methodological difficulties for those in the remaining group. The capacity for medical professionals on the LRECs to assess the validity of social surveys is unclear, but this does not stop them taking a view.

More recently, procedures have been established for Multi-centre Research Ethics Committees (MREC). The MREC system was introduced nationally in 1997 in order to avoid the extensive duplication and inconsistency of assessments under the previous arrangements. There remains the question about the compatibility of the research paradigms but the reality is that anyone wanting to undertake research involving access to specific patient groups is going to have to convince the REC of the validity and accept-ability of the study.

It is also necessary to identify and keep track of other surveys and research projects being carried out in the organization or with the same population. The risk of overlap and subsequent overload is quite high.

4.3.4 Obtain and plan resources

The obtaining and planning of the resources will have to be developed in more detail from the original proposal. This will cover staffing at all levels, equipment and informa-tion technology (IT) for data entry and analysis (see Figure 4.3). In many cases the staffing will be a combination of full-time, part-time and casual staff depending on the type of project and, in particular, whether the main survey method is the interview or the questionnaire. Staff will need to have a proper induction in order that they understand what the project is about and are motivated to do a good job and maintain quality standards.

With an interview survey there will be the need to find or provide 'comfort stations' so that interviewers can assemble their material and take breaks in order to maintain peak efficiency.

The provision of IT resources is covered in depth in Chapters 7 and 9. Here we want to emphasize that as part of the project management it is important that this is considered in the project planning and not left until after the data have been collected. The costing of IT should be included in the project costs with some account of replacement of hardware and software as well as operating costs which will be mainly staff.

The dependence on IT will be related to the complexity of the project, the balance between qualitative and quantitative methods, and the balance between primary and sec-ondary research.

Data processing and other tasks, whether manual or IT, may be contracted out completely or in part. This is more likely to be appropriate where:

- the market research contractor does not have adequate IT
- where the project survey method is a large-scale quantitative postal questionnaire with mainly closed questions
- where the survey is repeating a method which has been tried and tested.

In a project which does not meet these criteria we think that it is unwise to contract out since the coding and analysis need to be closely related in order to maximize the learning process either about (a) the design and management of the survey or (b) the analysis and findings.

The transcribing of focus groups and unstructured interviews should be done by the facilitators and interviewers. Thus the whole process of interviewing and analysis should be either in-house or contracted, not divided.

4.3.5 Develop survey instrument

The survey instrument or instruments have to be selected to supply the appropriate informa-tion for the objectives within the limitations of money, time and resources. This is covered in

No.	Activity / Task	Jan	Feb				Mar				
		25	1	8	15	22	1	8	15	22	29
1	FOOD CO-OPS ELEMENT										
a	**Form project development team**										
a1	Initial client scoping meeting	▓									
a2	Approach existing organizations		▓	▓							
a3	Hold briefing meeting			▓							
a4	Finalize programme of involvement				▓						
b	**Compile database of existing agencies/schemes**										
b1	Access already known sources										
b2	Contact organizations for updates			▓	▓						
b3	Sort out information into useful format					▓					
c	**Resident-led contact with agencies/schemes**										
c1	Residents contact – letter and phone (consultant support)										
c2	Selected visits to other projects									▓	
c3	Write up of outcomes										▓
d	**Organize events and activities**										
d1	Expo event										
d2	Resident-led survey										
d3	Results										
e	**Identify training needs and programmes**										
e1	Review of skills, awareness, gaps and solutions										
f	**Identify funding options**										
f1	General assessment of alternatives										
f2	Generation of specific funding initiatives										
g	**Prepare feasibility report**										
g1	Compile report										
g2	Present report and edit in the light of comments										

Figure 4.3 GANTT chart and costs.

Apr				May	STAFF	RP	MG/MB	JJ	GB	AB/VM	Cons't	Casual	Misc	TOTALS
5	12	19	26	3	RATE	695	625	415	360	285				DAYS
						0.2		0.3						
										1				
								0.3						
						0.2		0.2		0.5				
								1						
								0.3		1.5				
								0.2		1				
								0.3				150		
								0.5		1		350		
								0.5		1				
														0
										1.5		200	125	
										1.5		300	150	
										2.5				
														0
						0.4		0.5		0.2				
														0
														0
						0.5		1.5		1.5			50	3.5
														0

No.	Activity / Task	Jan	Feb				Mar				
		25	1	8	15	22	1	8	15	22	29
2	LETS ELEMENT										
a	**Form project development team**										
a1	Initial client scoping meeting					▓					
a2	Approach existing organizations					▓	▓				
a3	Hold briefing meeting						▓				
a4	Finalize programme of involvement								▓		
b	**Compile database of existing agencies/schemes**										
b1	Access already known sources										
b2	Contact organizations for updates							▓	▓		
b3	Sort our information into useful format									▓	▓
c	**Resident-led contact with agencies/schemes**										
c1	Residents contact – letter and phone (consultant support)										
c2	Selected visits to other projects									▓	
c3	Write up of outcomes										▓
d	**Prepare feasibility report**										
d1	Compile report										
d2	Present report and edit in the light of comments										
		▓	Continuous work activity								
			Intermittent work activity								

Figure 4.3 – continued.

Apr				May	STAFF	RP	MG/MB	JJ	GB	AB/VM	Cons't	Casual	Misc	TOTALS
5	12	19	26	3	RATE	695	625	415	360	285				DAYS
						0.2	0.3							
										1				
							0.3							
						0.2	0.2			0.5				
							0.5							
							0.2			0.3				
							0.2			0.5				
							0.3			0.5				
							0.5							
							0.5			0.5				
														0
						0.2	0.5			0.5			50	1.2
														0
						696.9	628.5	420.6	360.5	302				2408.5
						484346	392813	174549	129780	86070		Total staff costs		1267557
										Contract	0	1100	412.5	1512.5
										TOTAL COSTS				1269070

more detail in Chapter 6, 'Designing Surveys'. The first decision is whether the objectives can be met with secondary data alone (see Chapter 13, the Thailand case study) or whether primary data gathering is required (all the case study chapters include primary data collection other than Chapter 13). If primary data collection is required, then it is necessary to decide between:

- use of an existing survey instrument
- modification of an existing survey instrument
- development of a new survey instrument.

Options for design

One advantage of using an existing survey instrument is that it saves time and money. However, it is essential to make sure that the instrument has been properly validated. This may not be obvious from the published article found in the literature search, in which case it will be necessary to contact the authors for further information. The second major advantage is that the findings can be compared with the earlier applications. In many situations this 'benchmarking' provides valuable information. For example, The Short Form-36 health survey (Ware *et al.*, 1993; see also Bowling, 1997, p. 261) has been used extensively in the USA and UK and in many situations this 'benchmarking' provides valuable comparative information.

The main argument against using an existing survey instrument is where the objectives of the current project are not exactly the same as the project for which the instrument was developed. In this case there is the likelihood of collecting data which is not relevant and thus wasting resources.

Modification of one or more survey instruments is quite common. Rather than having to design all the questions in a survey, some can be taken from existing questionnaires where they have been tested and which are directly relevant for the existing survey. Even if the individual questions have been tested, there is still the problem that the combination and ordering of questions requires testing.

The advantage of developing a new survey instrument is that it should be relevant to the objectives and economical in scope. However, designing and testing a new instrument is highly skilled and resource intensive.

If it is important to develop a questionnaire or interview schedule that is as clear as possible for the population being sampled, then the language of questions may need to be adapted from standard English to the local vernacular. But this then loses standardization and so cannot be compared directly with other samples.

Ownership and consultation

The process of selection and design can be valuable in creating a sense of ownership by both commissioner and contractor. In the long run this is going to help the commitment to implementation of the recommendations. However, there is the danger that the development process will become prolonged and that the instrument will become too diffuse because all the participants want to include some questions which interest them. This has been the experience in developing lifestyle surveys which can be too long and too diffuse.

Coding and data entry and preliminary tabulations should be planned together at this stage as part of the survey design even though the activities take place later in the project.

Choose sample frame

The choice of survey method is not always determined by the ideal method of obtaining the required information. Sometimes there are practical constraints set by the means of identifying and accessing the sample. For this reason the issues of sampling and choice of method are intertwined.

Samples are selected from a sample frame or data-listing containing some or all of the population being studied. Examples are GP patient listings, the electoral register or the postal address file (PAF). Where populations are geographically dispersed (such as in rural areas and scattered village communities), accessing people face-to-face is operationally difficult and so postal surveys may be used. If the topic is impossible to handle in the postal questionnaire format (as for example in the detailed community care charging issues and attitudes cited in the Southwark case study in Chapter 11), then a telephone survey may be considered. Random population surveys by telephone are themselves problematic, however, owing to the shortfalls in the telephone directory sample frame (discussed in detail in Chapter 6).

Where specific patient groups are at the focus of the study – for example mothers who have given birth in the last 12 months – a sample frame may be available from the health authority but ethical approval will be required before such a list can be made available for survey research.

Another alternative is the use of the 'random walk' technique where an interviewer samples one in so many households along a route taking them through a neighbourhood. It has to be noted, however, that this produces a contact sample strongly biased towards households where people are at home most often, and who are prepared to answer the door to strangers. On average less than half the doors are answered even on a weekend daytime survey, as a result of people being out or not answering. Random walk is also not suitable for scattered communities.

People are sometimes sampled by exit or in-premises surveys, for example people leaving the GP surgery or visiting the pharmacy. This is an easy way of accessing a sample but again this sample frame is biased – towards the types of people most frequently using the premises. A sample obtained in this way will represent not 'users' but 'usage events' – it is intrinsically obvious but often forgotten that the chances of a service user being sampled through such a process is higher the more frequently they use it.

Some good survey texts discuss these potential pitfalls for the unwary researcher and we do not intend to go into more detail on the subject of sampling here. The key learning point, however, is that sampling is a potential minefield for the innocent and unwary and may undermine the validity of the whole survey – so 'think before you sample'.

Example: Home Care (3)

During the very short project time-scale the project director already had commitments overseas which could not be rescheduled and the consultant had limited
time available for this project and then was off sick. This meant that the principal
investigator did not get enough support on the technical and emotional levels. She
had been selected because she had long experience as a senior manager in
another social services department and her MSc dissertation had involved interview research with older people in residential and nursing homes. The second
interviewer had been a social worker and had experience of life-story work with
older people with memory loss and Alzheimer's disease. Without their experience and skills this project could not have been successfully completed.

The commissioners in SSD were too busy to help in arranging access and choosing the sample of respondents. An initial meeting with stakeholders in SSD had
demonstrated how little shared understanding there was about the research and
there was no follow-up support. The principal investigator had to spend a high
proportion of her time telephoning to explain what the research was about (lack
of briefing by SSD) and negotiating access. Without her combination of pre-
understanding of social services and research experience it is unlikely that the
project would have succeeded.

4.4 Data gathering (Figure 4.1–B3)

4.4.1 Pilot survey, analyse pilot survey, progress report on pilot survey, revise survey instrument

The importance of the pilot study will be dependent on the results of the literature search.
This will have shown how innovative the project is in terms of previous research on this
topic, and whether the survey instrument is repeated or modified or new. Innovation can lie
in any of:

- the survey methods
- the target group
- the research team's experience.

Generally, it is true that the more quantitative the survey method the more crucial is the
pilot study. If a large-scale postal self-completion questionnaire is being used, as for many of
the lifestyle surveys, the pilot survey must provide complete coverage of validating the
questionnaire, assessing the response rate, and testing the methods of coding and analysis. If
any of these requirements have not been met, then the whole survey may be completely
wasted or, even worse, the findings will be used without realizing that they are invalid.

With a qualitative study (see Chapter 5) it is possible to make adjustments as the project
proceeds without losing all the information or invalidating the study.

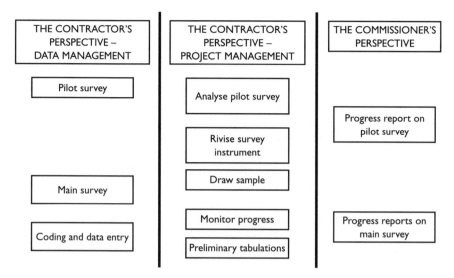

Figure 4.1–B3 Activities in a market research project – data gathering.

The commissioner of the market research project may need persuading that the cost and time of the pilot survey are justified. But reputable researchers must hold the line on the necessity for a full pilot.

The results of analysing the pilot may lead to conclusions that:

- the main study can proceed with no or minor modifications
- major modifications are needed, in which case another pilot must be carried out
- the project should be abandoned.

4.4.2 Draw sample, main survey

This should, all being well, be a straightforward implementation of the decisions made earlier in the 'Choose Sample Frame' activity. However, this does not always run smoothly. In Chapter 11, for example, the sample of clients for interview was drawn by Southwark Social Services Department from their database, but it was found that ethnicity was not recorded and so could not be used as a condition for sampling. Jackie Kimberley describes in Chapter 14 the day-to-day problems that she encountered in sampling residents in residential and nursing homes for her interviews.

In the case of a quantitative survey, the survey instrument will have been fully tested in the pilot survey (see Chapter 6). The emphasis in the main survey is, therefore, to ensure that the procedures for mailing and receiving postal questionnaires (see Chapter 15) or for preparing interviewers and receiving their completed forms (see Chapter 11) are completed on time to a high standard.

In the case where qualitative methods are being used, as described in Chapter 5, the conduct of the main survey is a more interactive and opportunistic process. Learning takes place as the data are gathered and there is usually scope for modifying the observations or amending the themes in the focus groups.

Monitor progress

Quality control requires the senior staff to involve themselves in all stages of the administration throughout the survey and to undertake follow-up visits to a selection of respondents. This is covered in detail in Chapter 6, Section 6.6.

The monitoring of progress should give attention to the feelings of the interviewers who may find that their job has stressful elements (see the Home Care case study below).

In M.E.L. Research's survey for the West Midlands Regional Health Authority in 1991, the views of people with HIV/AIDS were sought on the adequacy of their care programmes. The staff engaged in the fieldwork were experienced social researchers with a relatively strong track record of experience in social interviewing. Nevertheless, some interviewers found the experience of interacting with seriously ill and dying people particularly distressing. In the early stages of the project interviewers were unprepared for the experience and desperately needed to talk over their feelings with others after the interviews.

As the study progressed, a pre-interview counselling session was added to prepare interviewers for the experience and explain the symptoms and progress of the disease, which at that time was relatively untreated and often progressed rapidly. Arrangements were made for interviewers to formally debrief each other in order to share expression of feelings and experiences and help to cope with distress.

Example: Home Care (4)

The survey design was complex. Trying to combine quality of life and user satisfaction in one survey when previous applications in home care had been limited proved frustrating. A lot of compromises had to be made under pressure.

These pressures and compromises produced feelings of frustration and anger in the interviewers which were only considered after the very short period of fieldwork had been completed. Some of these feelings are clarified in these quotations from the debriefing of the interviewers:

Lots of negative feelings – anger, frustration, disappointment, guilt.

Guilt at not being able to do justice to older people.

Outrage that SSD wanted a Quality of Life schedule on one side of A4. How could they? So disrespectful.

Feel privileged to have been let into older people's lives ... admired their fortitude, resilience and humour.

On the topic of the quality of life investigation, I noticed in at least half the interviews clear changes of mood between the beginnings and ends of the visits (initial gloomy statements were being unwittingly cancelled out by subsequent buoyant remarks).

Barbara Jaggers's poem (Figure 4.4). is particularly effective in communicating the feelings of a sensitive interviewer of older people and captures some of the evidence which a questionnaire can never do.

You'd forgotten that old-fashioned look
they give you when you say you haven't time
to drink a cup of tea with them. Just like
visiting your mother, guilty wriggle,
a wish to hunker down, and tell it all. Well,

they're not going anywhere, they have
the time, and when they start talking
you remember time has lost its meaning
and all their history is in the now and here
inside this room, they're brimming over with

the echoes, warts and wishes of a life which
they unroll before you, endless carpet
running down the passage, down the steps
and down the street and century,
subdued and fearful pattern

turning soon to riotous and bold. You could
lap them up, swim around in them, those
revelations, except you've got these
sheets of paper, little boxes, knowing phrases,
sixty minutes of confinement, pushing

timeless life inside a written exercise. But
then, you're thinking, life's all barter, all
telling stories, so you make your visit lively,
come away elated or exhausted. Wonder later
what they wondered. If they wondered.

And you know
you will be mute some day, taste,
the half-light of a phrase, then
swallow it.

Barbara Jagger

Figure 4.4 Questionnaire time: survey of home care clients with memory loss.

Progress report on main survey

The monitoring will lead to the production of regular progress reports which will be used internally by the contractor, and summaries sent to the commissioner. The direct interest of the commissioner will vary: in some cases they will have adopted a *learning role* and be involved quite closely with face-to-face meetings; in others all they are interested in is getting a report of the findings.

Coding and data entry

This activity is covered in detail in Chapter 7.

Preliminary tabulations

This activity is covered in detail in Chapter 9.

4.5 Dissemination (Figure 4.1–B4)

4.5.1 List main findings and compare with literature

The preliminary tabulations in the case of a quantitative survey and the selected key responses in the case of a qualitative survey will be compared with those which were found in the literature survey and in comparative surveys. For example, in Chapter 16 Graham Flynn was able to compare the relative importance attached to the five service quality dimensions by the Toxicology Laboratory's customers with the well-known results of the PZB study (Parasuraman *et al.*, 1988). In Chapter 12, however, M.E.L. Research were unable to make direct comparisons because there had been no previous comparable research on Healthy Living Centres.

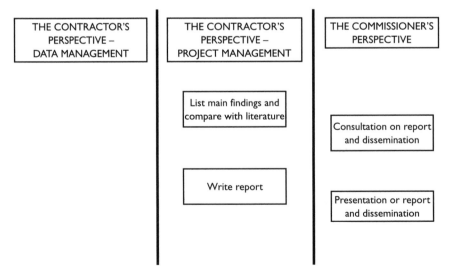

Figure 4.1–B4 Activities in a market research project – dissemination.

4.5.2 Consultation on report and dissemination, write report, presentation of report and dissemination

Usually, before the report is written there will be consultation on the form of the report which the commissioner will find most useful. This should not be confused with 'bending' the findings to suit the commissioner. In a sense, the consensus development conference (see Chapter 18) telescopes these activities into a single event.

In Chapter 15, Mary Parkes was the manager who had commissioned herself as MBA student to be the research contractor:

> After the MBA dissertation had been submitted, a short report was produced for internal circulation to planning groups, primary care teams and the commissioning group. A presentation was made to Aston students. A paper was presented at the Department of Health national conference on unwanted pregnancy.

In contrast, the project described in Chapter 11 with the 'complex client group' required a complex dissemination strategy. First, a summary version of the full report to Southwark Community Care Forum was circulated to elected members of the Social Services Committee and was, therefore, put on the 'public agenda'. Then the research team from M.E.L. Research gave a presentation to the joint Health Authority and Local Authority Community Care Liaison Group. The research proved to be a powerful catalyst for a political debate on whether the majority party had sensitively handled the issue of charges. In this book we have tended to present the techniques in a largely 'technocratic' managerial setting, but in the reality there is frequently a hot political pot boiling underneath.

The report, or reports, can vary greatly in length and content. Chapters 11 and 12 are taken from relatively short focused reports using bar charts and numerical tables to present the results. Chapters 14, 15 and 16 are taken from longer MBA dissertations which are required to include a comprehensive literature review and a full discussion of choice of methods. Often these are not of interest to commissioners.

Example: Home Care (5)

There was no time to provide progress reports for the commissioners. Decisions as to how to proceed had to be made 'on the hoof' by the researchers. Consultation took place before listing the key findings and writing the report. This was submitted as a draft. It was almost two months later before there was any formal feedback and that was at our instigation. After this, the ownership of the results and report still seemed to rest principally with the researchers rather than the over-busy commissioners. The researchers took the initiative in arranging a workshop with stakeholders to disseminate the findings and discuss how the research could be taken forward. This was particularly successful in bringing together people from within the department who did not normally have the opportunity to work together. The external stimulus appeared to prompt the creation of some productive internal partnerships within the department.

4.6 After the project (Figure 4.1–B5)

4.6.1 Further analyses

It is likely that the market research consultancy projects such as Chapters 11 and 12 will not be funded to carry out some of the more advanced analyses described in Chapter 9. However, if the contractor organization is carrying out a number of similar projects, then it may be productive to carry out further analyses in more depth and to compare results between projects. In the case of university projects, academic staff are encouraged to carry out more advanced analyses and seek publication.

4.6.2 Wider publication

As discussed in Chapter 1 there is a dearth of published market research studies, perhaps because of the increased competition in health and social care markets. Publication may be prohibited in the contract. On the other hand, some commissioners of research want to strengthen their organization's reputation through publication, as we see in Chapter 11:

> Southwark Community Care Forum was keen on national dissemination, both to promote its own profile within the field and also to stimulate the wider political and professional debate. SCCF therefore produced under their own 'covers' a copy of the report for sale at a nominal fee, and promoted its availability at local and London-wide conferences and events.

Some professionals and most academics see it as important to publish both for their careers and for public sector sharing of knowledge. Thus, Mary Parkes (Chapter 15) presented a paper at the Department of Health national conference on unwanted pregnancy. Graham Flynn (Chapter 16) has published a journal article and a working paper. Chapter 17 has been developed from a published journal article by the authors.

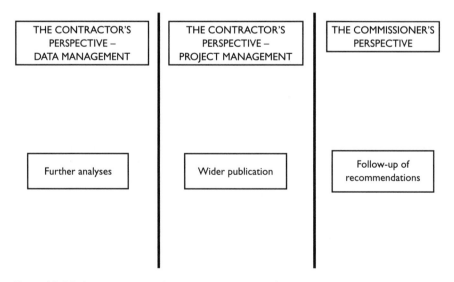

Figure 4.1–B5 Activities in a market research project – after the project.

4.6.3 Follow-up recommendations

If the market researchers are from outside the commissioning organization, then they may not be involved directly in following up the recommendations. This will then depend on a coalition of internal stakeholders being sufficiently committed to take the recommendations forward. Graham Flynn carried out a thorough review two years later (Chapter 16, Section 16.7) and presents a somewhat pessimistic view of progress:

> Collaboration opportunities have not been developed as a result of political obstacles and a lack of will to really drive them forward. There have been elements of work sharing and introductions, but larger projects such as the joint development of assays or the exploitation of new markets have failed to materialize.

In the South African health centre (Chapter 17) the outcome was more positive:

> This example shows that it is possible to improve patient care and access even in overloaded health facilities in developing countries. Key problems may be lack of operational management, and staff resistance to change, rather than scarcity of resources alone. Research can help clarify the issues . . . The simple methods used in this study elicited many . . . ideas, as well as helping to identify possible sources of conflict or resistance.

Researchers who are internal to the organization such as Mary Parkes (Chapter 15) and Jackie Kimberley (Chapter 16) are in a better position to act themselves or with colleagues on the recommendations.

Example: Home Care (6)

Our view was that there were two main possibilities for further work:

1   An action research project with one or more SSD area teams to develop quality of life and user satisfaction, not necessarily in one survey instrument, in order to influence practice. This might be carried out with several SSDs.
2   A more fundamental research study of ways of assessing quality of life and user satisfaction in home care with different research methods such as survey, observation, and including a control group of people who are not receiving services. This should cover a representative sample by age, gender, ethnicity and class. This would need independent funding as it would not provide immediate benefit to SSD but only after validation and testing.

In the event, the contracts section was successful in obtaining a significant amount of funding to take forward the work on measuring quality of life and service user satisfaction. This will be taken forward over a three-year period using the assessment tool developed in our pilot study. PSMRC was asked to advise on drawing up the specification and will be invited to tender in due course.

4.7 Overview

The detailed framework and schedule of tasks in Figure 4.1 is a clear, logical, plannable and systematic process. It is easiest done in cases of large-scale quantitative surveys where the methods are tried and tested, where experience has shown how long tasks will take and in what order. The whole process can be organized with a considerable degree of confidence. Chapter 6 sets out in detail the ways that surveys of this sort can be planned, designed and managed.

It should be noted, however, that this is but one form of market research – albeit the most common. Increasingly, however, there is growing interest in the use of exploratory, semi-structured qualitative methods that are by their nature not so sharply pre-defined, and where the course of investigation emerges only as the investigation proceeds. In the following chapter, Jill Jesson describes some of the methods in qualitative exploratory research and these fall less neatly in the schedule of events set out in Figure 4.1. An analogy may be seen in the contrast between building a house (where builder and architect can state with high confidence and precision the order in which things get done, the time and resources taken); and the way children on an adventure holiday experiment with ways of creating a shelter from the materials around them.

Systematic and exploratory surveys do nevertheless follow a broad common process summarized as 'get in, get on, get out' (Buchanan *et al.*, 1988). Chapter 5 shows that exploratory surveys have their own rules and discipline which within their own frame of reference are as systematic as in the structured large-scale quantitative surveys. In the past there has been a tradition of dismissing exploratory qualitative research as 'unscientific' but increasingly this has been displaced by a recognition that these forms of social research are essential as a way of assigning meaning to data, and their scientific validity is as credible as the methodology of the traditional survey.

Further reading

Bowling, A. (1997) *Research Methods in Health. Investigating Health and Health Services*, Buckingham: Open University Press.

Luck, M., Lawrence, B., Pocock, R. and Reilly, K. (1988) *Consumer and Market Research in Health Care*, London: Chapman and Hall.

Chapter 5

Observation, focus groups and narratives

Jill Jesson

In this chapter the reader will gain an understanding of:

- how to recognize when ethnographic observation methods are appropriate
- how to be clear about the ethical issues in doing observational research
- how to understand the need for clarity in fieldwork diaries
- how to analyse data
- when to use a focus group
- how to design a theme plan and set up and carry out a focus group
- how to analyse the data
- in what circumstances a narrative method could be used
- the validity of the narrative technique.

5.1 Introduction

This chapter explores three research methods that are traditionally known as qualitative methods: observation, focus groups and narrative.

Observational techniques have been used in the scientific pursuit of knowledge and can be traced back to the Mass Observation studies in the 1930s. In anthropology and sociological studies participant observation has developed its own momentum and theory and practice as ethnography. Ethnographic studies emphasize the cultural and social context of a group, community or organization. Recently the technique has been adapted by the nursing profession, using ethnographic observation to develop critical thinking, reflection and experiential learning. Structured observation continues in scientific quantitative research, but there is no reason why the two techniques cannot complement each other.

Focus groups are a relatively new technique to social and health research, but the method has been used and developed extensively from market research techniques. Some scholars have described focus groups or in-depth discussion groups as 'quick and dirty method', a comment which reflects the positivist paradigm. For this reason data obtained from focus groups have been less acceptable to the referees and editors of scientific journals, with the result that many interesting publications circulate as 'grey literature'. Good-quality modern textbooks do now include focus groups as an acceptable method.

Narratives or stories is the latest technique to be taken up by qualitative researchers. There are similar concerns about scientific credibility, but in 1998 a complete edition of *Social Science and Medicine* (1998, Vol. 38, No. 6) was dedicated to papers in which narrative played a prominent theme. In 1998 an Open University text of readings in health and social care was published containing an interesting mix of documents based on observational, narrative and in-depth interview (Allott and Robb, 1998).

5.2 Observational methods

Key concepts

Observation
- a research method in which the investigator systematically watches, listens to and records the phenomena under observation.

Range of researcher roles
- complete participant
- participant as observer
- observer as participant
- complete observer.

Type of observation
- unstructured – record as much as possible, no definite format
- semi-structured – using a pre-specified schedule and count occurrence plus open comments permitted
- structured – observing events according to a pre-specified schedule.

(Bowling, 1997)

5.2.1 Rationale for using observational methods

Observation is a well-established and accepted research method which can be used in a variety of ways in both qualitative and quantitative research paradigms. Most qualitative researchers will be familiar with the method from classic published ethnographic studies, such as Goffman's *Asylum* (Goffman, 1961) or Humphrey's *Tearoom Trade* (Humphrey, 1970). Opportunities to undertake truly ethnographic research in the Goffman style are scarce, because the researcher is expected to immerse themselves into another culture for a considerable length of time. But that does not mean that an observation technique cannot be part of a research practice. After all, the nature of the project determines the role.

It is not intended to rehearse the entire description of observational roles in this chapter, since most good research method books cover the technique in detail. There is an excellent discussion from a psychological perspective in Robson (1995) and for comparison from a medical model perspective in Bowling (1997). A summary of the key roles is presented in Figure 5.1.

Regular and structured observation takes place in health and social care practice every day. Clinicians and physiotherapists observe individual patients as part of forming a diagnosis and therapeutic response. Epidemiologists observe the course of a disease. Social

1. Role of the observer		
Full participant	Partial observer	Outsider
2. Portrayal of the role to others		
Overt: people know that they are being observed and who is the observer	Observer role known by some but not others	Covert: people do not know that they are being observed or that there is an observer
3. Portrayal of the purpose of the research		
Full explanation to everyone	Partial explanation or explanation to some but not all	Covert: no explanation, or deception and false explanation
4. Duration of observations		
Single observation, maybe one hour	Several observations over a period, at random or regular intervals	Long-term continuous period of months or even years
5. Focus of the observations		
Narrow, single elements ignoring anything else	Selected elements and their interactions	Broad holistic view

Figure 5.1 Key elements in observational research.

Source: Adapted from Marshall and Rossman (1989)

workers observe at case conferences. In education, classroom observational studies are common. Observation, like interviews, can be more or less structured depending on what is appropriate in the particular circumstances. Even when not carrying out any research, a researcher will usually be observing what takes place at meetings, case conferences or committees – it helps to develop a feeling for the atmosphere and culture of an organization, as well as showing who is important or dominant.

A working practice developed in our own research team requires a 'theatre report' to be delivered from any one who has attended a conference or seminar. The aim of the practice is to develop observational skills in all the researchers, whether they are working on predominantly quantitative or qualitative projects. The 'theatre report' describes the scene, who was there, in terms of gender, ethnicity, age and other social characteristics; whether there were any supporting organizations displaying promotional literature, who were the speakers, what was the main message in the papers presented and so on. This semi-structured observation is developed through practice.

The researcher as research instrument

Some research method texts describe the observation technique in terms of researcher roles, where the researcher is the instrument. Others take a more structured approach, recommending the design of a measurement instrument. Thus there are two opposite types, open participant ethnographic observation and a structured quantitative style, but the two techniques can be incorporated in one study. In studies where the researcher systematically watches people and events to find out about behaviours and interactions in natural settings, it is implicit that the researcher is the research instrument. In this instance the method will involve observing, asking questions and possibly analysing documents. Observations are recorded in a field notebook, supplemented with interviews, they help to place behaviour in context, to see the discrepancy between what people do and what they say they do. The participant observer has to become involved in a new culture, to see and experience life as they do, but also to retain objectivity in order to see what needs to be seen. Since it is impossible to record everything that is seen the researcher inevitably has to be selective and to rely on memory. Thus the research instrument may have a bias and be accused of subjectivity.

The participant observer shares the everyday life of the people under study, either openly in the role of researcher or covertly in some disguised role, observing things that happen and listening to what is said, over a fairly long period. The use of the covert role has been a source of controversy for over thirty years. Covert research has been described as a 'morally hazardous enterprise' (Dingwall *et al.*, 1992). The ethical issues of a covert role are discussed later.

A variation of the observational role has been developed from the classical ethnographic one of complete absorption, to one using observation as a technique in critical thinking, reflection and experiential learning in nursing (Wallace, 1996). Wallace describes how she used the learning from an ethnographic study of fifty trained nurses over a five-year period, based on in-depth reflective interviews and grounded theory analysis, to develop a deeper understanding of nursing practice. The participants described examples of how they had deviated from traditional rule-bound behaviour, such as taking verbal orders for drugs, or becoming emotionally involved with patients. The recognition of the importance of feelings acknowledged through the self-reflective process could then be addressed by teaching nurses management techniques for their emotional labour.

In a less demanding role the researcher may use observation for comparative purposes in a triangulation methodology. In an organizational study, observation can help uncover differences in patterns of care, language, labelling of patients, differences in decision-making practices or evaluating the implementation of procedures. For example, Jackie Kimberley (see Chapter 14) interviewed residents in elderly care settings and was able to observe the way in which carers related to residents whilst she was on the premises. She wrote:

> Observation can be enlightening as demonstrated when the author asked questions about whether staff 'knock and wait' before entering residents' rooms. Some residents said 'yes' to this even though on a couple of occasions the author experienced staff interrupting interviews by walking into rooms, usually preceded by a cursory knock, but without waiting for a response.
>
> (Kimberley, 1997, p. 38)

In this example observation was a minor element of a structured interview method, but was a useful technique to validate what residents and carers said they did.

5.2.2 Structured observation

Some authors are uncomfortable with the ethnographic free-ranging unstructured participant observation technique. For example, Herbert advises students:

It is wise to make observations according to some predetermined schedule. This is an important precaution against the bias that would arise if the observer merely recorded whenever something obvious or interesting happened.

(Herbert, 1997)

In situations where the researcher has a clear idea of what they are looking for a more structured approach can be adopted, maybe using a recording proforma with a two-dimensional matrix, for example when observing a small group meeting. Along one dimension there could be the names of the participants, along the second might be types of behaviour to be observed, for example: introducing novel ideas, assessing suggestions raised by others, positive or negative behaviour, keeping the meeting to the agenda, being supportive of people who feel under attack. When one of the people being observed displays the relevant behaviour a tick is placed in the appropriate box (Phillips *et al.*, 1994).

Another way of structuring observation is to take time sampling, such as hourly or every fifteen minutes, to observe what is happening in a situation at fixed intervals (see Figure 5.2), or event sampling, looking at critical incidents and recording when they occur.

Key features in the observational process

- choosing the setting
- getting into an organization or setting
- gaining/negotiating access to the group
- building rapport with the group
- recording observations
- retaining objectivity and not going native
- getting out

Date	Time	Place	Activities/comments
12/7/82	10.00	Benefit office	Long queue
	10.15		People despondent
	10.30		Staff calm
	10.45		
	11.00		Queue longer
	11.15		Fewer staff
	11.30		
	11.45		Disruption in one office
	12.00		

Figure 5.2 A page from a time sampling field notebook.

Advantages and disadvantages

ADVANTAGES

- the participant observer is likely to feel empathy towards the group, and uncover the hidden and the secret
- the observational technique can be adapted to the situation
- observation can form the third part of a triangulation methodology.

DISADVANTAGES

- a non-participant role is unlikely to uncover the secrets
- sampling may be permissive rather than systematically chosen
- the participant observer may go native and lose track of the objectivity required
- the participant observer needs to establish rapport, which takes time
- people may change their behaviour if they know they are being observed (observer reactivity)
- care is needed in how the information is revealed and published.

5.2.3 Bias, validity, reliability and ethical issues

There are obviously important ethical considerations to be made about the decision of the role to be taken in any given study. In addition to the well-rehearsed debate about covert research and the moral 'rightness or wrongness' of the approach, there are considerations related to the impact that knowledge of being observed has on the group or organization.

The British Sociological Association's *Statement of Ethical Practice* describes a set of obligations to which researchers should adhere as a principle for guiding their conduct with research participants. The document states:

> There are serious ethical dangers in the use of covert research, but covert methods may avoid certain problems. For instance, difficulties arise when research participants change their behaviour because they know they are being studied . . . However, covert methods violate the principles of informed consent and may invade the privacy of those being studied . . . Participant or non participant observation in non public spaces or experimental manipulation of research participants without their knowledge should be resorted to only where it is impossible to use other methods to obtain essential data.
>
> (British Sociological Association, 1996)

Validity

Hammersley has written extensively on ethnographic observational methods. He states that there are two main considerations to bear in mind when examining ethnographic descriptions. First, how valid are ethnographic data? Second, how convincing is the relationship between them and the claim they are presented to support? (Hammersley, 1990). Data are usually recorded as field notes, so the reader has to consider to what extent there has been any observational reactivity caused by the research process or the characteristics of the researcher.

To avoid observational reactivity serious consideration has to be given to the impact of obtaining informed consent, because 'informed consent' may well jeopardize the validity of the findings. Observation in itself becomes an ethical dilemma. Health research ethical guidelines emphasize the importance of gaining informed consent from respondents (Kimmel, 1996; Smith, 1997). But, informing subjects about the purpose and procedures of a study has been found in some cases to alter the spontaneity and responses to questions.

5.3 Focus groups

Key concepts

A focus/discussion group
- a focus group is an in-depth discussion with between six and ten people, facilitated by a researcher
- the method seeks information from the interaction of the group challenged by a combination of probing and direct inquiry techniques

Moderator/facilitator
- is not an interviewer; the role is to gently lead the discussion.

Theme plan
- the theme plan is a one-page checklist of all the issues that must be covered by the group.

5.3.1 Rationale for the focus group study

The key feature of a focus or discussion group is the group setting which enables the opinions of each person to be considered by the other members in an environment that is friendly and supporting – the interaction. Focus groups have been described as a form of group interview that capitalizes on communication between research participants in order to generate data (Kitzinger, 1996). Yet it can be misleading to think of the process as an interview because the method produces a synergy that is lacking in an individual interview. However, if the group members do not interact with each other, but each one directs their remarks at the group moderator, this can become face-to-face serial interviewing.

The moderator uses the characteristics of the group to elicit useful information, so it makes sense to draw together participants who share a common interest relevant to the topic under discussion, although they may otherwise have different social characteristics such as ethnic origin, age or sex.

Focus groups are becoming an increasingly popular method for assessing health education messages, exploring public understanding of illness and behaviour in community development projects. There are a number of reasons for choosing to use the focus group method. The following section provides illustrative examples of real commissioned research involving focus discussion groups.

Some examples of use

To stimulate and generate new ideas about the topic under discussion. These ideas may never arise in a one-to-one interview and would not arise at all in a structured interview unless the designer had already thought of them, e.g. Luck *et al.* (1992) were commissioned to carry out a study of the ways in which Asian mothers coped with minor childhood ailments. The origin of the study was concern by a health authority at the high level of antibiotics prescriptions issued by inner city GPs to Asian families. The evidence was in the PACT data (Prescribing Analyses and Cost – issued to all GPs by the Prescription Pricing Authority (PPA)). The researchers carried out an exploratory research project to identify the attitudes, health knowledge and perceptions of Asian parents about the management of their children's respiratory ailments . The study involved focus group discussions and in-depth interviews. The information was used to make a health promotion video in Asian languages on treating minor respiratory ailments.

To explore new topic areas, e.g. The Brinnington Community 2000 project was a community development initiative set up by Stockport Metropolitan Borough Council. To ensure that a community-driven agenda was not dominated by professional researchers, their role being restricted to facilitating, or by other paid professionals, the residents were trained to carry out their own research through running focus groups. In all, seven focus groups were held with a broad representative cross-section of the Brinnington population, thereby allowing the views and aims of the residents to emerge in a free-ranging but controlled environment. The residents then used that basic information in the design of an interview schedule; they did some interviewing themselves, ran a Youth Audit and analysed the results (Brinnington Community 2000, 1997).

In the developmental phase of research, where the information will be used to design a structured questionnaire. For example, in 1989 the Department of Health commissioned a survey of consumer views, experiences and expectations of community pharmacies in the West Midlands. This study explored the views of both the general public and high users of pharmaceutical services (Jepson *et al.*, 1991a). The initial ideas for the design of a structured questionnaire came from focus groups of people with a specified range of characteristics. There were seven high-user patient groups, people with asthma, diabetes, a stoma, coeliac disease, frail elderly, young women with families, and carers. The outcome was a range of core ideas and key concepts, use patterns and expectations from the service provided by community pharmacy.

To reveal differences in attitude. The group setting provides an insight into the dynamics of attitudes and opinions, the flexibility or rigidity with which a view is held, or how a firmly held belief can be modified by differing views. This idea was used in a review of the local health services in community development projects in Newcastle upon Tyne where the researchers wanted women to speak for themselves, to present a diversity of views (Newcastle Inner City Forum and CHC, 1983).

To reach people who are often marginalized in society or who are unlikely to respond to other research methods. For example, a health authority wanted to evaluate to what extent outreach work on health promotion on safer sex was being taken up by women who work in saunas (Luck *et al.*, 1991). The study in itself was an exploratory exercise to examine the use of discussion groups in setting the agenda in health promotion strategies. The discussions covered a range of views on sexual health and HIV held by women working in saunas and massage parlours. The information was then used by the health authority to clarify their own views on female perceptions of HIV as an issue in overall personal health and to evaluate their HIV outreach work.

To develop a research tool or pre-test an intervention instrument. For example, focus groups were used to pre-test the design of health promotion materials for an intervention to increase the consumption of fruit and vegetables amongst primary school children. The researchers wanted to adapt a fruit and vegetable fridge chart, that had been successfully tested in the USA, for use with British children. The researchers had to be sure that the fruit and vegetables would be familiar to the target population and representative of the British diet. Eleven focus groups in all were held; the various groups were made up of sixth form secondary school children, junior school children, Brownies aged 7, the Women's Institute, an Asian women's group and a group of unemployed men on a re-training scheme. The procedure involved an initial meeting to distribute the charts, a two-week trial at home, a brief questionnaire and a video recording of the focus group discussion. Participants were asked to complete a short questionnaire to consolidate their thoughts about the issue and then to discuss in a group context what they liked and disliked about the charts, how often they had used them, whether any fruit and vegetables which they had eaten were missing from the sticker sheets, and which fruit and vegetables were eaten most often (Boaz and Ziebland, 1998).

In addition the method can help to develop insights into an issue. The group format allows an opportunity to observe directly the group process, not only learning how people would behave in a particular social setting but also understanding something about the process of decision making.

5.3.2 Setting up – theme plan and recording

There are no set rules directing how many focus groups should be run to achieve a desired outcome, it depends on the purpose of the study. In the West Midlands consumer expectations of community pharmacy study we ran one focus group for each patient group, a total of seven were held (Jepson *et al.*, 1991b). Some information was common to all seven groups, but other issues emerged from the sessions, and were substantiated or enlarged on in subsequent groups. *You have gained all that you can from your focus group when you can anticipate the outcome of the discussion.*

Focus group – key features in the process

- invite seven or eight participants with a facilitator (in some cases a second link-person can be very helpful)
- arrange the room setting – informal arrangement of chairs around a small table
- record on audio tape and take brief notes
- duration: one hour for discussion plus start and finish
- analysis: transcribe tape and extract data by themes
- write report.

Moderator

The role of the moderator, or facilitator, is the most important factor in producing useful information from the group. The moderator is playing a role, which might have to change with the nature of the group process, from being fairly passive with an alert and lively group, to more interventionist and directive in a sluggish group who cannot find any enthusiasm for the topic. The moderator sets the ground rules for the process, emphasizing that this is not an interview, that everyone is expected to participate, but no one person has the 'correct' answer. The moderator has to create an environment which is supportive, in which sensitive issues, beliefs, experiences and insights can be exchanged. Problem solving can be facilitated through challenge, clarification and exploration. Consensus may not always be the objective, so at some point it may be feasible to play devil's advocate or make a provocative statement to test reaction amongst the group. The moderator must be generally knowledgeable about the topic, remain alert during the discussion to draw out new or unanticipated ideas, guide the meeting to cover the theme plan, and ensure that all members participate and the discussion is not dominated by one individual or set of ideas.

Theme plan

The theme plan is the research instrument. The plan is a set of questions designed to encourage participants to talk. It is usual to have a number of subject headings that introduce a general topic, which then moves into the specific as the discussion moves around the group. Since this is a guide only, should anyone raise an unanticipated or new point then the moderator can ask them for more detail or to elaborate. The moderator must ensure that all the themes are discussed before closing the session, so the theme plan also serves to mark the time.

5.3.3 Data management, transcription and analysis

Each group session should be recorded in some way, either by audio tape or video, and a transcript made of the recording as soon as possible after the group has met. This task can be handed on to a typist but the best understanding comes where the moderator leads the group, hears the tape and carries out the analysis. With each listening the ideas and analytical skills are honed in to the material.

The discussion group method produces *qualitative* information rather than quantitative data. It reveals what exists and not how many. The first stage of analysis with the transcript is some form of data reduction (see Box for range of options), then drawing up hypotheses or theories and verifying them against the data, before drawing conclusions. Analysis using grounded theory is becoming more popular (Robrecht, 1995) but basic first stage results can be achieved from theme and content comparison.

Options for data reduction

- summarizing and paraphrasing
- search for patterns, anomalies, linkages
- selecting some themes and excluding others
- subsuming specific instances into larger patterns
- quantification into numbers of ranked order
- using highlighting pens, or cut and paste.

Analysis is a subjective process drawing on the material arising from the data reduction phase but it must have an appropriate conceptual framework. Display of original data is usually in narrative text, using appropriate quotations, tables or boxes. However, different authors present their data in a number of ways. Two extracts illustrate the point. In the Newcastle upon Tyne health service review, the authors provided the comments and wrote:

> We have not attempted to spell out in detail the implication of what the women are saying. Clearly there is a case for some change in services, their method of delivering and the attitude of professional workers. We hope that readers will draw some of their own conclusions on these points.
>
> (Newcastle Inner City Forum and CHC, 1983)

In the consumer expectations of community pharmacy study only key phrases were used and published in a working paper. From a group of seven people recruited through the Colostomy Welfare Group we learned a lot about public perceptions of the pharmacist as a very busy person under pressure dispensing prescriptions.

Q. Would you like your chemist to be more medically oriented?
   – they should know a bit more about illnesses, if they have got the means to treat them.
   – I think they should get an update every so often.
   – difficulty is there is only one pharmacist.

- he's under constant pressure at the moment, he's only got the assistant and odd people to help him.
- if he had somebody who was almost as knowledgeable to do the prescriptions.
- to be there at the same time, not a locum replacement.
- they can't issue prescriptions and be talking at the same time.
- surely they go to refresher courses anyway?
- are the counter assistants knowledgeable?

(Jepson *et al.*, 1991b)

Advantages and disadvantages

ADVANTAGES

- provides a good way to explore attitudes and beliefs where the researchers have little preconception as to what these might be
- a good way of generating and developing ideas and concepts prior to a more quantitative survey
- can be set up quickly and does not require extensive preparation provided that the facilitator is well briefed
- can be motivating for the researchers by hearing in concentrated form the opinions of people
- may stimulate participants to be creative and spark off new ideas.

DISADVANTAGES

- groups can be difficult to organize, may be costly in time and payments to participants
- it can be unsuitable for high-risk issues, where personal disclosure can be seen as threatening
- the discussion may get hi-jacked by one or two strong personalities (discussion hog)
- the group process may inhibit some members from being frank and encourage others to exaggerate
- experienced group facilitators are hard to find and take time to train
- transcription of discussion is time consuming (expensive)
- analysis of text is a skilled task
- the method produces qualitative information which some researchers dislike
- is often dismissed as quick and dirty by some researchers in medical and positivist perspective.

5.3.4 Bias, validity, reliability and ethical issues

Given the many criticisms to which the focus group method has been subjected it is important to demonstrate to what extent the findings are objective, reliable and valid. One way is to make the primary data and analysis available to anyone else to confirm or challenge.

Validity

The information is valid if it measures what it says it measures. The findings should have a truth that goes beyond the research context. Validity from the focus group method cannot be measured in the same way that quantitative data can, because the method operates not only at the individual level but it also involves group dynamics.

The iterative nature of the method through several groups and through analysis of the data opens it up for allegations of bias. In qualitative research methods, where the interviewer is a variable, there is always an opportunity for moderator bias to creep into the process and the outcome of a focus group discussion. It should be emphasized that we are trying to understand the process of opinion forming in a group setting, in understanding the underlying motives or prejudices that influence opinion. Ideas, attitudes and opinions are dynamic, representing a given moment in time. The structured survey can also be accused of the same lack of scientific credibility.

Another way to demonstrate validity is through the use of a validating checklist. A validating checklist could cover methodological details such as: participant recruitment, who, where, how, when and details of the group process. It is often the case that the first group acts as a model for subsequent groups by letting the moderator have some insight into what may be likely to emerge. As each group progresses this view could be confirmed or challenged. Greenhalgh *et al.* (1998) used triangulation of methods to study the views of Bangladeshi people with diabetes. Beginning with in-depth interviews they used six focus groups to validate their development of social constructs. They recorded the group's response on video tape. As a follow-up method they developed the new qualitative technique of structured vignette.

The commissioner of a qualitative focus group report should be aware of what it does not do. The method helps to establish the range of attitudes without asserting any representativeness of these attitudes in the wider population. It generates creative and fruitful hypothetical ideas, but does not claim to make broad generalizations. Such an output could be achieved by a follow-up survey to test and substantiate the hypothesis.

5.4 Narratives and stories

Narrative
- an account, or story of events or experiences.

Story
- a narrative of a chain of events told or written in prose or verse.

Narrate
- chronicle, describe, detail, recite, recount, rehearse, relate, repeat, report, set forth, tell, unfold.

Hermeneutics
- the science of interpretation

Vignette
• short narrative description of people, interactions or situations which illuminate a point or theory.

(*Collins Concise Dictionary*, 1989; *Collins Thesaurus*, 1986)

5.4.1 Narrative as a method: introduction

The standard research methods of surveys cannot explore the circumstances of a person's life, cannot describe the varied experiences or search out those contextual meanings that underpin decisions that have been taken and choices made. Surveys can only 'quantify the known' or scratch the surface layers of attitudes, knowledge, beliefs and self-declared behaviour in a limited way that is pre-structured by the agenda of the research instrument – the questionnaire.

Whilst an in-depth semi-structured interview does give the opportunity to overcome some of the surface limitations of the survey, it is still set in a framework that has been bounded by the pre-set format or agenda of the interviewer. The face-to-face interaction is still a socially constructed interaction with a purpose. Sometimes the pre-set agenda of such a purposeful interaction can be difficult for the respondent to grasp. For example, in trying to understand some of the power relationships in residential homes for the elderly, Kimberley (1997) (see also Chapter 14) used a structured interview schedule to interview the frail elderly residents, but found that several of them did not grasp what it was she was trying to lead them to say, or maybe they could not recall at that particular moment in time, or were afraid of the consequence of upsetting a carer on whom they relied so heavily. Kimberley noted:

> It was sometimes difficult to get residents to answer the questions directly (indicated by the number of don't knows or not declared). But why should we expect residents to have clear-cut answers when our own experience of filling in questionnaires often tempts us to tick boxes which do not reflect our own experiences.
>
> (Kimberley, 1997, p. 131)

5.4.2 Rationale for a narrative method

One way of overcoming the problem of accessing the hidden is to use a far less directive method of enquiry, such as the use of stories, or narratives. In a non-directive method, intervention by the researcher is at a minimum, the aim is to stimulate and encourage the respondent to share a personal view and experiences. Narratives allow a respondent to talk through their version of an incident or time in their life that is memorable. The stories we make about ourselves are accounts, attempts to explain who we are and to understand our own experience of the world. The cultural context of stories helps to provide the listener with social categories, a glimpse of common sense beliefs, folk knowledge, or an interpretative frame of reference from which personalized meanings and conceptions of the self are constructed. It is important to remember that experience is not always remembered in a linear fashion.

To use the narrative method invites the respondent to speak for and about the self, it employs his or her choice of metaphors, his or her context, selection of events and selection of explanations for events. The respondent can control both the information that is expressed and the information that is withheld. Thus the narrative construction becomes his or her own and through it he or she informs the audience about the way in which events have been subjectively internalized but the meaning was socially externalized. This could be issues to do with the ageing process or the diagnosis of a chronic illness.

The method has been adapted from the field of cultural studies. Bruner (1991) argued that life experiences and memories are organized primarily in a narrative form which is culturally transmitted and culturally defined; culture influences why a story is told, how and when it is told, and how it is interpreted by the interviewer/listener. In telling their story a person gives out a virtual text – the story is not the actual text – because narrative framing occurs, and the virtual text that the listener constructs for herself is according to what the utterances mean to her. It is the virtual text that the listener will recount when asked to repeat the story at a later date.

5.4.3 Narrative devices

Plot
- a narrative structure that imposes an order (possibly chronological) upon events and organizes these events into a meaningful whole.

Narrative movement
- the chronological function of the plot.

Movement
- enables a story to go somewhere by arguing events and experiences in a temporal order directed towards some destination or goal.

Narrative framing
- selects and highlights certain details out of the field of experience.

(Thompson, 1997)

The use of stories or narratives is becoming more popular in social research as we endeavour to understand why people behave as they do, and to understand what meaning they give to social phenomena as they experience them, as opposed to how we think they are experienced. The narrative methodology can be a useful research tool in giving 'voice' to people who may have been silent in the past, for example men, feminist researchers, children and consumers who have begun to develop their own methods for expression. In simple short narratives a small group of men have collected their thoughts on concepts such as masculinity and their puzzlement at a perceived inability 'to be a father' (Ryan, 1995). The stories show how some men are reluctant to take on the sick role and admit to weakness, men tell the story of illness and what it means to a man:

> Despite feeling dreadful most of the time, I still did not feel it was possible to take any time off work as I still did not see myself as properly ill . . . Physical weakness is a daily challenge to my sense of myself as a man.
>
> (Tolson, 1995, pp. 54–55)

In a similar way, feminist researchers have told the stories of socialization and powerlessness in male-dominated worlds. The narrative technique has been employed as a significant means of discovering the social experience of previously silent women. Cotterill and Letherby wrote:

> Life histories in our view 'tell it like it is' from the lived experience of the narrator. They are invaluable because they do not fracture life experiences, but provide a means of evaluating the present, re-evaluating the past and anticipating the future.
>
> (Cotterill and Letherby, 1993)

Graham reminded us that narratives, stories told in the first person, have always had a place in the social construction of knowledge about the world. It is a popular tradition that stands in contrast with the more controlled process of structured survey research, where the position of women has been masked, invisible or rendered irrelevant by studies designed from a male perspective and man as the objective (Graham, 1984).

> It is through the telling of stories about ourselves and the events around us that we define reality, explain who we are to one another and set the stage for future action. As we listen to the stories others tell us we learn what is important to them, what they believe is memorable, who in their stories is what kind of person and what kind of values justify decisions and actions.
>
> (Smith, 1987)

A novel and innovative use of the narrative technique was used to uncover the values held by a range of workers and users of the NHS (Patton, 1999).

Over seven one-day workshops NHS managers, staff and users were asked to write down and then present a story that encapsulated an important aspect of their experience of the NHS. The time for each story varied, but ranged from 30 seconds to 10 minutes.

The analysis of the stories generated an interesting range of core values: mismatched expectations, disparity in care, working the system, abuse of power and being valued.

The issue of validity and reliability was not raised.

The practice

The methodology of narratives has been explained in terms of a qualitative in-depth reflective practice. To undertake a narrative project needs regular visits to the respondent. It requires more attention paid to developing rapport with the respondent over time, respect and understanding between responder and interviewer. Data recording can be by tape recording supported by manual note taking. The tapes would be transcribed and then submitted to analysis.

5.4.4 Interpretation and analysis

In the typical standard structured interviews the respondent becomes a 'repository of data' (Graham, 1984), while the power of interpretation and analysis remain with the analyst. A major difference in narrative analysis is that the respondent begins to make their own analysis of events and reasons. In theoretical or policy-directed studies the researcher may still retain the final interpretation in the light of wider knowledge of purpose. For example, in a study of elderly people in residential care the narrative might cover the events leading up to moving into the residential home, moving on to describe their experience of living in the home. An analytical framework might include criteria based in Critical Incident Technique (CIT) categories covering communication, listening behaviour, caring and sensitively giving information, facilities and actual treatment. Examples could then be presented as vignettes.

Analysis of narrative text draws on a hermeneutic framework (the science of interpretation). The first step is to read the text in its entirety. Next, read the text again looking for patterns and differences within the interview and across interviews if several have been held. For example, if the stories of several elderly residents have been told, it will be possible to identify key incidents or historical events which shaped their lives, their health or happiness in life. The key feature of analysis lies in discerning the construction of personal history that underlies a respondent's goals, and his or her interpretations of outcomes.

The analysis takes time, because it is a reflexive process whereby the researcher uses a framework of interpretation based on background knowledge, underlying assumptions, interests and objectives. This method is a prime example of the researcher as instrument where the ability to make insightful linkages between background knowledge and narrative text is permissible.

The final stage is to develop a broader understanding of the cultural, societal and or historical processes from one case to the general. To carry out a useful interpretation of textual data one device is to draw up a set of binary themes, e.g. in the example of elderly residents to identify themes such as:

- doing things for others versus doing for self
- being together with others versus being apart
- being appreciated versus not being appreciated
- being helpful versus not being helpful
- giving pleasure versus receiving pleasure

5.4.5 Bias, validity, reliability and ethical issues

The main criticism of anyone using the narrative method is that the work might be dismissed as subjective and largely intuitive – a creation that is artistic but not scientific – by those of a more positivist scientific background. One response to this assertion is to draw on Graham's argument, that interviewers can be too interventionist, structured interview schedules can produce brief, stilted and often unhelpful answers which fracture experiences. In narratives the emphasis is on the telling rather than the asking, guiding the plot but not necessarily imposing a framework.

So long as the listener understands that people never tell the whole story, they highlight specific characteristics which reflect back on their self – the self owns its own narrative, it is created and constantly re-created, constantly re-adapted over time and reformulated through ongoing experience, then validity and reliability are no greater problem than in survey methodology.

Advantages and disadvantages

ADVANTAGES

- participants give the evidence in their own voice in their own way
- written descriptions can be produced by a large number of people at the same time, e.g. class of children
- stories may allow you to examine change over time and across contexts, the study often gives more useful information than simply the sum of its parts
- participants often benefit personally from the self-reflection that accompanies the process.

DISADVANTAGES

- life histories can be presented for analysis as a vast amount of rambling data
- remembrance can colour the past (although this in itself may be useful). There are sometimes confidentiality problems which may prevent the use of data
- participants may find themselves revealing more than they might wish
- analysis of sequential events is difficult to do well
- the methodology can be dismissed as subjective, the data as anecdotal
- stories rely on good listening skills in a researcher
- analysis is dependent on researcher knowledge and abilities
- the process demands strong and trusting relationship between researcher and participants over time so that life can be reflected and slowly drawn out.

5.5 Summary

This chapter has described the theoretical techniques of observation, focus discussion groups and narrative. By drawing on examples from published research to show practical application of the techniques I have demonstrated the contribution that can be made to an understanding of the reality of people's lives. The main criticism of qualitative research methods is that they are subjective and therefore less scientific than the qualitative methods. By careful design and attention to issues of validity and reliability the researcher can demonstrate that such methods do produce valid insights into social, health and community care settings.

Discussion topics

- which research methods would be appropriate and possible to explore the daily life on a hospital ward or in a residential home?
- how would you demonstrate the generalizability of the findings?
- what ethical considerations would you need to take into account?

Further reading

Abbott, P. and Sapsford, R. (1994) 'Studying policy and practice: the use of vignettes', *Nurse Researcher* 1: 81–91.

Bowling, A. (1997) *Research Methods in Health. Investigating Health and Health Services*, Buckingham: Open University Press.

Greenhalgh, T. and Hurwitz, B. (1999) 'Narrative based medicine: why study narrative?', *BMJ* 318(7175): 48–50.

Luck, M., Lawrence, B., Pocock, R. and Reilly, K. (1988) *Consumer and Market Research in Health Care*, London: Chapman and Hall.

Mattingly, C. and Garro, L. (1994) 'Narrative representations of illness and healing', *Social Science and Medicine* 38(6): 771–774.

Riessman, C.K. (1993) *Narrative Analysis*, London: Sage.

Social Science and Medicine (1998) 'Narrative representations of illness and healing', [Special Issue], 38(6).

Chapter 6

Designing surveys

Mike Tricker and Julie Green

In this chapter the reader will develop an understanding of:

- the conceptual and practical strengths and weaknesses of alternative survey designs and survey techniques
- the practical skills which are involved in questionnaire design
- the problems and pitfalls which are likely to be encountered in survey designs and, more importantly, how to avoid them.

This understanding should not only help in designing more effective surveys, but also in critically assessing the tools and techniques used by other researchers. It will also highlight how these tools may constrain the interpretations which can be placed upon research results. The contents of this chapter reflect the authors' hard won practical experience in designing, managing, undertaking and analysing many large-scale surveys during the past twenty-five years as well as the experience of the case studies described in later chapters.

6.1 Introduction

As discussed in the previous chapters, before beginning a market research project a researcher needs to consider:

- what information already exists
- what additional information is likely to be required
- when this information is needed
- where, how and when to obtain it
- what factors will need to be controlled or held constant
- what measurement techniques should be used.

The practical experience described in the case study chapters in Part 3 also suggests that it is likely to save time and effort if provisional decisions are also made at this stage on:

- how the data are going to be processed for analysis (see Chapter 7)
- what methods of analysis are going to be used (see Chapter 9)
- who are the audience for the report (discussed in Chapter 4).

In practice therefore it will be important to consider each of these issues *before* making decisions about the nature and scope of data gathering.

Clearly, in most practical situations a researcher's control over the quality and relevance of data sources depends in large measure on the scale of the investigation and the resources available to complete it. If resources are limited it may be necessary to rely on secondary rather than primary sources. However, many research questions cannot be answered by data derived from secondary sources and will therefore require a specific purpose-designed primary survey. These are topics such as those relating to:

- individual opinions
- attitudes
- preferences
- motives governing behaviour
- measures of user satisfaction.

An additional reason for choosing survey approaches rather than relying on secondary data sources is that the research 'instruments' (interview schedules or questionnaires) can be designed to reflect the precise research objectives. Many secondary data sources, in contrast, will be collected for more general purposes and are likely to be several months or even years out of date.

Nevertheless, with so many public and private organizations using surveys as a means of gathering information there is clearly a danger of 'over researching' sections of the population and provoking a resistance amongst potential respondents. Surveys should therefore *only* be used to collect information which is *not* available in any other way.

6.2 Resource allocation

Having decided that a questionnaire survey *is* necessary, a balance has to be struck between:

- the need to obtain information of sufficient detail and precision to enable the research questions to be answered, and
- the resources available to collect the information.

In order to strike this balance, surveys will need to be carefully 'tailored' so that the research objectives can be achieved with the time and resources available. This usually involves estimating the time, staff and money which will need to be allocated to planning, collecting, processing and analysing the data (see Chapter 4).

In planning the allocation of available resources a researcher is faced with choices on:

- the range of topics to be included
- the amount of data on these topics to be collected
- the number of responses required
- where, when and how to obtain these responses
- the degree of precision required in the data.

Clearly, decisions on these issues can only be made by reference to the research objectives (see Chapters 3 and 4). Indeed, practical experience suggests that a lot of time and effort can be saved by starting at the end of the process and working backwards rather than starting at what appears at first sight to be the beginning. Ideally, this would involve trying to visualize the intended audience for the final report and the information which will need to be presented to them, and then working backwards through each of the research stages – checking all the time that what is planned will contribute to the achievement of the specific research objectives (Kotler and Andreasen, 1996).

6.3 Choice of survey methods

The case studies in Part 3 of this book illustrate that there is a wide choice of alternative survey methods. These include:

- structured versus semi-structured approaches
- self-completion versus interview methods, and
- face-to-face approaches versus 'distance' methods such as postal questionnaires, telephone interviews or Fax back surveys.

Factors which are likely to influence the choice of methods which are used in practice include:

- The nature of the target population
    - is it dispersed or localized?
    - are potential respondents young or old?
    - what are the literacy levels?
- The nature of the information required
    - is it sensitive or not?
    - is it interesting or dull?
- The issues being investigated
    - are they complex or simple?
    - are they sensitive?
    - are they likely to raise concerns about confidentiality?
- The overall length and complexity of the final questionnaire
    - will respondents' interest be sustained through to completion? or,
    - is their interest likely to flag?
- Access to financial and other resources including
    - availability of trained interviewers, and
    - access to potential respondents.
- Time constraints:
    - is speed of completion of the report a crucial concern?

Given the resource constraints, the nature of the target population which is being investigated and the complexity of the issues which are being explored, the aim is clearly to select a method which is likely to provide data of an acceptable quality from a high proportion of respondents within the time and resource constraints.

In most situations the major choice will be between face-to-face interviews and 'distance' methods (see Table 6.1). These alternatives are discussed in later sections.

Table 6.1 Factors influencing the choice of survey methods

	Face-to-face interview	Telephone interview	Mailed questionnaire	Focus group
Level of information				
Descriptive	Yes	Yes	Yes	No
Explanatory	Yes	Yes	No	Yes
Type of questions				
Behaviour	Yes	Possible	No	No
Attitude	Yes	Possible	Possible	Yes
Knowledge	Yes	Yes	Yes	No
Type of information				
Sensitive/personal	Yes	Yes	No	No
Sequence of questions				
Simple	Yes	Yes	Yes	Yes
Complex	Yes	Yes	No	No
Duration				
Under 20 minutes	Yes	Yes	Yes	No
Over 20 minutes	Yes	No	No	Yes
Number of questions				
Less than fifty	Yes	Yes	Yes	Yes
Over fifty	Possibly	No	No	No
Speed of response				
Short time-scale	Yes	Yes	No	Yes
Longer time-scale	Yes	Yes	Yes	Yes

In practice, face-to-face interviewing by trained specialist staff is likely to be the most expensive approach but it may be essential where:

- the population a researcher is interested in is not experienced in filling in 'forms', or
- information being sought is complicated or 'sensitive', or
- questions are inevitably 'open ended' rather than 'closed', or
- responses are required from a representative sample of the target population within a short time-scale.

6.4 Methods of data collection

6.4.1 Interview-based surveys

Experience suggests that successful use of interview-based questionnaires depends on establishing a 'rapport' with the respondent. How easy it is to establish and maintain this rapport will depend on a number of factors including:

- the respondent's interest in the subject of the survey
- the context in which the interview is being carried out, and
- the skill with which an interview is carried out.

It follows that one of the most important parts of interviewer training and briefing will therefore be aimed at developing effective ways of:

- *engaging* a respondent's interest and attention
- creating and *sustaining* a 'rapport', and
- leaving a respondent feeling that something worthwhile has been achieved by *disengaging* effectively.

In order to achieve this, interviewers need to be relaxed and fluent and be able to find their way around the questionnaire or schedule of questions easily and confidently – this in turn will help to inspire confidence amongst respondents. While these aspects are partly a matter of training and practical 'hands on' experience, careful attention to the detailed design and layout of the questionnaire to ensure that it 'flows' is likely to be crucially important in achieving these objectives.

6.4.2 Exploratory interviews

In addition to their use for the main survey itself, interviews may also be used:

- as a complement to qualitative methods (see Chapter 5) to explore issues and firm up ideas/research questions which will influence the survey design, and
- as part of the 'pilot testing' of the methods which it is intended will be used in the main survey.

Both these stages may be critical to the success of the whole research project and so it is usually preferable that these should be carried out by the principal researchers themselves rather than delegated to someone outside the core team. Some of the most experienced and respected market researchers (such as Robert Worcester of MORI) believe that it is vital for the principal researchers to witness at first hand the full range of a respondent's reactions to questions in order to make effective judgements about whether these questions are working or not (Worcester, 1995).

Arguments which are often cited in favour of using interview-based approaches rather than postal questionnaire surveys include:

- the possibility of getting higher response rates
- the 'richness' of the data obtained, and
- the possibility of using 'probes' and 'prompts' to elicit a fuller response.

These are powerful arguments, since *how* something is said may be just as indicative of a respondent's attitudes, opinions or beliefs as *what* their formal response was. However, interviewers will need to be trained carefully in the appropriate use of probes and prompts in order to ensure that a spurious variability is not introduced into the data as a result of the different approaches adopted by individual interviewers.

6.4.3 Postal questionnaire surveys

In private sector market research, postal questionnaires often produce very low response rates, but this need not necessarily be the case. Thus, the survey of users of Family Planning Services described in Chapter 15 produced a response rate of 60 per cent. Experience also suggests that even higher responses can be achieved by:

- paying careful attention to the 'marketing' of the survey
- preparing the ground carefully
- paying careful attention to presentation of the questionnaire
- tapping into the factors which are likely to motivate respondents to participate
- providing a 'help line' facility so that potential respondents can clarify areas of uncertainty
- using postal reminders a short while before and after the suggested return date
- using telephone 'chasing' to boost responses in under-represented categories of responses, and
- making the return arrangements as user friendly as possible.

One of the ways in which barriers to returns can be minimized is to provide Freepost envelopes. The cost per returned questionnaire will be higher than if postage stamps had been attached, but this is usually more than compensated by the fact that the researcher will only have to meet the postage costs of the questionnaires which are returned.

An important part of the wider marketing of a postal questionnaire survey will be the attention which is paid to the languages used by the target population. This is likely to be particularly important where the researchers are likely to be seen as 'outsiders', and where the survival of community languages is an important issue.

Example: The importance of taking account of language

In a survey designed to assess the effectiveness of a support service provided to community groups in Wales, potential respondents were sent two questionnaires – one in Welsh and one in English. A bilingual telephone 'help line' was also provided. These steps helped in producing a very high response rate and produced several spontaneous compliments from Welsh-speaking respondents, some of whom even completed the English version of the questionnaire in order to make things easier for the English researchers!

(Millward et al., 1995)

6.4.4 Telephone interview surveys

Experience suggests that telephone interviewing methods offer the possibility of retaining many of the advantages associated with face-to-face interviewing whilst gaining other distinctive strengths (Lavrakas, 1993). In particular, interviews can be conducted quickly, easily and cost-effectively over a wide geographical area. They are also likely to be extremely useful where 'fear of opening doors' is an issue, such as in some inner city areas and where old people are concerned.

In recent years, UK household telephone ownership rates have increased dramatically and have reached levels comparable to the USA. As a result, an estimated 93 per cent of private households and 95 per cent of those living in them are contactable by telephone at home (Office of National Statistics, 1995; Noble *et al.*, 1998).

One of the most important advantages of telephone surveys is that close supervision can be maintained on the interviewers to ensure uniformity of approach and high standards of interviewing. Thus, rigorous quality control can be ensured over the entire process – including sampling, respondent selection, interviewing, questionnaire completion, coding and data entry. Another advantage is that the responses can be keyed directly into a computer with the screen in front of the interviewer thus saving on data input, increasing accuracy and speeding up the analysis and delivery of results (see Chapter 7).

A number of studies have been carried out which have compared the response rates achieved by telephone and face-to-face interviewing approaches. One of these which was specifically designed to test the feasibility of using telephone interviews in carrying out surveys of social attitudes, found that:

- the overall response rate for telephone interviews was about 7 per cent less than for face-to-face interviews, and
- the response rate to 40-minute interviews was lower than for 20-minute interviews (Sykes and Hoinville, 1985).

In this study, few differences were found in the answers obtained from face-to-face and telephone interviews – even for potentially sensitive questions. However, other studies (e.g. Frey, 1989) have found a higher rate of non-response to sensitive questions. This has been explained by the anonymity of telephone interviews discouraging respondents from relaxing and opening up.

In 1995 the Survey Methods Centre of SCPR carried out a review for the Health Education Authority (HEA) which was designed to assess the feasibility of using telephone interviewing methods for some of their routine surveys (Purdon and Thomas, 1995). This concluded that, provided satisfactory solutions to certain problems were found, then the HEA would gain significant advantages by using telephone interviewing methods. Three particular problems were identified:

1   The difficulties in drawing unbiased probability samples from the population comprising the residents of all telephone-owning private households.
2   Non-response bias (Collins *et al.*, 1988).
3   Difficulties in weighting the survey data to give estimates for total household population.

However, the study showed that re-weighting of data obtained from telephone surveys to give accurate estimates for the whole population is now relatively easy and that non-response bias and 'mode' effects can also be minimized by the application of methods already available to researchers. The final problem of drawing probability random samples of telephones has proved more awkward until fairly recently.

The usual sampling frames for many telephone surveys are the printed or computerized directories. These sources suffer from a number of disadvantages – not least because they can be out of date and incomplete because of unlisted 'ex-directory' numbers. In 1996, according to British Telecom, the proportion of numbers not listed was around 36 per cent in Great Britain as a whole, but was as high as 50 per cent in major cities. If these unlisted numbers were randomly distributed, it would still be possible to draw an unbiased sample from the directories, but this is clearly not the case, since such ex-directory numbers are more likely to be those of younger females resident in urban areas (Thomas, 1991).

A technique known as Random Digit Dialling (RDD) tries to solve the problem of unlisted numbers by using a two-stage random dialling method. This sampling technique, which is used extensively in the USA, is relatively new in the UK, where its application has been inhibited in the past by the variability in the length of telephone numbers, codes and prefixes, and by British Telecom's view that it should act as gatekeeper to defend the privacy of the increasing proportion of ex-directory subscribers.

The problems of the numbering system have recently decreased, as the system has moved towards a standardized number for all subscribers (only 2 per cent of private households in Britain now have non-standard numbers) and a number of experiments have been carried out to test ways of implementing satisfactory RDD systems in the UK (Noble *et al.*, 1998).

Methods for recording responses to telephone interviews

Many telephone surveys still use pencil and paper methods to record responses and this is likely to be perfectly adequate for a small survey where resources are limited. Interviews may be conducted by the interviewers either from the survey base or from their own homes with them being reimbursed for their time and telephone calls.

However, large-scale formal surveys are more typically conducted from centralized call stations which have special computer-assisted telephone interviewing (CATI) equipment for managing and recording interviews. With this system, the interviewer sits at a computer workstation that controls the administration of the questionnaire and may also control the sampling process. CATI systems can prompt interviewers with introductory spiels and selection procedures and can also have the 'skips' and 'filters' programmed into them. The responses are entered directly by the interviewers into computer-readable data files.

A major advantage of CATI systems, compared with face-to-face individual interviews, is that they offer more effective quality control (see Box). Immediate guidance and feedback can be given by a supervisor to the interviewers and the supervisor can monitor an interview as it is being conducted – as long as the interviewer has the agreement of the respondent for another person to listen in. Overall, therefore there should be fewer problems of interviewer error.

The advantages of CATI

- improved data quality
- fewer problems of interviewer error
- the flow of questions is directed (i.e. if a given response elicits a skip to another question, then the computer goes directly to the next relevant question)
- data can be processed and analysed almost immediately.

The major disadvantage of this approach is that it requires a large amount of investment in hardware and programming before the commencement of a survey. However, installations are now standard equipment in most major market research companies.

6.4.5 Other approaches

Various forms of interviewerless interviews have been conducted for a number of years. In such approaches a recorded voice asks respondents to answer questions by pressing numbers on the key pad of their telephones. The information obtained is downloaded directly and analysed by computers. Responses to open-ended questions can also be recorded on to audio tape and listened to by the researchers.

Automatic speech recognition (ASR) approaches have also been piloted in market research applications (Syedain, 1994). The potential benefits of such techniques could be far reaching in that large telephone surveys could be completed at very short notice, and it would no longer be necessary to engage a large force of human operators.

Current and emerging technologies such as videophones and the availability of video over the internet and via digital TV services, will give new opportunities for remote 'face-to-face' interviewing. With this equipment the interviewee will be able to see the interviewer and will also be able to see the interviewer's visual surroundings. There may therefore be a convergence of distance and face-to-face approaches. These approaches will, however, need to be used carefully in order to ensure that new forms of bias are not introduced – not least because of systematic variations in the rate at which such technology is adopted.

6.5 Designing questionnaires and interview schedules

6.5.1 The design process

The experience of the case studies in this book indicates that the successful design of effective questionnaires depends on a combination of skill, experience and common sense. In particular, our experience indicates some broad rules apply:

- a 'good' questionnaire will be designed and tailored specifically to suit the study's aims and the nature of the potential respondents
- the construction and design will need to be clear and unambiguous
- questions should be as few in number, as briefly worded, and as unambiguous as possible
- the design should be such that it will minimize the risk of errors arising from misunderstanding or uncertainty on the part of respondents or interviewers or those responsible for coding and preparing information for analysis.

Finally, since participation in a survey will usually be voluntary, questionnaires and the contacts with potential respondents need to be designed in such a way that they will encourage respondents to co-operate and enable accurate and reliable responses to be obtained. In effect, this involves a fairly straightforward 'selling job' in which the perceived relevance of the survey to the potential respondents will be of critical importance. Successful performance of this selling job will involve explaining in a succinct and easily understood way:

- the purpose of the survey
- how it is proposed to use the information gathered
- how the particular respondent came to be selected, and
- why it is important that they should take part in the survey.

In customer care terms, the implications of this are that researchers need to pay very careful attention to every aspect of their 'encounters' with potential respondents at every stage of the 'perceived transaction period' – from the initial approaches to the 'disengagement' and the numerous 'moments of truth' in between (Norman, 1991). The overall aim at each of these stages is to present a positive image of the researcher and the organization he/she represents or is associated with, as well as the survey itself.

6.5.2 Stages in the design process

The process of designing and drafting questionnaires can be broken down into a number of discrete stages:

1 Identify broad coverage and general content. This will usually be indicated by the statement of the research problem itself and, where applicable, by the research hypotheses.
2 Identify specific information required – including information needed to classify respondents, and to identify and control for possible intervening variables (such as gender, age, income, ethnicity), which might obscure a direct relationship between the factors on which the research is intended to focus.
3 Decide on the sequence of questions required to provide each item of information. Drawing up a flow chart like that in Figure 6.1 may be useful here. The aim is usually to get as close as possible to a fairly natural conversational 'flow' in which topics follow on in a logical manner. Experience suggests that if this is achieved the respondent is likely to feel more at ease.
4 List possible/desired categories of responses/answers. Again, this will require reference back to the research objectives and projection forwards to the types of analysis which it is intended to carry out in order to achieve these objectives.
5 Add instructions for interviewers/respondents (e.g. 'skips', filters and recording instructions).
6 Carry out 'pilot' testing in conditions which are as close as possible to those likely to be encountered in the main survey.
7 Review the experience of the pilot test in order to identify aspects which did not work satisfactorily.
8 Refine the design to correct for these weaknesses and to plug gaps.
9 Carry out further pilot testing if this is considered necessary.

6.5.3 Useful pointers

Experience suggests there are no fixed rules for the design of effective questionnaires. In practice, as discussed in Chapter 4, developing most questionnaires involves the adaptation of approaches which have been found to work in other contexts. For example, the survey of service users described in Chapter 11 relied on a questionnaire which had been designed and

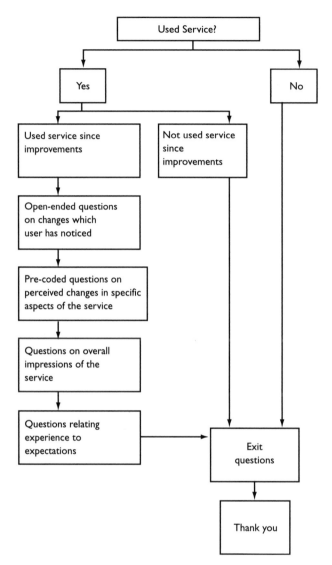

Figure 6.1 Flow chart sequence of questions.

piloted in a similar project in another area and was adapted to reflect the particular circum-stances of this study. Experience suggests however, a number of basic 'pointers' which are worth bearing in mind:

1   The *flow*, *structure* and overall *length* of the questionnaire should be such that it is capable of engaging and keeping the respondent's interest and attention.
2   The first few questions set the *tone* of the questionnaire/interview and therefore should, as far as possible, be:
    •   directly relevant to all potential respondents
    •   interesting

- short
- non-controversial, and
- easy to answer.

In this context it is worth bearing in mind the adage which is sometimes used in customer care training programmes: *You never get a second chance to make a first impression.*

3   Longer, more complex questions (such as those designed to gauge attitudes towards different aspects of the issues under study) generally work best if they are spread throughout the questionnaire.

4   Sensitive or personal questions are likely to provoke less resistance if they are located towards the end of the questionnaire, and the reasons for asking them are explained.

5   The layout of the questionnaire should be such that it:
- facilitates the interview and recording process (i.e. permits fluent questioning and allows speedy and accurate recording of responses)
- sets out clearly coding procedures
- facilitates direct data entry from the questionnaire.

A well-designed layout will minimize the risk of errors occurring at each of these stages.

6   'Filters' or 'skips' should be used to clearly indicate which sections of the questionnaire are to be answered by a particular respondent (again, flow charts may be useful here in planning and checking the routing). Experience also suggests that putting filter instructions alongside the boxes or spaces in which answers are recorded can help to make a significant saving in time. In self-completion questionnaires, visual (rather than verbal) skip instructions can also add interest and variety and help to sustain the interest of respondents (see Figure 6.2).

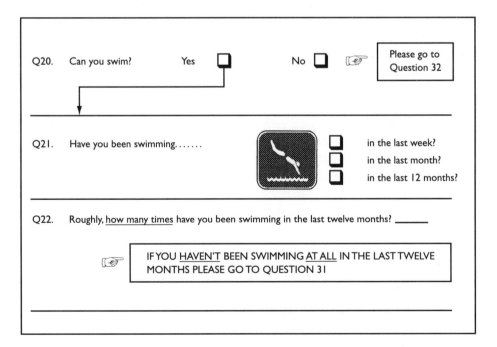

Figure 6.2 Example of use of a verbal and visual skip and a filter.

A clear and consistent layout is likely to be crucial in ensuring that interviewers and respondents adopt a consistent approach to asking questions and recording responses. Experience also suggests this will help to inspire confidence amongst respondents – which is vital if they are to take a survey seriously.

6.5.4 Common problems and pitfalls (and how to avoid them)

The experience of the case studies in this book indicates that no questionnaire design is ever 'right' or 'wrong'. However, there are several common problems which can be avoided by careful planning and attention to detail.

1   *Layout* – one of the mistakes which is sometimes made is to attempt to cram questions into the minimum number of pages in the belief that questionnaires which are only a few pages long are somehow more likely to achieve a better response. Experience suggests this is likely to prove to be a false economy. One of the basic rules of effective graphic design is that a design should be able to 'breathe' if the viewer is to absorb the 'message'. Our experience suggests that the same is true of questionnaires and that it is therefore important, if at all possible, to allow plenty of space around and between questions.
2   *Sensitivity* – particularly sensitive areas will need careful handling in order to obtain frank and honest answers. For example, a series of indirect questions may need to be used where a direct question is unlikely to prompt an honest response (see Box below).

Overcoming problems of sensitivity

Hoinville and Jowell (1978) draw upon a classic paper entitled 'Asking the embarrassing question' published by Barton in 1958 to illustrate a number of established techniques for eliciting sensitive information. In this paper Barton took as his example the extremely delicate issue of whether a respondent has murdered his wife.

First, he says, there is the *casual approach*: 'Do you happen to have murdered your wife?'

Second, there is the *numbered card approach*: 'Will you please read off the number of the card which corresponds with what became of your wife?'

Third, comes the *everybody approach*: 'As you know, many people have been killing their wives these days. Do you happen to have killed yours?'

Finally, there is the *other people approach*: 'Do you know any people who have murdered their wives?' (pause for reply and then ask) 'How about yourself?'

Clearly, today this example appears facetious and sexist, but it does serve to illustrate the point that if a question cannot be asked directly then there is a wide range of indirect questions which could be asked and which are arguably more likely to elicit honest and frank responses.

(Adapted from Hoinville and Jowell, 1978, pp. 31–32)

---

3   *Retrospective and prospective questions* – collecting information on past events and patterns of behaviour often depends on the ability of respondents to remember and describe the details accurately. In practice, respondents may be unable to recall the circumstances of mundane issues and, as a result, there is a risk that they may omit or distort details. Reliable attitude measurements are particularly difficult to obtain when the subject concerns past events. Similar problems are likely to be encountered with questions which ask respondents to forecast their future behaviour or feelings, and in this context 'Diary' approaches, of the kind which are often used in travel and expenditure surveys, are likely to provide more reliable data.

4   *'Leading' questions* – practical experience indicates that there is a natural tendency for respondents to give the answer they think the interviewer or survey designer would like to hear (see Chapter 14 for a powerful illustration of this tendency). The effects of this tendency may be minimized by careful attention to the 'balance' of a question (Figure 6.3); by use of indirect questions and by preceding questions which are the focus of interest by a series of more general questions.

A question which is likely to lead towards a positive view:				
7. Do you like this service?	Yes ☐	No ☐	Don't know ☐	Prefer not to say ☐
A more balanced question:				
7. Do you like or dislike this service?	Like ☐	Dislike ☐	Don't know ☐	Prefer not to say ☐

Figure 6.3 Examples of leading questions.

Examination of questions used in many surveys will reveal some that are either blatantly or subtly leading. In auditing the findings of other people's surveys it is important therefore to consider the extent to which the balance of responses reported may be a function of the wording of the questions asked.

5   *'Catch all' questions* – over-long and complex questions which attempt to cover several issues or which contain complex language or 'jargon' are unlikely to provide reliable information (Figure 6.4). Clearly the bundle of issues which such questions refer to need to be 'unpacked' and a series of questions relating to these individual aspects need to be asked.

9. Would you agree that the staffing configuration of this hospital is conducive to optimal patient throughput?	Yes ☐	No ☐

Note: this question is also blatantly leading

Figure 6.4 Example of a 'catch-all' question.

6   *'Double-barrelled'* questions – will also lead to ambiguous answers which are open to mis-interpretation (see Example below).

Example: The problems in interpreting responses to 'double-barrelled' questions

During 1993 and 1994 a series of surveys were carried out for the Local Government Commission in the non-metropolitan counties in England in order to identify local people's preferences for alternative structures of local government. Amongst the options under consideration was the transfer of responsibility for personal social services from the county authorities to smaller unitary district authorities.

Amongst the questions asked was one which invited respondents to indicate which of the following factors they felt should be most important in deciding the local government structure in their area:

Ease of contacting the Council	1
Accountability	2
Historical or traditional boundaries	3
Cost and quality of services	4
Level of information about the Council and its services	5
Access to Local Councillors	6
Responding to local people's wishes	7
Sense of local community	8
Size of population covered	9
Access to the Council	0
Other	X

....

Don't know/no opinion   Y

In the first few surveys by far the most common response was for respondents to select the criteria 'Cost and quality of services' as their first choice. The interpretation placed on this by the Commission in some of its reports was that most people wanted 'low cost services'.

When it was pointed out that this was in fact a 'double-barrelled' question and therefore this interpretation was not sound, the questionnaire was revised and some surveys were repeated. In subsequent surveys these two criteria were uncoupled and the results indicated that in fact the number of respondents selecting 'quality of services' was far greater than those who selected 'cost of services'.

(Tricker, 1994)

7   *Interviewer and respondent 'bias'* – unless a clear, consistent layout and design is adopted, interviewers and/or respondents will tend to adopt their own interpretations and procedures which may lead to inconsistent responses and inaccurate recording of information.

8   *Ambiguity* – clearly, many words have a range of alternative meanings (Figure 6.5). It is important therefore to ensure that the specific meaning which a researcher wishes to attach is clear from the phraseology of the question itself.

Questions	Potential responses
Q9 When did you last see your dentist?	Respondent 1 'I had a check-up a month ago' Respondent 2 'In the supermarket last week'
Q10 What will be the length of your residence in Australia?	Respondent 1 'Two years' Respondent 2 '10 metres'

Figure 6.5 Examples of potential responses to ambiguous questions.

6.6 Building in quality assurance and quality control procedures

There are several procedures which can be built into each of the stages of a survey which can help to improve the reliability and validity of the data obtained. These include:

- pre-tests of the questionnaire itself
- pilot testing of the questionnaire and the proposed survey procedures
- selecting, training and briefing the interview team
- monitoring responses during the survey itself
- a range of checks built into the analysis stage.

6.6.1 Pre-tests of a questionnaire design

A simple checklist which has proved useful in 'auditing' a questionnaire design is included in the Box below.

A checklist for assessing questionnaire contents

- *Relevance* – Will the questions provide the data which is relevant to the research problem and will this data enable the research objectives to be met? (The researcher needs to avoid the danger of being 'seduced' into including interesting but essentially irrelevant questions.)

- *Comprehensibility* – Will questions be understood and meaningful to the respondents who are being contacted and are they phrased in an appropriate manner? Is the wording ambiguous?
- *Appropriateness* – Will questions provide data in a form which is suitable for the particular form of data analysis which is required? (If a researcher plans to use techniques which require interval scaled data it won't be appropriate to collect nominal or ordinal scaled data or vice-versa.)
- *Comprehensiveness* – Does the range of questions adequately cover all the various aspects of the research problem? Is anything important missed out? Will they provide all the necessary data in the appropriate degree of detail? Are the relevant classificatory variables and those needed to enable the data to be disaggregated or stratified (e.g. by type of respondent, location etc.) included?
- *Feasibility* – Is the questionnaire too long or too complex? Will it be feasible to obtain all the necessary answers?
- *Completion and return arrangements* – For self-completion questionnaires, are the return arrangements clear and as painless as they can be? Have all the potential obstacles to completion and return been removed or minimized?

The simple process of reading questions aloud can also be very helpful in identifying problems such as over-long or clumsily worded questions.

Before proceeding to pilot testing it can often be useful to simulate a number of interviews. This might involve members of the design and/or interviewing team role playing different types of respondents in a range of different interview situations. This process can be useful not only in identifying faults in the design but can also form a valuable part of the briefing and training for the survey team.

6.6.2 *Pilot testing*

The pilot test should ideally aim to test out every aspect of the survey including:

- sampling procedures
- initial approaches to potential respondents
- the questionnaire itself
- quality control and monitoring arrangements
- the coding frame for responses to open-ended questions, and
- analysis procedures.

The scale of the pilot test will depend on its primary purpose. If it is primarily aimed at testing the questionnaire design and the survey arrangements then a relatively small sample (30–60) will usually be sufficient (see Example below). If it is also intended as a means of identifying categories for pre-codes for the questions to be used in the main survey, then it may be necessary to increase the size of the sample.

Example: Procedures adopted for testing a questionnaire design

In the survey of users' views on the quality of service provided by the Toxicology Laboratory described in Chapter 16, the draft questionnaire was tested out on staff from the Toxicology Department and the Trust's Clinical Audit Department as well as being piloted with internal customers within the Trust. These tests produced a large number of recommendations for improvement – including a reduction in length, simplification of the instructions and adjustments to the phraseology of questions.

(Source: Chapter 16)

The review of a pilot test will need to include consideration of:

- The response rate – both
  - overall, and
  - within specific categories or 'strata'.
- Responses to individual questions in order to assess
  - whether these appear to have been understood
  - whether they have been answered as intended
  - whether the responses make sense in terms of the survey objectives
  - whether pre-coded categories are adequate or whether there is a need to increase or reduce these, and
  - whether sufficient space has been allowed for recording responses to open-ended questions.

If the changes made as a result of the pilot test are substantial, a further pilot test should be carried out before proceeding with the main survey.

6.6.3 Selecting interviewers

It is a mistake to assume that the results of any survey are ever entirely free from bias. Experience suggests the perceived purpose of the survey, the personal characteristics of individual interviewers and the reputations of the organizations commissioning and undertaking the survey will all exert some influence on the pattern of responses. In some cases this effect may be substantial. Thus, one survey of sexual harassment at work found that men who were interviewed by male interviewers were twice as likely to report that they had sexually harassed someone at work compared with those who were interviewed by female interviewers (Lavrakas, 1992). Moreover, experience indicates that it will often be far easier for certain kinds of interviewers to secure interviews with particular categories of respondents. For example, female interviewers are likely to find it easier to interview Moslem women than male interviewers. It will be important, therefore, to consider these possible effects when recruiting an interviewing team and to match the personal characteristics of interviewers and their language skills to those of potential respondents in order to achieve a satisfactory response and obtain reliable data.

6.6.4 Training interviewers

Although many of the instructions given to interviewers are likely to be very similar from survey to survey, details and the context will vary. Most surveys will therefore require the development of a project-specific training manual. Some of the items which will need to be covered are summarized in the Box below.

Items which may need to be covered in interviewer training and briefing

- confidentiality agreement – a written agreement for interviewer to agree and sign
- notes on the reasons for the survey, sampling procedures, scope and coverage etc.
- copies of introductory letters sent to potential respondents
- notes on how the survey is to be monitored
- notes on procedures for completion of call sheets (see Figure 6.6)
- instructions on reading questions, as worded (standardization)
- style and manner – need to speak in a clear and pleasant manner even when refused
- notes on the importance of following skips on the questionnaire
- explanation of the use of prompts, if used
- guidelines on probing for answers, keeping probes neutral and avoiding leading respondents etc.
- procedures for introducing the survey using a set introduction
- advice/guidance on how to handle 'gatekeepers' – such as receptionists, secretaries, personal assistants etc.
- set answers to common queries, such as:
    - what is the purpose of the survey?
    - who is paying for it?
    - how much is it costing?
    - who do you work for?
    - what are you selling?
    - how did you get my telephone number/address?
    - how do I know you are authentic?
- guidelines on appropriate responses to shows of reluctance from respondents
- testing procedures – (pre-pilot) dry run, trial interviews etc.
- piloting procedures
- refusal training
- organizing work/shifts
- payment arrangements/employees' information etc.

TELEPHONE CALL SHEET

NAME OF SURVEY

Organization (if appropriate): ....   Interview No: ....

Contact Name(s): ....   Tel. No: ....

....   Tel. No: ....

Attempts	Date	Time	Outcome (contact name, ring back etc.)	Interviewer
1				
2				
3				
4				
5				

Additional information:

Response:

Completed	☐		Answer machine	☐
Refused	☐		Call back	☐
Engaged	☐		Language barrier	☐
Number unobtainable	☐			
			etc., etc.	

Figure 6.6 Example of a telephone call sheet.

Some of the case studies described in subsequent chapters have attempted to recruit and train local residents to carry out some of the interviewing work (see Chapters 12 and 17). These efforts have often been part of a deliberate strategy aimed at building skills and capacity within the local community and ensuring that part of the research funding is channelled back into the local economy. In some situations, however, it will be important to weigh the benefits against the risk of reducing the apparent 'objectivity' of the research in the eyes of key stakeholders.

6.6.5 The role of the supervisors

Training alone will not ensure maintenance of high-quality interviewing. Supervisors can help to enhance interviewer performance by:

- providing advice on interviewing techniques
- listening in to a selection of interviews
- distributing interview/call sheets
- providing general feedback
- checking completed questionnaires
- monitoring a proportion of completed interviews – including checking with a sample of respondents that they did complete an interview for that particular survey and that the interviewer did adhere to the guidelines and code of practice (see Figure 4.2 for an example of where this went wrong)
- checking response rates
- maintaining energy, morale and enthusiasm amongst the interview team.

6.6.6 Monitoring responses

While a survey is in progress, response rates and the nature of responses will need to be examined both overall and for specific groups and strata within the population. If certain groups or categories are under-represented then steps may need to be taken to boost the response rate and/or to increase the size of the sample within these categories, and/or to weight the responses accordingly at the analysis stage.

In this context, telephone interviewing has a big advantage over other modes since the survey processes and the processing of the survey data are centralized. As a result, data collection processes can be closely monitored and controlled and consistently high-quality data can be produced.

In a typical telephone interview survey, the telephone call sheet is an essential quality assurance instrument. This is designed to provide a record of every attempt to contact individual respondents as well as the final outcome. In this way a 'history' of each telephone number can be built up which, for example, can identify the times of day when there has been no response, or an answer machine has been switched on (see Figure 6.6). Even if a researcher is conducting a small telephone survey personally it is still advisable to use a telephone call sheet as it is so easy to forget the outcome of calls made a few days previously.

In larger surveys, experience suggests that interviewers should be given a relatively small number of telephone call sheets at the start of each session/shift and that further sheets should be released only as needed in order to minimize the risk of systematic non-response bias. Experience indicates that respondents who are harder to contact in a survey of the general population are more likely to be younger and male, while those who are easier to contact are likely to be older and female. This means that there is a constant risk of compromising the ability to make reliable generalizations from the achieved sample unless systematic attempts are made to contact respondents at different times of the day and different days of the week. At the end of a session or before the beginning of the next session, the supervisor will need to monitor the responses achieved – both overall and for individual interviewers.

CATI systems can also control the monitoring of the sample as there is an on-screen facility equivalent to a call sheet built into most systems.

Comments made on the telephone call sheet are likely to be useful, not only for the supervisor who sorts the sheets, but also for other interviewers who may subsequently have to call that number. A decision needs to be made on how many rings the interviewer allows before hanging up. If dialled a number of times previously, it may be appropriate to let the telephone ring for longer. The call sheet is only attached to the relevant questionnaire after the interview has been completed.

6.6.7 Follow-up interviews

In Britain, commercial market research companies carrying out face-to-face interview surveys are required by the Market Research Society code of practice to carry out follow-up interviews with a small proportion (generally one in ten) of respondents. These follow-up interviews are designed to establish, first that the respondent was in fact interviewed, and second that the proper procedures were adhered to. For this reason, such follow-up interviews are often presented to respondents as customer care surveys.

6.6.8 Building checks into the analysis stage

As part of the ongoing analysis of survey results it can also be useful to compare the results obtained by different interviewers for key variables. If all members of the interviewing team are using a standardized approach and there is no interviewer bias there ought to be no significant differences in the patterns of responses obtained by different interviewers.

6.7 Conclusions

The case studies included in this book illustrate the fact that there are no rigid rules for designing a questionnaire-based survey. Questionnaire design is in essence a 'craft' and the skills involved will be refined by practice and experience. Experience suggests, therefore, that often the most practical way to proceed is to explore and test alternative approaches or to adapt approaches which have been found to work in comparable contexts. In the course of their initial literature searches and preliminary enquiries researchers may, therefore, wish to search for and obtain copies of the questionnaires and interview schedules which other researchers have used. However, it is vital that the design process is approached in a self-critical manner. This requires sensitivity to the situation of the potential respondents and, above all else, a generous measure of common sense.

Chapter 7

Data preparation

Rob Tinsley and Julie Green

In this chapter the reader will develop an understanding of:

- what is involved in data preparation
- what factors should be considered in designing a data preparation system
- what software tools are available to assist the researcher
- which tools are best suited to particular purposes.

7.1 Introduction

Instead of viewing data preparation as a necessary evil – an obscure, inconvenient activity carried out by anyone with the necessary keyboard skills, we can now see it in its proper position – as the second most important activity in any research programme. Swift (1996) observes that data are 'constructed by researchers' rather than being 'found in the world' (p. 153). An important stage in this process of construction is coding and keying in of data. Getting data preparation right cannot add anything in terms of realism, but getting it wrong undermines the quality of the whole enterprise.

In this book the necessity for an integrated approach to market research has been given prominence (see Chapter 4, Figure 4.1). Data preparation should not be overlooked in this context. We think that the staff who will be responsible for data preparation should be encouraged to become personally involved in the planning and design of the research at an early stage. Later on we will see what can happen when data is simply handed over to a data processing manager or (worse) data processing personnel who have no previous concern in the project.

It is ironic that new developments in data processing software (such as all-in-one packages) may well achieve the objective of seamless integration of the data preparation function yet, we suspect, may at the same time encourage further downgrading of its status. The danger is that such tools make data preparation appear 'transparent' to those who commission research and who may not be aware of the assumptions being made and their implications for data quality.

This chapter provides a brief synopsis of an enormous subject but will, we hope, give the reader some idea of the fascinating range of possibilities.

For the purposes of this chapter we use the term 'data preparation' to mean *the process of converting data into a format in which it can be read by a computer*. In social sciences this usually means numeric or text types of data. We include any data transformation (coding) that may be necessary prior to the actual digitization process (keying-in).

7.2 What factors should be considered?

The following questions will need to be resolved:

- what can be afforded?
- which data need to be entered?
- is ethics an issue?
- what form should each variable take?
- what coding is required to achieve this?
- who should enter the data?
- when and where should this be done?
- what checks are necessary?
- who will correct the errors?

Let us consider these questions one at a time.

7.2.1 Can we afford it?

Some researchers have plenty of time and are generously funded for the size and complexity of their task. But the rest of us are usually trying to meet tight deadlines within limited budgets. Careful planning is needed to identify the resources required and the costs incurred by various activities. It is important not to forget to include both fixed and variable costs. Draw up a plan, although you will not necessarily be able to stick to it but it might help. Apply this process to both time and money constraints (see Figure 4.3 for a GANTT chart with costs associated).

In the UK a data manager's time probably costs about £20 an hour (do not forget to include time spent at meetings, training and supervising others, coding etc.). Coding and data preparation staff probably cost between £5 and £10 per hour. Commercial quotes for data entry alone (keying-in) are based on the total number of keystrokes required to enter all the data. A skilled operator makes up to 2000 keystrokes per hour. Suitable software for data entry may already be available within your organization. Costs range from £20 for a simple spreadsheet to £2000 for sophisticated optical mark reading (OMR) tools.

7.2.2 Which data need to be entered?

For almost all projects some use of a computer will be required. Having made this decision the temptation may well be to enter everything on to the computer but this will almost certainly incur unnecessary costs. It is more sensible to limit what is entered to what is actually needed. Kotler and Andreasen (1996) suggest that the most efficient way is to work backwards from the reporting stage, never doing more than is necessary to produce the required output. It is our experience and that of the case studies in this book that many stakeholder groups will more readily accept conclusions and reports based on simple analytical techniques such as cross-tabulation illustrated by bar charts and seem unimpressed by multiple regressions and other more complicated techniques.

This decision about what to include and what to leave out is obviously going to be easier for a data manager who understands the project thoroughly. Some questions on a questionnaire may have an open-ended 'comments' or 'other' category. However, there would not be much point in coding and entering this information if it could not contribute anything or if only one respondent filled it in. In addition, answers composed of long text strings will always be time consuming to enter verbatim. There may be some obvious way to reduce the data by extracting what is relevant. Of course it is possible to go too far and be too parsimonious by leaving out data that may be needed to throw light on something at the analysis stage or help to explain a pattern which emerged.

7.2.3 Is ethics an issue?

In the UK, the Data Protection Act 1998 removed the former distinction between computer-held data and other forms of data. This means that it is no longer the responsibility of the data processing manager to ensure that legal niceties are observed since no change in legal status is occasioned by transfer to the electronic storage medium. Nevertheless, data staff should be aware of the legal position regarding personal data (all personal data about identifiable individuals are covered by the provisions of the Act) and resist any attempts to circumvent obligatory procedures. This is discussed in detail in Chapter 8.

Ethical obligations may be moral rather than legal in character. Assurances are often given during the course of data collection that 'information will not be passed on in a form that allows the source to be identified'. In this case the source may include both organizations and individuals. It is important that researchers should act responsibly in such matters if public confidence and co-operation is to be maintained.

A further ethical issue exists with regard to leaks. Employers who use casual labour for coding or keyboard work are particularly at risk, especially if staff might be personally affected by the issues which are being researched. Part-time journalists, members of political pressure groups or people who are in contact with these groups may also be tempted to leak information. Part-time staff should be screened carefully and all workers should be made aware of the need to respect confidentiality.

7.2.4 What form should each data item take?

The traditional data file is a rectangular table or matrix in which each row represents a *case* (or respondent) and each column represents a *variable*. For the purposes of this book a *variable* is an attribute which can be determined or measured and which once measured takes the form of a set of *variable values* (or *values*) each of which refers to a single subject or respondent. Each cell within this matrix consists of a single item of data. What form should it take? Data may be stored either as text ('male', 'female'; 'type1', 'type2'; 'I find hospitals depressing') or as numeric values (1, 2, 3 . . .). Reducing data to numbers reduces the effort of keying in but introduces an intermediate 'coding' stage.

A hierarchy of 'levels of measurement' for variables was developed by Stevens in 1946:

- *Nominal*. Are the measurements the same or different? Permissible statistics are frequency and mode. Example: male, female.
- *Ordinal*. Is the measurement greater or less than others (i.e. some form or ranking)? Permissible statistics are median and percentiles. Example: dependency index with categories − (1) no assistance required, (2) needs assistance with activities of daily living including shopping, (3) needs assistance with personal care activities of daily living including toilet.

- *Interval.* Are the intervals for differences between measurements of equal size? Permissible statistics are mean, standard deviation, product moment correlation. Example: body mass index.
- *Ratio.* Are the ratios between measurements of equal size? Permissible statistics are coefficient of variation. Example: age, height.

The main value of this hierarchy is in determining the type of analysis that can be carried out. According to the strictest statistical rules only measurements at or above the interval level may be subjected to the more rigorous statistical tests such as correlation and regression analysis, factor analysis etc. (often called *parametric* tests). An exception occurs in the case of

---

Q41. Which of the following best describes you? Tick one answer only.

Single, never been married	☐
Married or living as married with partner	☐
Widowed	☐
Divorced or separated	☐

Figure 7.1 Example of a question giving rise to data at the nominal level.

Q2. Which type of bread do you eat most often?

White	☐
Brown	☐
Wholemeal	☐

Figure 7.2 Example of a question giving rise to data at the ordinal level.

Q20. At what age did you get your first full-time job? ....

Figure 7.3 Example of a question giving rise to data at the interval level.

Q5. How many pints of milk did you drink yesterday (approx)? ....

Figure 7.4 Example of a question giving rise to data at the ratio level.

dichotomies when such distinctions have less meaning. You can treat male versus female just the same as if it were really measured at the interval level. You must assign numerical values but the values actually used are irrelevant. See Chapter 9 on data analysis for more exceptions and further details on this subject.

7.3 Coding and data entry

7.3.1 What coding will be necessary?

Imagine that you have a completed questionnaire in front of you. You have what is often called 'raw data'. For every question asked you must decide on appropriate coding. Codes form the link between raw data and the computer. Gender is relatively easy to code. One option is to enter the value as text 'male', 'female'. The trouble with this is the degree of redundancy. A more usual approach is to enter an abbreviation 'M' or 'F'. However, since gender is a dichotomous variable it can legitimately be subjected to (powerful) parametric tests. If this is required then numeric values such as '0' and '1' should be used. In order to avoid ambiguity a 'value label' can be created. This is a descriptive word or phrase that supplements or replaces the coded value in printed tables and charts.

A more complex problem would present itself in the case of discovering what languages are spoken in a population. Respondents are to be asked an open-ended question: 'what languages do you speak fluently?' It is anticipated that any individual respondent will speak up to five languages and that in all up to ten languages will be spoken – the main ones being English, Welsh, Gujerati, Urdu, Hindi, French and German. We need to know how many people speak each language – how can this be coded?

Variables like this are known as 'multiple response' and there are two ways to code them. (Note that each requires that several variables be created from this single question.)

- *Multiple dichotomies method* – Create a separate variable for each of the ten languages. Each takes the value 1 or 0 according to whether that language is spoken.

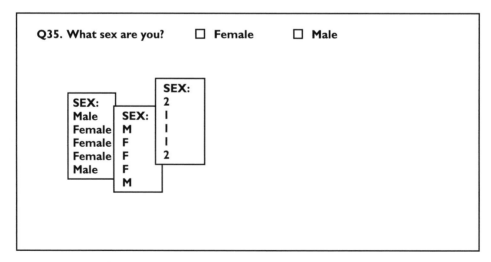

Figure 7.5 Alternative ways to code gender.

Q17. What languages do you speak fluently?

1._____
2._____
3._____
4._____
5._____

multiple response method

Lang 1	Lang 2	Lang 3	Lang 4	Lang 5
English	Gujerati	None	None	None
English	None	None	None	None
Gujerati	None	None	None	None
English	None	None	None	None
Hindi	Gujerati	Urdu	English	German

English	Gujerati	Hindi	Urdu	German	etc.
1	1	0	0	0	
1	0	0	0	0	
0	1	0	0	0	
1	0	0	0	0	
1	1	1	1	1	

multiple dichotomies method

The multiple dichotomies method is better suited to an alternative question form:

Q17. Which of the following languages do you speak fluently?

English	☐
Gujerati	☐
Hindi	☐
Urdu	☐
German	☐
Other	

Figure 7.6 Coding multiple response questions.

- *Multiple response method* – Create five or six variables called language 1, language 2 etc. Create codes for each of the 10 languages (1, 2, 3 . . . , 10). You can create 'value labels' linking languages and codes to avoid confusion at the analysis stage.

Since both these methods record all the available data there is no need to create codes for 'English only' etc. at this stage. These can easily be calculated later. The astute observer will also have noted if information about the languages themselves and the number spoken by any one person is indeed known in advance (say from pilot work) the question itself could easily have been changed to suit the proposed coding scheme.

Some responses to open-ended questions, interviews, focus group discussion and narratives, which are described in Chapter 5, require more sophisticated coding schemes based on 'content analysis'. Coding may then be based on use of certain words or concepts and attitudes expressed (Seidel and Kelle, 1995) (example: GP mentioned in negative context). In these cases it may be most effective to transcribe the text verbatim and perform coding afterwards using special purpose software.

In some cases it may be appropriate to make use of existing classification and coding schemes. This is commonly done in the case of social class, occupation etc. Suitable schemes include the Standard Occupational Classification (SOC) defined in some detail by the former OPCS (1990).

Where an answer has been overlooked or omitted by a respondent, special codes are needed to represent these 'missing values'. This must be a code that could not be mistaken for a real value. Traditionally 9, or 99, or 999 have been used.

Whatever coding schemes are used this should be carefully recorded in a 'coding manual'. This should also contain a detailed record of the procedure for dealing with ambiguous or nonsensical responses.

7.3.2 Who should enter the data?

This is an area where technology is making a big impact on the range of choice. A number of choices are available:

1   *Entry by the interviewer during the interview itself.* This method saves multiple recording and as a result reduces the risk of error. This approach is now a common feature of telephone interviewing using computer-aided telephone interviewing (CATI; see Chapter 6) and it

---

Q41. Which of the following best describes you?

10	**Single never married**
11	**Married or living as married with partner**
12	**Widowed**
13	**Divorced or separated from partner**

Q42. How many children are there in the household?

10	**Number of children aged under 1**

Figure 7.7 Coding manual.

is also now common for information from face-to-face interviews to be entered directly into a lap-top computer by the interviewer.

2   *Subsequent entry by the interviewer.* This gives an opportunity to review ambiguities.

3   *Data entry by untrained staff.* This is likely to be relatively cheap and convenient, but it may be less accurate and slower.

4   *Data entry by trained, skilled specialists either in-house or from an agency.* This may be more expensive, but is likely to be more accurate and flexible. However, there may be a security risk if the work is undertaken off the researcher's own premises.

5   *Data entry by optical character reader (OCR) direct from questionnaire scripts.* This is a relatively cheap and easy way of entering data which relates to pre-coded categories. However, the set-up costs may be high and there may be a high proportion of errors and ambiguities if respondents have not followed the procedures accurately which will have to be cleaned up later. Responses to open-ended and supplementary questions still have to be coded.

6   *Data entry by the respondent over the internet by e-mail or web page.* This method is still in its infancy. It promises to be cheap and easy but may be limited in reach and insecure. Response rates may also prove to be poor but there is little good evidence yet.

A further issue applicable to methods 2–4 concerns the type of data entry interface used. At one time keyboard operatives used a simple text editor or word processor to enter the data for each case as a continuous set of numbers. This is rarely done today. Simple spreadsheets also use the matrix approach but with slightly more flexibility and less risk of the operator losing track since variable names can appear at the head of each column.

Where a database package or purpose-built data entry software are used more options are available to reduce the risk of error:

•   the computer prompts the operator for the next value using the variable name
•   responses are entered into an online form that mimics the layout of the questionnaire itself.

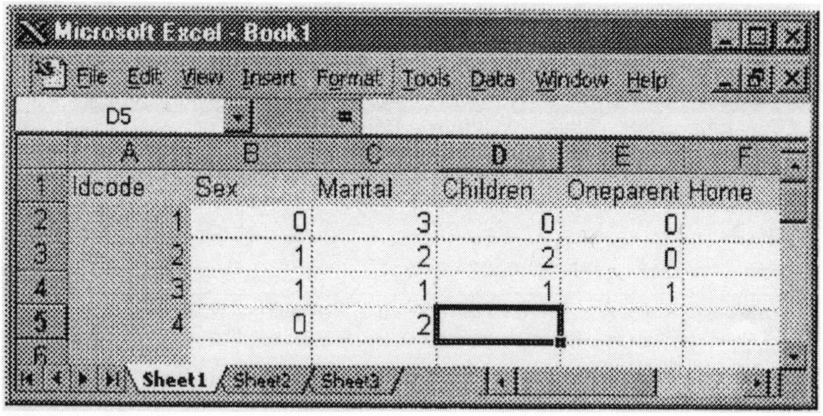

Figure 7.8 Entering data using a spreadsheet.

7.3.3 How will checking take place?

No matter how careful you are, errors are bound to occur at all stages of the research process. Some errors can be detected and corrected quite easily but others will escape even the most thorough checks. Both coding and keying procedures should be subject to continuous monitoring so that the level of accuracy is known. Staff working on these functions should be properly trained and encouraged to take a pride in the accuracy of their output. Where possible, they should also be encouraged to try to identify errors made during the preceding phases of research (ambiguity of question phrasing is an obvious example). Data entry staff may be able to spot coding errors if this is done separately.

At one time it was fairly commonplace to duplicate the data entry procedures in order to verify the accuracy. A special programme was then used to identify discrepancies which were then investigated and corrected. In most cases, however, this is unnecessary unless a very high degree of accuracy is paramount or operators are suspected of being particularly error prone.

Recommended checks for any project are as follows:

- hand checking of a sample of the coding*
- data entry staff should be made familiar with the coding process (if possible) so that obvious errors can be spotted and corrected at the data entry stage
- hand checking of a sample of data entry*
- checking for out-of-range values
- subjecting all variables to frequency counts and thoroughly investigating suspicious outliers.

*Borque and Clark (1994) suggest that 10–25 per cent should be checked.

Some data entry software may not permit inappropriate values to be entered. This then alerts the operator to a potential error before it is made. Although this clearly reduces the level of error, unless these messages can be logged and recorded it also means that the errors which have been made will be virtually undetectable. This type of safeguard may therefore encourage sloppy work. You should make up your own mind about the implications of this for your own project.

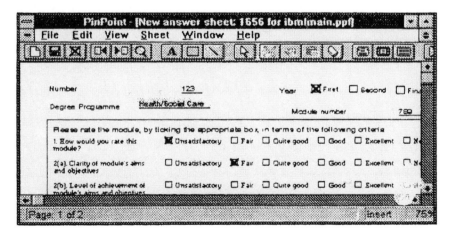

Figure 7.9 Entering data using an online form.

7.4 What software tools are available?

A very large range of software tools are available to assist you in the data entry task. These range from traditional general-purpose database and spreadsheet tools such as Dbase or Excel to fully integrated do-everything packages that help you design the questionnaire, enter the data and undertake sophisticated analysis (Research Solutions' Pinpoint package is an example). Some integrated software is specialized in function. CATI software tools are an example of the latter.

Another variation takes the form of traditional analysis tools (such as SPSS and SAS) which have been supplemented over the years by stand-alone data entry software (SPSS Data Entry, SAS FSP FSEDIT). A recent refinement are OCR/OMR packages that read in data from questionnaires via an automatic scanner. The software of these systems will interface with major data analysis tools including Pinpoint and SPSS (Principia Products' Remark OMR is an example).

For internet-based survey work, web authoring tools such as Microsoft's Word 97, Publisher and Frontpage, or Adobe's Pagemill will be of assistance in producing a suitable questionnaire although these tools need to be combined with specialized 'common gateway interface' (CGI) software (which must be installed on your web server) if awkward data-handling problems are to be avoided. Integrated software such as Principia Products' Remark Web Survey combine both elements in one package.

The level of investment needed varies markedly. At the time of writing (August 1999), a basic spreadsheet package costs as little as £20, e.g. Ability Spreadsheet. A database package from the same software house also costs £20. Borland Dbase 7 costs £81. Excel is no longer available separately but only as part of Office 97 (full price £385). Microsoft Access costs £272. SPSS Data Entry Builder (which has questionnaire design and production capability) costs £595 ex vat. Remark OMR costs £280 ex. vat.

Basic web authoring tools range from £80 to £120 (Adobe Pagemill, Microsoft Frontpage). Integrated web survey packages cost around £218 ex. vat, Remark Web Survey; SNAP all-in-one package, £995 ex. vat; SNAP Scanning – OCR, £2,995 ex. vat; SNAP Internet, £795.

7.4.1 Which tools are best for particular purposes?

We all appreciate good tools that are well adapted for a specific purpose. That being said, the best tool is the one that is to hand. A screwdriver makes a good hammer when you are up a ladder and the real hammer is in a toolbox in the garage. It is very tempting to rush out and buy the very latest software, but do you really need it? Will it be more trouble than it is worth? Even the most user-friendly software can take a long time to learn to use properly. A good rule of thumb is to always use what you feel comfortable with. Let your data entry staff use what they feel comfortable with – this will usually be what they have used before. Most packages allow easy interchange of information. The exceptions are likely to be value and variable labels so it is best to enter these into the analysis package itself rather than at an earlier stage. Apart from that there is really no reason not to use the Excel spreadsheet in Microsoft Office for data entry (if you are doing this in-house) and something else for analysis. In fact, you will probably get a much better understanding of the data and what you are doing with it if you take this route. This ought to be more 'future proof' as well, since you have more scope for upgrading without having to start from scratch.

Having said that, there is no doubt that fully integrated software has strong advantages in that it is usually:

1   *User-friendly.* Offering ease of use for the inexperienced researcher.
2   *Seamless.* Allowing direct transfer between questionnaire design, data entry, analysis and report-writing phases which may in turn lower marginal costs and speed up this work.
3   *One stop.* Offering an easier decision and lower initial costs than buying equivalent functions in separate packages.

The main disadvantages of integration are lack of:

1   *Upgradability.* It may not be possible to upgrade one function separately.
2   *Standardization.* It may not be possible to contract out the data entry function or export data to a client using different software.
3   *Continuity.* There will be additional costs of training staff to use unfamiliar software.

7.5 Conclusions

This chapter has provided a brief overview of data preparation issues, tools and techniques. Hopefully, this has made it clear just how many factors need to be taken into account in a properly formulated data preparation job, and how important and critical this task is within the research process. From this it should be clear that there really is no single best way. Most of the time in research, as in anything else, you just get your head down and get the job done. Cutting corners and performing miracles is all in a day's work. Nevertheless, we hope we have made it clear that you should be aware that you are cutting corners, know which corners are being cut and what effect it could have in degrading your data. Go too far and cut too many corners and you run the risk of making the whole thing pointless.

Example 1: West Birmingham Health Authority

The authority's survey of elderly ethnic minority residents has proceeded as far as the data collection phase. This has been carried out extremely conscientiously by Research Nurse Sarah X. The completed interview questionnaires now sit in an upper office in Y Hospital. What are they going to do next? ZZ, a clerical officer with considerable experience of database management, is given the task of putting the material on to the computer. He sets up the database structure and starts work. As far as possible entries are copied verbatim from the scripts. That way the richness of the data is preserved while leaving scope for any reduction or approximation at the analysis stage. This task is easily manageable on any computer. Field widths of up to sixty characters permitted multiple responses to a question to be recorded where necessary.

All proceeds well until the database is handed over to the University for analysis. Then it is discovered that the task of separating out key responses from surplus data is beyond the every-day programming abilities of the data analysts. Moreover, the fields contain numerous errors, inconsistencies in spelling etc. that further complicate the task.

Example 2: Health and social care and the internet

Many local authorities hope to use the Internet to communicate with citizens in their area. X social services department carries out a small preparatory study of potential users before launching its web site. The survey comprises a self-completion questionnaire of twenty-five questions dealing with existing usage, equipment, software and potential usage for information about social services. One hundred scripts are returned completed.

The research team are working with extremely limited resources. One officer has been seconded to the project half-time for two months. There is a budget of £1000 to cover consumables. The latter has been almost entirely consumed by the costs of printing and sending out the questionnaires.

The decision is taken to carry out the programme of data entry (and analysis) in-house using existing software. Microsoft's Excel (cost £50) is chosen as a package with which the officers and their clerical support are already familiar, thus eliminating purchase and retraining costs. This package will also be used for the analysis. Only simple frequency counts and descriptive statistics are required. Data are entered into the spreadsheet as a traditional matrix. A variable name is entered at the top of each column and each set of responses occupies a single row. Formulae can then be entered at the foot of each column to calculate totals, means or to determine frequencies.

This project also involves data collection via the Internet from a questionnaire on the local authority's existing web site. This data arrives via e-mail as individual messages with elaborate headers, footers, variable names etc. Substantive data are manually transferred to Excel using the standard Windows cut and paste function.

Example 3: Are you eating properly?

The contact list for the telephone survey of eating habits contains names and telephone numbers and space for recording details of the outcome of contact attempts including time, etc. The interview schedules were numbered, they contained interviewer identification details but no details as to the respondent's identity. There was no recorded link between the interview questionnaire and respondent identities. This ensured maximum confidentiality and obviated the need to register under the Data Protection Act 1984.

This survey requires that 'occupation of head of household' be classified as it is expected that eating habits will vary measurably according to social class. Coding is carried out according to a detailed classification given in Appendix B.2 of Classification of Occupations 1980 (OPCS/GSS 1980), pages cv to cxvii. This classification details occupations individually in fourteen closely typed pages. Most occupations are readily identified though problems arise over occupations such as 'engineering'. For this occupation interviewers always obtained additional information (such as qualifications) since the term embraces both motor mechanics (IIIM – skilled manual), electrical engineers in management positions (II – intermediate) and self-employed chemical and electronic engineers (I – professional).

The data are now keyed in by three operatives. One is an experienced freelance data entry specialist, the other two are students with some typing experience. All use Dbase. On completion of the job some error checking is carried out. It is found that the experienced operator has made errors in four entries per 1000 key strokes whereas the two students made 60 and 100 errors respectively per 1000 key strokes. Moreover, the experienced operator worked at twice the speed and has tagged dubious entries with post-its for further clarification. The decision is taken to double enter and correct the work of the two students. Meanwhile the experienced operator is employed on defining variable labels and value labels in the appropriate SPSS code.

Further reading

Sapsford, R. and Jupp, V. (eds) (1996) *Data Collection and Analysis*, London: Sage Publications and Open University.

Chapter 8

Processing personal data: the legal framework

Graham Pearce

In this chapter the reader will develop an understanding of:

- the legal framework of the Data Protection Act 1984
- recent developments arising from the European Union directive
- the relevant issues in the Data Protection Act 1998, including the definitions of key terms
- how the Acts affect data processing in market research in health and social care.

8.1 Introduction

Health service professionals, local authorities, voluntary bodies and social researchers increasingly rely upon the use of personal data, a process that has been accelerated by rapid developments in information technologies. This has been accompanied by a growing concern that the processing of personal data could undermine the privacy enjoyed by the individual citizen. Many organizations need to process personal information about their clients but the storage and use of personal data poses numerous dangers. For example, GPs and social service departments retain information about their patients and clients which is vital in providing treatment and care. Similarly, epidemiological researchers are reliant upon the co-operation and trust of individuals in gaining access to personal data about lifestyles and medical histories. But such data are highly sensitive and their use needs to be carefully controlled to protect the rights and freedoms of individuals. In most cases a common sense approach to the use of personal data will suffice, for example data should be collected fairly and lawfully, they should be secure and individuals should have the right to gain access to their data and establish for what purposes it is being processed. These principles form the basis of data protection law in the UK and it is important that those involved in the processing of personal data are aware of their legal obligations. The purpose of this chapter is to provide an outline of the principles governing the operation of the present UK law on data protection and to highlight the particular steps which those carrying out health and social research involving the use of personal data need to adopt.

8.2 The legal framework

8.2.1 The Data Protection Act 1984

For many years the Data Protection Act 1984 has provided the framework for the safeguarding of personal data and has required the users of personal data to register with the Data

Protection Registrar, who has overall responsibility for data protection in the UK. The Act was targeted at safeguarding the automatic processing of personal data (using computers) and placed an obligation on data users to comply with a set of data protection principles based upon the Council of Europe Convention on Data Protection (Council of Europe, 1981) and which are fundamental to data protection law. The principles comprise a mixture of obligations on those who are responsible for the processing of personal information, together with rights for individuals who are the subject of data processing:

- the information to be contained in personal data shall be obtained, and personal data shall be processed, fairly and lawfully
- personal data shall be held only for one or more specific and lawful purposes
- personal data held for any purposes shall not be used or disclosed in any manner incompatible with that purpose or those purposes
- personal data held for any purpose or purposes shall be adequate, relevant and not excessive in relation to that purpose or those purposes
- personal data shall be accurate and, where necessary, kept up to date.
- any individual shall be entitled
  a   at reasonable intervals and without undue delay or expense
      i   to be informed by any data user whether he holds personal data of which that individual is the subject, and
      ii   to access to any such data held by the data user, and
  b   where appropriate, to have such data corrected or erased
- appropriate security measures shall be taken against unauthorized access to, or alteration, disclosure or destruction of personal data and against accidental loss of personal data.

The aim of registration was to provide the public with information about the purpose of processing by the data user, help individuals gain access to their personal data and enable the Registrar to ensure compliance with the data protection principles.

Following registration, data users have been able to process data, providing that they remained within the limits of the registration. The Act stated that subject to certain exemptions, data subjects have the rights of access to their data, to have inaccurate data rectified or erased and to compensation in respect of inaccurate data or because of the loss or unauthorized disclosure of their data. In effect, data subjects have had the right to find out who holds their personal data, how those data are used and may elect to limit the transfer of data to data controllers with whom they do not have a contractual relationship.

8.2.2 The European directive and the Data Protection Act 1998

The existing legislation with which many data users have become familiar has recently been revised in the wake of a 1995 EU directive on the protection of individuals with regard to the processing of personal data and on the free movement of such data (European Union Council and the Parliament, 1995). The purpose of the directive is to harmonize existing data protection law at a high level across the European Union and thereby remove existing barriers to the free flow of personal data between member states. This is to be achieved by the adoption of a coherent and enforceable set of administrative laws and independent scrutiny which will apply to all organizations, public and private (Bainbridge and Pearce,

1996; Pearce and Platten, 1998). The principles underpinning the directive are similar to the extant UK law and reflect the Council of Europe Convention.

The EU directive has now been transposed into UK law through the 1998 Data Protection Act, the full provisions of which will come into force in 2000. In addition to reforming the 1984 Act the opportunity has been taken to amend legislation which relates to data protection issues. For example, the rights of access provided by the Access to Personal Files Act 1987, which deals specifically with health, educational and accessible public records (housing and social services records) has been repealed and is brought within the new legislation. Further regulations relating to the operation of the Act were introduced during 1999.

Formal registration to the Data Protection Registrar, who now takes on the title Data Protection Commissioner, will in future not have the same importance as under previous law since it is intended that data subjects will be better informed of the users or processors of his or her data. The exemptions to notification will not, however, release data controllers from the obligation to make information available about their processing at the request of any individual. In each of these respects the new Act will not significantly disturb existing arrangements. However, the Act will have a significant impact in certain areas since it will extend the law to the processing of manual data. *Personal information held on paper will no longer fall outside the law.*

8.2.3 Definitions

For those charged with the processing of personal data it is important to grasp the language used in the latest data protection legislation (Bainbridge and Pearce, 1998a). The new Act distinguishes between *data* and *personal data*. In addition to data that are intended to be automatically processed, data recorded or intended to be recorded as part of a *relevant filing system* are within the definition of data, so that certain manual files are included within the scope of the Act. *Relevant filing systems* are defined as sets of information structured by reference to individuals or criteria relating to individuals in such a way that information relating to a particular individual is readily accessible. *Personal data* includes data relating to an individual who can be identified from those data and any other information which is either in or likely to come into the possession of the *data controller*, who is responsible for determining the purposes and manner of processing. The *data subject* is the individual who is the subject of personal data.

A *data processor* is any person who processes data on behalf of the data controller, other than an employee of the data controller, for example a computer agency or IT company employed by a health trust. However, the processor's role may not be restricted to the analysis of data, it may also relate to the collection and recording, retrieval, erasure and even destruction of personal data, all of which fall within the exhaustive definition of processing. Processors, therefore, include not only IT specialists who manipulate data but also those individuals who collect personal data from data subjects. However, unlike the data controller the data processor is not required to notify either the Commissioner or the data subject of his/her processing activities, but the data controller has special responsibilities for managing the activities of the processor, in particular the security obligations imposed on the processor, normally by way of a contract.

The Act pays particular attention to the processing of 'sensitive personal data', which is subject to specific conditions and which have particular significance for health and social service practitioners and researchers. They include data such as those revealing racial or ethnic origin, political opinions, religious or other beliefs, trade union membership, physical or mental health and sexual life. Information relating to criminal offences, proceedings and sentences also fall within this category.

8.2.4 The principles

The principles conform to those in previous UK legislation, with the exception of an additional principle which prohibits the transfer of personal data to a country outside the EU unless adequate data protection safeguards are in force. This provision will not prevent all data transfers to third countries, but social and health researchers undertaking comparative studies using personal data in EU and non-EU states should be aware of the potential limitations (Greenfield and Pearce, 1998). Similarly, a foreign-based health care provider operating within the EU may be unable to transfer data on patients to the parent company. The data protection authorities are likely to adopt a pragmatic approach to this provision and even if the third country does not afford adequate safeguards transfers may still be possible, where the controller adduces sufficient safeguards, or where the data subject consents.

Unlike the 1984 Act a duty is placed upon data controllers to inform data subjects when the data are obtained and in other cases, for example where data have been disclosed to a third party. The information to be provided to the data subject is, however, to be limited. Particular emphasis is placed upon security measures and data controllers must take reasonable steps to ensure the reliability of staff having access to personal data. In addition, data processors must provide security guarantees relating to both technical and organizational measures. Processors must act under a written contract which confirms that the processor will only act on the instructions of the data controller and which imposes security obligations.

8.3 Data processing

The 1998 Act requires that to be fair and lawful at least one of the following conditions must apply if personal data are to be processed:

- the data subject has given his consent
- it is necessary for the completion of a contract to which the data subject is a party or for taking steps at the data subject's request for entering into a contract (this would include, for example, the relationship between a health professional and a client)
- it is necessary for compliance with any legal obligations to which the data controller is subject, other than a contractual obligation (health and social service agencies are subject to national laws)
- it is necessary to protect the vital interests of the data subject or another, for example where the data subject is physically unable (ill health) or legally incapable of giving consent (young children)
- it is necessary for the administration of justice, the exercise of functions conferred on any person under any enactment, exercise of state functions and the exercise of a public nature exercised in the public interest by any person
- it is necessary for the purpose of the legitimate interests pursued by the data controller

or to the third party to whom the data are disclosed except where the processing is unwarranted in any case by reason of prejudice to the rights and freedoms of the data subject.

In the latter case of 'legitimate' processing, which potentially offers data users considerable discretion, the Secretary of State may clarify the circumstances in which the condition is or is not to be taken as being met. However, the extent of these conditions implies that the processing of personal data by health and social service agencies will, in all conceivable circumstances, be permitted.

Much of the personal data processed by public and voluntary organizations and social researchers may be regarded as 'sensitive' and the 1998 Act distinguishes between these and other forms of personal data. For example, local authority social service, education and housing departments hold data on disadvantaged families, the homeless, adoptions and fostering and child offenders. Similarly, health professionals have access to highly confidential personal data relating to health and sexual behaviour. Such information is often shared, quite legitimately, between different departments in local authorities and care services and may be disclosed to other agencies. However, the sensitivity of such data requires additional safeguards.

Additional conditions over and above those to be applied in the case of 'normal' data must be applied in respect of the processing of sensitive data and the Act requires at least one of the following conditions to be met, that:

- the data subject has given explicit consent to the processing
- processing is necessary for employment law rights or obligations
- processing is necessary to protect the vital interests of the data subject or another where consent cannot be given by the data subject or the data controller cannot be expected to obtain the consent of the data subject
- processing is necessary to protect the vital interests of another person in a case where consent by or on behalf of the data subject has been unreasonably withheld
- processing is carried out subject to appropriate safeguards by non-profit bodies or associations which exist for political, philosophical, religious or trade union purposes. Processing must relate only to individuals who are members or who have regular contact in connection with the body's or association's purposes and which does not involve disclosure to a third party without consent
- the information contained in the data has been made public by deliberate steps taken by the data subject
- processing is necessary in respect of legal proceedings, legal advice or legal rights
- processing is necessary for the administration of justice of functions conferred by or under any enactment or function exercised by the Crown, Minister or government department
- processing is necessary for medical processing (includes preventative medicine, medical diagnosis, medical research, provision of care, and treatment and management of health care services) and is undertaken by a health professional or person under a duty of confidentiality equivalent to that owed by a health professional.

The processing of data relating to offences and convictions is not provided for in the Act and such data may only be processed, unless otherwise exempt, where necessary for the administration of justice or statutory functions.

Although the obligations relating to the processing of sensitive data may appear at first sight exacting, in practice the range of conditions available suggests that neither local authorities, health agencies or other organizations in the public or voluntary sectors will be fettered in their data-processing activities.

8.4 Rights of data subjects

The rights of data subjects are significantly extended by the 1998 Act (Bainbridge and Pearce, 1998b). As before, data must be obtained fairly and lawfully, for example individuals must not be deceived into providing personal data. In addition, data subjects must now be informed if their personal data are being or are intended to be processed. More information is to be provided to data subjects by the data controller, including the identity of the controller (whose identity may well be obvious), the purpose or purposes of processing and an outline of security measures. In the vast majority of circumstances the data controller will have informed the Commissioner of the processing activities and security measures and no further information is required to be given. If information has not been obtained directly from the data subject the data controller is under a duty to ensure that the data subject is informed within a reasonable time, providing that the effort involved is not disproportionate.

In addition to these specific obligations, the data controller has a duty to respond to a request for information about processing in the form of a 'data subject access request'. This requirement is more extensive than existing practice. Data controllers must provide a description of the information that they hold on an individual to that person, together with a description of the purposes of processing and recipients, as well as a description of the logic in any automatic decision taking. The latter may be relevant, for example, in the case of authorities using automatic procedures in determining housing allocations or health care priorities, where the data subject should have the right to make representations in order to safeguard his/her legitimate interests.

There are particular provisions to deal with those circumstances where compliance with a subject access request would lead to the disclosure of data relating to another individual. An example would be the release of adoption or care records held by a social services department. In these circumstances the local authority may be obliged to refuse access because the individuals involved have either refused consent to access or cannot be traced.

Individuals may also give notice to the data controller that they wish the processing of their information to cease for a specific purpose or in a specified manner on the grounds that, for specified reasons, it is unwarranted as causing or likely to cause substantial damage or substantial distress to him/her or another. However, this right is restricted, for example it excludes those circumstances where the data subject has already granted consent, where processing is necessary in relation to a contract, is against the public interest or is in accordance with the legitimate interests of the data controller.

Data subjects also have the right to have inaccurate data rectified, erased or destroyed and blocked if a court is satisfied that they are inaccurate. This extends to data which contain opinions about the data subject and which are based upon inaccurate information. In cases where it is deemed practical, courts may require data controllers to notify third parties to whom inaccurate data have been disclosed. It is important, therefore, that controllers log all disclosures of data to third parties.

Individuals may seek financial compensation in respect of damages arising from a contravention of any requirement under the Act. This right is similar to the previous legislation. However, it is wider in scope, and includes any contravention, while previously it was limited to certain specific acts or omissions.

8.5 Notification

Under previous legislation all organizations were required to register their data processing activities (apart from manual processing) with the Data Protection Registrar, unless exempt. The 1998 Act modifies existing procedures, registration is replaced by notification of the particulars of data-processing activities and a general description of security measures. Manual processing is exempt from notification although the data controller may choose to notify such processing. If manual processing is not notified the data controller is still obliged to make available the information that would have previously been in the registered particulars to any person on request. Moreover, all data controllers are required to comply with the data protection principles.

The Act, therefore, removes the link between registration and enforcement, and while the failure to notify is an offence, the Commissioner has no powers to refuse to add a data controller to the register merely on the grounds that the processing will not comply with the data protection principles. It also seems possible that the Secretary of State may take the opportunity to simplify procedures for data processors through the appointment of 'data protection supervisors' who will be responsible for ensuring that the data controller in an organization complies with the law in an independent manner. It might appear, therefore, that the powers of the new Commissioner have been reduced but this would be misleading. For example, in addition to assessing the adequacy of third country transfers and assisting data subjects to secure their rights, the Act makes provision for certain categories of processing, including some types of sensitive manual processing, not to be undertaken until the Commissioner has made an assessment to ensure that the processing complies with the law. The extent of such prior checking is likely to be limited, for example to highly sensitive personal information or processing which can cause significant damage or distress or significantly prejudice the rights and freedoms of data subjects, but it is indicative of the enhanced function of the Commissioner.

8.6 Processing of manual data

Most organizations hold considerable quantities of personal information, in both paper files as well as on computers, some of which may extend back over many years. Personal health records held in doctors' surgeries are an example and the Access to Health Records Act 1990 provided individuals with the right to inspect their medical records. Under the 1984 Act, personal data held in paper files were exempt, but the new Act extends the data protection principles to the processing to all data contained in structured and accessible filing systems. Files or index cards containing information about clients and employees will be covered by the new provisions but general correspondence files will be excluded. These provisions have given rise to particular concerns among a range of organizations about the cost and effort involved in ensuring that existing manual records fulfil the data protection principles in terms of both their accuracy and security and the meeting of subject access requests. Indeed the extension of data protection to manual records was strongly resisted by the UK government during discussions on the EU directive. For example, the Department of Health suggested that the costs to the National Health Service could be £2 billion (Department of Health, 1994).

In view of these potential difficulties the EU directive provided member states with the opportunity to delay the introduction of certain requirements of the new law in respect of manual filing systems – the so-called transitional arrangements (Bainbridge and Pearce, 1999). The Act makes full use of these provisions in respect of data quality and processing. However, it does not extend to the right of access of data subjects and a right to rectification, erasure, blocking or destruction of inaccurate or incomplete data and a right to require the data controller to cease holding exempt manual data in a manner incompatible with the data controller's legitimate interests. Effectively, data controllers are given until 2007 to take all reasonable steps to meet all the requirements of the Act in respect of manual filing systems that were in place at the time the Act came into force. This will provide organizations like the NHS, which spends in the order of £2.8 billion (Audit Commission, 1995b) on data processing, with sufficient time to amend their practices. Indeed, many organizations that still rely upon manual processing will be encouraged to rationalize existing systems and introduce new and more efficient data-handling procedures with long-term benefits for both themselves and their clients.

An indefinite time limit applies to the processing of eligible manual data and relevant automated data only for the purposes of historical research – for example, historic health data – subject to certain conditions being observed.

8.7 Conclusions

It is difficult to be sanguine about the ability of legal instruments to safeguard personal data. Nonetheless, the latest Data Protection Act provides a combination of obligations on data users and rights for data subjects that appears reasonable in terms of the costs and benefits involved. The vast majority of provisions in the Act are unlikely to impose additional requirements on data users beyond those involved in satisfying the 1984 Act. However, it would be wrong to conclude that the new legislation will not bring about significant changes in the law and practice of data protection. Indeed, those who have become used to the 1984 provisions will find the transition to the new law exacting. Moreover, it is apparent that while the basic principles of data protection law are fairly comprehensible there are numerous exemptions to these general provisions, including the transitional arrangements, which complicate the overall picture.

In general, the requirements regarding data subjects' rights of access to their data and the emphasis given to security have been sharpened while the conditions relating to third country transfers emerge as a largely new theme in UK law. The main concern over the extension of data protection law to manual records has been finessed through the long lead time given to organizations to meet their new obligations. These developments have been accompanied by a redefinition of processing, to include activities ranging from collection to disposal, restrictions on the processing of sensitive data, a new right to prohibit processing where it will cause distress or damage, restrictions on decision making by automatic processing and enhanced rights to have personal data rectified.

Each of these new provisions will effectively help reinforce the rights of data subjects. It is clearly too early to judge the long-term impact of these new conditions and certain aspects will almost certainly produce unforeseen consequences as well as uncertainty, for data users and the Data Protection Authorities. At the same time advances in information and communication technologies, in particular the use of the World Wide Web, will increasingly challenge traditional legal approaches to the safeguarding of personal data and the long-term effectiveness of the Act will need to be judged in this emerging technological context.

8.7.1 Checklist

Guidance for data controllers

1   Organizations engaged in market research studies, whether in the public or private sectors, need to be aware of the core principles which underpin data protection legislation. They should build data protection into their data-processing activities.
2   The requirements are not onerous. Those engaged in collecting personal data, for example by telephone or through household surveys, should ensure that data subjects are informed who the data is being collected for, the purposes of data collection and how the data are to be used. Every effort must be made to ensure that individuals are aware of how their data are to be employed.
3   If the data are to be used in connection with other surveys, either completed or planned, then the data subject must be informed at least about the scope and purpose of such studies.
4   Data subjects must be informed about any intentions with regard to the disclosure of their personal data to third parties, for example businesses, local authorities or central government departments.
5   Where there is a possibility that personal data may have to be transferred to states in 'third countries' (outside the EU), then the data subject should be given this information and asked for explicit consent to such a transfer. Transfers to third countries may take place, providing that the data controller adduces appropriate safeguards.
6   Most organizations responsible for market research studies will already be registered with the Data Protection Commissioner (hitherto the Registrar) but it is for researchers to check their registrations to ensure that their processing activities are included. These comprise the categories of persons on which data is to be collected, the types of data to be collected, for example age, sex, address, qualifications, data sources, disclosures to third parties and (if relevant) details of data transfers to third countries.
7   Data controllers need to ensure the security of personal data at all stages of processing and organizations need to prepare a statement setting out the broad measures which have adopted to meet this obligation.
8   Since they are obliged not to retain data for a period beyond that which is reasonable, organizations need to consider for how long data are to be retained and how they are to be disposed.
9   Each of these measures will help ensure that organizations are in a position to respond effectively to any future data subject access request.

The respective responsibilities of data controllers and processors

1   The responsibilities for data protection of the various parties which may be involved in market research exercises needs to be clarified.

2   These distinctions are important since it is the data controller who has the prime responsibility for ensuring that processing is undertaken fairly and lawfully.
3   The activities of data processors, including security measures, must be in accordance with the instructions from the data controller and these should be specified in the form of a contract between the controller and processor, which must be in, or evidenced in, writing.
4   The identity of the data controller must be clearly defined.

Example

A local authority decides to commission a market research company to undertake research on its behalf and that agency, in turn, employs another organization to collect and/or analyse the data.

- if the local authority is the decision-making body responsible for designating the objectives of the study and the methods to be adopted, including the survey design, it is regarded as the data controller
- where the local authority has commissioned the market researchers to devise the survey, including the questionnaire, then the latter will be held to be the data controller. If preferred, the local authority and the market researchers could act as joint data controllers.

The importance of sensitive data

1   Especial emphasis is placed on the need to safeguard sensitive personal data. Where data subjects are being requested to provide data, for example relating to health, political or religious beliefs, it is vital that they be informed of their rights.
2   Consent to the processing of sensitive data must be freely given, preferably in writing, it must be explicit and the data subject should be informed about the specific uses to which the data may be put. Each of these requirements must be observed.
3   Where epidemiological research is being undertaken in the 'public interest' this may be used to avoid the Acts' requirements relating to sensitive data. However, individuals need to be informed about how their data are to be used.
4   There is a strong case, again on public interest grounds, in favour of linking data sets together, for example medical and social service records. However, this is not acceptable and organizations intending to adopt this approach, without the consent of the data subject, should ensure that the data are anonymized before merging is permitted. Apart from transgressing data protection law, such practices would breach the common law duty of confidentiality.

Transitional arrangements

1   Although the Data Protection Act was granted Royal Assent in 1998, its provisions are not likely to come into full effect until 2000.
2   The Act provides for a two-stage transitional period covering manual and automatic processing.

3 A partial derogation applies to the processing of manual data until 24 October 2007.
4 A complex system of derogation will apply to automatic processing already under way on 23 October 1998 until 24 October 2001.
5 In the case of the processing of new information, or new processing of old data, the new law appears to apply in its entirety.

Further reading

Bainbridge, D. and Pearce, G. (1998a) 'Data protection: data controllers and the new Data Protection Law', *The Computer Law and Security Report* 14(3): 259–326.

Bainbridge, D. and Pearce, G. (1999) 'Data protection: the new UK data protection in law and the transitional arrangements', *The Computer Law and Security Report* 15(4): 343–347.

Pearce, G. and Platten, N. (1998) 'Achieving personal data protection in the European Union', *Journal of Common Market Studies* 36(4): 529–547.

Chapter 9

Analysing data

Rob Tinsley

In this chapter the reader will gain an understanding of:

- how data analysis fits into the research process
- the main stages in data analysis
- the main techniques of analysis
- a range of software tools for data analysis and current costs.

9.1 Introduction

Data analysis lies at the very heart of the investigative process. For researchers it represents the 'moment of truth' when the relative worth of their efforts is revealed. Will carefully constructed hypotheses be supported or refuted? Will a contextually rich database give the expected insights into cause and effect? Because the stakes are high, data analysis tends not to suffer from the general neglect and resource poverty that attends some other important functions. But as Nie *et al.* observed as long ago as 1975:

> The wide dissemination of statistical packages such as SPSS, containing large numbers of complex statistical procedures, have, almost overnight, made these techniques available to the social science community. There is little doubt that social scientists are using them, and there is equally little doubt that in many instances statistical techniques are being used by students and researchers who understand neither the assumptions of the methods nor their statistical or mathematical bases.
>
> (Nie *et al.*, 1975, p. 3)

These authors also note the tendency for researchers to employ 'the crudest form of empiricism' by resorting to grand fishing expeditions among their data. We do not think that these observations are any less true today. In fact, the problem has arguably been made worse by the increasing availability of computing power and the introduction of more 'user-friendly' computing environments. These days anyone can do analysis but if they do it badly then effort and resources put into the project by sponsors, research staff and respondents will be wasted!

The three main stages in data analysis are:

1   *The search for error.* Before the analysis is carried forward there must be sufficient error checks. This is to avoid 'red herrings' where apparently interesting findings actually arise from errors in coding or keying-in data.

2   *Finding out about the sample.* The findings of the study with respect to the primary data sample should be based on valid effects that have been observed. Researchers are sometimes led to overemphasize trivial differences or associations either in their enthusiasm for particular theories or because there is a need to produce interesting findings of any sort whatever.

3   *Finding out about the population beyond the sample.* Inferences are made as to the implications of the findings for the population from which sample data has actually been collected. Justifiable conclusions have to be made as to the degree to which the sample is 'representative' and researchers must explain the precision to be expected from their forecasts.

In this chapter we will consider what issues need to be addressed in order to avoid such pitfalls. We start by describing some of the analytical techniques that are available and then move on to consider how they can be successfully applied in each of the above tasks. The final part of the chapter looks at some of the software tools currently on the market.

A short chapter like this cannot presume to give a thorough grounding in statistical techniques. For this reason readers are recommended to supplement their reading from texts such as Sapsford and Jupp (1996). Beginner's texts or even software manuals can also prove helpful and we have found the clear explanations in early editions of SPSS manuals (such as Nie *et al.*, 1975) to be particularly useful.

Although we recommend a systematic approach to analysis we do not want to suggest that researchers are necessarily excluded whose projects are characterized by:

> no design . . . no well-worked-out set of hypotheses to be tested, no data gathering instruments purposely designed to secure information relevant to these hypotheses, no set of analytic procedures specified in advance.
>
> (Becker *et al.*, 1961, p. 17)

We hope that there is something of value in this chapter for every type of research and every type of researcher.

9.2 Techniques for analysis

Analysis is the process of reducing complexity by summarization. Although a wide range of statistical techniques are available to the analyst it is nevertheless true that for most purposes the process necessarily begins with a few relatively simple ones. In many surveys these same few techniques will be all that are required. We will start by describing the most basic type of simplification – the frequency count. We then go on to consider some slightly more sophisticated techniques. Those who are already fully conversant with the basic range of statistical techniques may skip this section.

9.2.1 Basic techniques of summarization

The frequency count

This is the most basic type of statistical reduction. We simply count all instances of a particular response (e.g. '10 respondents ticked white sliced bread') (see Figure 9.1). Usually

SEX					
Value label	Value	Frequency	Per cent	Valid per cent	Cumulative per cent
Male	0	49	49.01	49.01	49.01
Female	1	51	51.01	51.01	100.01
	Total	100	100.0	100.0	

Valid cases 314   Missing cases 0

Figure 9.1 Frequency count.

this is done for all possible combinations of responses. The most popular response in any set is known as the *mode*. A refinement is for the count to be expressed as a percentage of the sample. For values which are ordered in some way we can use these percentages to calculate the *median* which is the numerical value of the 'middle' case and therefore subdivides the sample into two equal parts.

Applies to: Single variable measured at nominal level (gender), or at higher levels where values are discrete and not too numerous. ('On how many days per week do you drink alcohol?')

Mean

For a variable which is measured at the ordinal, interval or ratio level it may be more appropriate to summarize the distribution of values by calculating an imaginary 'average' or *arithmetic mean*. The mean is the most common measure of central tendency. This is often supplemented by the *standard deviation* which indicates to what extent values are dispersed around this central value – the smaller the standard deviation the tighter the cluster. *Skewness* indicates deviation of values from the symmetrical bell-shaped curve of the normal distribution. Together with the *maximum* and *minimum* the above measures are known collectively as 'descriptive statistics' (see Figure 9.2).

Applies to: Single variable measured at the ordinal (rating), interval (temperature) or ratio (age, height, weight) levels.

Variable	Mean	Std Dev	Minimum	Maximum
AGE	42	5.62	18	73

Figure 9.2 Descriptive statistics.

Cross-tabulation

Essentially this is a frequency count in two dimensions. It summarizes the relationship between two variables. The values for one variable appear as columns and the other as rows. Thus a table representing gender and car ownership has four cells. The left-hand cell in the upper row shows the number of men who do not own cars. The right-hand cell in this row shows the number of men who do own cars. In the lower row the left-hand column indicates the number of women who do not own cars and the right-hand the number of women who do. Each cell in such a table will usually show row and column percentages in addition to the frequency count (see Figure 9.3).

> **Applies to:** Any two variables for which frequency counts are appropriate (gender by number of days drink alcohol).

Cross-tabulations of more than two variables may be made. In this case a separate two-dimensional table is produced for each value of the additional variable (see Figure 9.4).

9.2.2 Correlation and regression

Correlation

Where it is desired to examine the relationship between two variables measured at the ratio, interval or ordinal levels, correlation analysis represents a more powerful if less intuitive method of summarization than cross-tabulation. Pearson correlation analysis produces an index known as r (taking a value somewhere between -1 and $+1$) which indicates the extent to which these variables appear to move together or are *associated* in the jargon. A value of $+1$ indicates the most complete degree of moving together when one variable goes up the other

AGEBAND BY AREA

		AREA	Page 1 of 1	
	Count Row % Col %	CORBY	SBHAM	
		1.00	2.00	Row Total
AGEBAND				
UP TO 24 YEARS	24.0	212 50.1 14.5	211 49.9 13.8	423 14.3
25 TO 34 YEARS	34.0	289 51.5 20.4	272 48.5 17.7	561 19.0

Figure 9.3 Part of output for two-way cross-tabulation.

Q83X03 DOCTOR VISIT 12 MONTHS BY R6 SEX
Controlling for....
FACTORD Value = 1.00 UNABLE TO WASH DRESS

		R6		Page 1 of 1	
	Count				
	Row %	FEMALE	MALE		
	Col %				
		A	B		Row Total
Q83X03					
	0	20	3		23
NO VISITS		87.0	13.0		
		42.6	13.0		32.9
	1				
		4	1		5
		80	20		
		8.5	4.3		7.1

Q83X03 DOCTOR VISIT 12 MONTHS BY R6 SEX
Controlling for....
FACTORD Value = 2.00 UNABLE TO SHOP COOK

		R6		Page 1 of 1	
	Count				
	Row %	FEMALE	MALE		
	Col %				
		A	B		Row Total
Q83X03					
	0	31	37		68
NO VISITS		45.6	54.4		
		27.0	37.8		31.9
	1				
		11	9		20
		55.0	45.0		
		9.6	9.2		9.4

Figure 9.4 Part of output for three-way cross-tabulation.

goes up to a similar proportionate extent (but not necessarily by the same amount). A value of −1 means complete disagreement – they move in opposite directions. If values for such variables are plotted on a graph the result is an exact straight line, hence they are said to be linearly associated. A value of zero for r means they do not move together at all and are not associated. Various other types of correlation (Spearman is probably the most well known) have been devised that are applicable to ordinal data.

Applies to: Any pair of variables measured at the ordinal, interval or ratio levels.

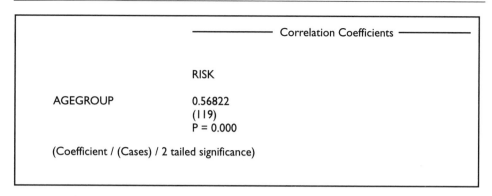

Figure 9.5 Output for Pearson correlation.

Linear regression

This is similar in many respects to Pearson correlation, giving similar results but rather more information about the nature of inter-relationships. The principal outputs are an index similar to Pearson's r (and also known as r but taking a value between 0 and 1) and a regression equation. The latter takes the form:

$$y = bx + c$$

where y is a variable whose value is dependent on that of another variable x, b is a coefficient or weighting applied to x and c is a constant.

Applies to: Any pair of variables measured at the ordinal, interval or ratio levels.

Multiple linear regression analysis

This technique summarizes the degree of association between a single 'dependent' variable and a group of 'independent' variables acting in combination. This is useful where it is posited that an effect is due to several causes (e.g. if it were hypothesized that drinking alcohol is caused by both age and gender). Outputs are similar to those for simple regression; an index r and an equation of the form:

$$y = b_1x_1 + b_2x_2 + b_nx_n + c$$

In addition, information relating to the possible contribution of each variable at each step of the calculation may be produced (see Figure 9.7).

Applies to: Any variables measured at the ordinal, interval or ratio levels.

Variable(s) Entered on Step Number
1. AGEGROUP

Multiple R	0.56822
R square	0.32288
Adjusted R square	0.31709
Standard Error	1.42674

Analysis of Variance

	DF	Sum of Squares	Mean Square
Regression	1	113.56575	113.56575
Residual	117	238.16534	2.03560

F = 55.78978 Significance F = 0.0000

Variables in the Equation

Variable	B	SE B	Beta	T	Sig T
EST1	1.015398	0.135944	0.568222	7.469	0.0000
(Constant)	-0.025462	0.364103		-0.605	0.5463

Figure 9.6 Part of the output for a bivariate linear regression analysis.

Variable(s) Entered on Step Number
2. HISTORY

Multiple R	0.58415
R square	0.34124
Adjusted R square	0.32988
Standard Error	1.41332

Analysis of Variance

	DF	Sum of Squares	Mean Square
Regression	2	120.02316	60.01158
Residual	116	231.70793	1.99748

F = 30.04361 Significance F = 0.0000

Variables in the Equation

Variable	B	SE B	Beta	T	Sig T
AGEGROUP	0.668420	0.235321	0.374052	2.840	0.0053
HISTORY	0.431057	0.239744	0.236772	1.798	0.0748
(Constant)	-0.228707	0.377977		-0.605	0.5463

Figure 9.7 Part of the output for a multiple linear regression analysis.

9.2.3 Advanced methods

Readers will no doubt be aware that the methods already described are by no means at the cutting edge of statistical science. Much more advanced and complex procedures have long been available and are constantly being improved and extended. These techniques serve various specialized functions for instance:

- to identify the distinguishing characteristics of certain groups – *discriminant analysis*
- to identify groups of respondents that differ from each other in certain respects – *cluster analysis*
- to construct new indices that combine the essential features of several existing variables – *factor analysis*
- to investigate and model changes in a variable or group of variables over time – *trend analysis*.

9.2.4 Graphical presentation

Many of the techniques described above can be adapted to make use of graphical presentation of results. The value of this is not so much for the purposes of report writing but to assist in the analysis process itself. For example, frequency counts may be more easily interpreted when presented as a *bar chart* or *pie chart*. Three-dimensional histograms may similarly be useful to help interpret cross-tabulated results. A *scatterplot* may be utilized to supplement bivariate correlation and regression analysis.

9.2.5 Statistical significance

Statistical significance tests constitute an important element in many analyses and most of the above techniques make use of them either to supplement the output itself (e.g. when applying a *Chi square* test to a cross-tabulation) or to delimit the analysis itself (e.g. carrying out multiple regression).

Use of a significance test always presupposes the presence of some element of randomness, either in the selection of the subjects of study or in their assignment into categories (e.g. interviewers, coders or into control and treatment groups). The basis of these tests is always that there is a probability of x per cent that such and such effect occurs by chance as a result of this random selection or allocation process. It is conventional for x to be set at 0.05 although other values, typically 0.1 or 0.001, signifying greater or lesser certainty are sometimes used.

Significance is determined in practice by comparing an index based on the strength of the relationship and sample size with values given in standard tables for the type of distribution to which the measure is expected to conform. There are many such distributions but the ones which principally concern us in this chapter are:

- *Student's 't'* – for comparing the means of two samples and testing associations.
- *Chi square* – for testing the effects observed in a cross-tabulation
- *F distribution* – for testing hypotheses, overall equations and individual terms in a multivariate regression analysis.

9.2.6 Statistical terminology

Every complex activity has its own special language. In writing the above we have made use of a number of specialist terms such as *distribution*, *dependent* and *independent*. We hope their meanings have been made sufficiently clear in the text. It is now necessary to introduce some additional terms.

Quantitative and qualitative

These terms may be applied both to a type of study (see Chapter 5) and a type of variable. In the context of this chapter, a quantitative study is one that concerns itself with making relatively precise measurements of a sample and inferring from them to a strictly defined population. A qualitative study, by contrast, concentrates on extracting meaning (especially as to cause and effect) from the sample itself.

When applied to variables the term quantitative may be taken to infer something that is measured at the interval or ratio level such as height or weight. Quantitative variables are also usually assumed to conform to the normal distribution. A qualitative variable is measured at the nominal level like place of birth or at the ordinal level like preference.

Parametric and non-parametric

These descriptions are often applied to statistical techniques. Parametric techniques include the calculation of means, Pearson correlation and regression analysis. They can only be applied to quantitative data. Non-parametric techniques include frequency counts, cross-tabulation (which can be applied to any variable) and Spearman's correlation which can be applied to ordinal variables. That at least is the theory. In practice, we find that the rules on the use of parametric techniques are often violated with respect to the requirement that the data should conform to the normal distribution (Nie *et al.*, 1975) and some consider it acceptable to apply them to ordinal data (Labovitz, 1970). Given the greater power of parametric tests we think this approach is acceptable. Even so, we reckon that it is advisable when deviating from the official route both to be aware that one is doing so and to proceed with caution. This applies particularly to the interpretation of the results of the analysis.

9.3 The process of analysis

9.3.1 Deciding on the general approach

In many studies it may be advisable to limit the analysis of the sample data to what is actually required to satisfy the objectives stated at the outset. As noted before, Kotler and Andreasen (1996) actually suggest that the most cost-effective approach is to work backwards from the proposed output (research report or presentation) doing only what is necessary to provide the information required. This has the merit that there is little opportunity to devote time, effort and resources to investigation of interesting phenomena or pet theories. It has the demerit that it reduces flexibility to attend to unforeseen outcomes. Nevertheless, we would not argue with the suggestion that the requirements of the audience to be addressed should be a primary consideration. Many stakeholder groups will prefer that findings and conclusions are based on a straightforward analysis illustrated by bar charts, pie charts and simple two dimensional tables (see e.g. the figures in Chapters 11 and 12). Where this is so there can be little point in producing complex analyses based on multivariate regression or factor analysis. Similarly, if the output needs to be presented in a single page report or short verbal presentation at a meeting then the comprehensiveness of the analysis could be restricted accordingly.

The foregoing should not be taken to imply that analysis should not always be systematic. Findings, especially those known to be controversial or unexpected, should always be thoroughly investigated both to suggest explanations and to reduce the risk that may arise from errors.

General description

The first task of the analysis proper is to describe the characteristics of the sample to some extent. We can identify four main stages:

1   *Presenting basic profiles.* Basic information on factors such as the proportion of females to males, age distribution and ethnic origin of the respondents in the sample will need to be provided as well as information relating to more specialized matters with which the study is concerned such as whether a nurse is employed by a GP or an NHS Trust. Frequency counts and descriptive statistics are likely to be the main techniques used at this stage of the analysis.

2   *Identify simple inter-relationships.* Simple relationships between variables will need to be identified. These may be either relationships that are hypothesized from previous research literature or from pilot work or they may be purely a matter of conjecture. The main techniques used are likely to be cross-tabulations and correlation analysis.

3   *Investigating the nature of effects by subgrouping.* Interesting effects observed during the previous exercise can be investigated further by the addition of further variables to the analysis as a means of subdividing the sample. For instance, if a relationship is found to exist between country of birth and some medical condition, it may be useful to know whether this is equally true for all ages and sexes. This process may bring to light interesting variations between different sexes etc., but more importantly, may show that an apparent effect of ethnicity is really attributable to gender or age. The main techniques which are likely to be used are multi-dimensional cross-tabulation and descriptive statistics, the latter being calculated separately for each subgroup.

4   *Investigating the nature of effects by multivariate techniques.* The effects observed by correlation analysis or cross-tabulation of the variables are not necessarily causal. In fact, the chain of causation may run in the opposite direction from what might be supposed or an association may be due to the influence on both variables of some third variable which is the real cause. A matrix of correlation coefficients which summarizes the association between each pair of variables often provides evidence where one pair of variables are weakly associated but share a much stronger association with some other variable. Such effects are also revealed by multiple regression analysis which may demonstrate that a variable such as age has no association with eating behaviour once gender has been taken into account. The latter being indicated by a reduced partial correlation coefficient for age once gender is added into the analysis.

Judging the magnitude of the effects

This stage aims to judge which effects in the sample are worth noting and worthy of further investigation and which can be ignored. Also, to assess when associations between variables are strong enough to take note of. Sometimes, of course, the answers are obvious but between the extremes there are grey areas! The answer, of course, is that it all depends. In particular, it depends on whether the difference in the observed association is what you expected or whether you just happened upon it. It also depends on the context and whether it has a particular bearing on the real reasons for making the study.

One approach which is commonly used to judge the importance of a research finding is to rely on estimates of statistical significance. That is to say, anything which is identified as statistically significant is considered to be large enough to be important. This is a tempting shortcut which may prove useful as a rule of thumb to 'bookmark' interesting effects. We do not recommend you to use it in any other way, however. An effect may be statistically significant without being otherwise important or notable in any practical sense.

The best advice is to treat each instance on its merits. If it seems to you that a result which indicates that 35 per cent of the females in your sample have a particular characteristic compared with 40 per cent of males is an important distinction, then by all means say so. If you think that a correlation which explains a quarter of the variance in something is a big step forward, and that you have a convincing rationale for believing this, then by all means say so. But it is also important not to lose sight of the fact that the other 75 per cent of this variance has not been accounted for.

Rationale and causation

In the foregoing discussion we mentioned causation several times. The objective of science is not just to describe nature (in summary form) but to uncover chains of causation: not just knowing what happens, but knowing *how* it happens and *why* it happens. If, for example, people born in rural India and now living in the UK suffer a greater incidence of diabetes than other groups, is this because they consume more raw sugar than previously? A number of issues would need to be investigated before such a hypothesis could be accepted:

- does the supposed cause and effect show the necessary association?
- does the supposed cause precede the supposed effect in time?
- does the supposed mechanism have a plausible theoretical explanation?
- can the supposed mechanism be substantiated empirically?

It may not always be possible to answer all these questions, but nevertheless every effort should be made to identify both cause and rationale to each observed effect.

The following three sections outline some of the processes which are likely to be used at each of the three main stages of data analysis.

9.3.2 The search for error

This section describes the initial phase of data analysis. The first task in any analysis should be to identify any weaknesses in the data. The process cannot be too thorough, though real world considerations dictate that some form of cost–benefit analysis should be applied. Otherwise you might overdo it. The more serious errors should always be identified and corrected before the next stage of analysis commences. For some errors actual correction may not be possible but the nature and possible impact of these errors should be noted for reference purposes during the remainder of the analysis.

General consistency checks

These are concerned with the detection of errors from recording, coding and keying-in. The main techniques are frequency counts, descriptive statistics and correlation analysis:

- the general patterns in the distribution of values should be examined using frequency counts (histograms are useful here) and descriptive statistics (mean, standard deviation, maximum and minimum). Any unexpected or exceptional effects, such as out-of-range and outlying values, should be checked against existing records such as original questionnaires
- tests can also be made to ensure that skip and filters in questionnaires have been followed correctly either by cross-tabulation of relevant variables or by computing new variables using conditional (Boolean) logic.

Reliability checks

These are intended to detect errors that arise due to differences in interviewer technique and from the effects of learning or fatigue. The effectiveness of these checks is dependent on interview subjects having been randomly assigned between interviewers and time periods in the first place. Extra variables representing these factors (interviewer, observer, time of day, day of week, week, month, etc.) will have been included in the data. Values may then be cross-tabulated or subjected to t-test as appropriate to identify significant differences in the results obtained by different interviewers or by the same interviewer over time.

Validity checks

These are intended to detect errors due to misunderstandings in interpreting or filling in the answers to questions, inappropriate coding etc. No matter how much care is devoted to the design of the data collection instruments, such errors are bound to occur. Devices such as duplicated (or similar) questions and the use of triangulation (the same phenomenon being investigated using more than one data collection method) allow this danger to be quantified. The relevant variables can be subjected to cross-tabulation or correlation analysis as appropriate. Errors of validity can also occur within the analysis itself.

9.3.3 Finding out about the sample

In this chapter we have deliberately made a distinction between 'the sample' and 'the wider population' by treating them completely separately. We accept that this is unusual but we have done it for what we think is a good reason. In our experience very few samples can be considered to be entirely random in nature, indeed many samples make no pretence at this. In such instances it is vitally important to make a distinction between what is known and that which is merely inferred. As far as the sample itself is concerned the findings are a matter of fact (or as near to fact as one can reasonably get).

9.3.4 Finding out about the population beyond the sample

It is very rare for a research project to concern itself only with the sample of respondents with whom it has contact. Almost invariably an objective is to draw some conclusion about a much wider population or universe of organizations, subjects, customers, clients or users etc. We will start by considering the meaning of *statistical significance* and then proceed to consider how this can be used for purposes such as testing hypotheses and making generalizations. Independent learning and testing phases offer a way for those engaged in purely exploratory work to give additional validity to their findings. Finally, we consider the implications when research findings support or conflict with the work of others.

Statistical significance

Most techniques of data analysis contain or are associated with tests of statistical significance. In the present context we can say that two conditions must be met before such tests can have any meaning at all:

1   There should exist both a sample which the data describes and a population which is the true subject of study.
2   The sample forms part, and is representative of, this underlying population in all respects with which the research is concerned. This condition is usually satisfied by selecting the sample at random or with some approximation to randomness.

Within this narrow context, a statistically significant result is one in which the observed relationship in the sample has a low probability of being due to chance. This probability will be dependent on the size of the sample as well as the strength of the relationship observed. It is conventional to accept a level of probability of 0.05 or 5 per cent as setting the boundary. Any relationship which is significant at 0.05 will occur by chance in five out of 100 random samples even though there is no relationship at all in the underlying population. In other words, you can be 95 per cent certain that some such effect (however small) is present in the population from which the sample was drawn.

Testing hypotheses

It is advisable to construct *a priori* hypotheses if at all possible This is done either from knowledge of previous research in the field or on the basis of pilot work. This procedure is much to be preferred to the production of *ad hoc* findings of a purely exploratory nature. A *hypothesis* is a proposition stated in such a way that it is capable of being disproved. For example, suppose we believe that housing conditions have an impact on health (see 'Improving the quality of housing' in Acheson (1998, pp. 52–53). Many researchers find it convenient to construct a *null hypothesis* – in this case that no relationship between housing and health exists in the underlying population – and test that instead. This may seem a rather odd thing to do but there is method in the apparent madness. Whereas a null hypothesis is disproved by an exception, the original hypothesis (as stated) never could be. We can test the null hypothesis by carrying out a Chi square test on the appropriate cross-tabulation or by applying a *t*-test to a correlation analysis (whichever is appropriate to the way these variables were measured). If the result is significant at the 0.05 level of probability the null hypothesis is disproved and the association between housing and health is supported.

Where a quantitative relationship is hypothesized the testing process is slightly more complex and conceptually slightly different. A null hypothesis is set up to the effect that no difference exists between the sample on which the hypothetical model is based and that on which it is being tested. The test itself consists of making a comparison between the original distribution of values that gave rise to the hypothetical relationship and that which exists in the test sample. The resulting index or ratio is compared to figures given in standard tables which indicate whether it is of sufficient magnitude to be significant at the required level. If it is large enough, then the null hypothesis is disproved. The two samples are not the same. In this case the original hypothesis is disproved also.

The probabilistic nature of the testing process leaves room for doubt as to whether the conclusions are correct. A *Type I* error arises when the hypothesis is in fact true but the test indicates that it should be rejected. A *Type II* error, by contrast, arises when the hypothesis is false but the test indicates that it should be accepted. In each instance the probability of making such an error is equal to the level of significance.

Exploratory work

The testing of *a priori* hypotheses is probably much less common in research analysis than purely exploratory work. Validity can never be as great as with *a priori* hypotheses since there is a much greater possibility that any effects will be the result of chance.

In its crudest form, exploratory research produces endless series of descriptive statistics, correlation analyses and multi-way cross-tabulations that encompass every conceivable permutation and combination of variables in the hope of finding something significant. This method is known technically by the deliberately disparaging term of *data dredging*. It is a method which, though it has the virtue of thoroughness, nevertheless tempts fate because if the data set is complex enough the exercise is bound to produce something. Something, moreover, that will not be replicated elsewhere. For this reason data-dredgers are recommended to subdivide their samples by a random process and satisfy themselves that any interesting effects are duplicated in both subsets before they permit themselves to generalize from these results.

Learning and testing

This represents a convenient compromise between the two approaches outlined above. In this approach, the sample is subdivided at random and the first group is used for an unashamed data-dredging exercise (the learning phase). The resulting hypotheses in the shape of quantitative models (regression equations etc.) are subjected to testing on the remaining data set (the test phase). Though this method appears fairly foolproof and is undoubtedly superior to exploratory work used alone, the method still suffers from the drawback that biases of question design or interviewer technique will corrupt to both data sets equally. Moreover, if large numbers of hypotheses are produced there is a high probability of Type II errors occurring.

Comparison with other work

An important stage in the process of generalization is that at which the research findings are related to and compared with an existing body of knowledge. For some studies it may be the only way to establish a wider validity for the findings. In our experience researchers tend to suffer from a considerable terror that their results will be pre-empted or that their conclusions will be insufficiently controversial to be accepted as truly original. In reality, the exact opposite is true. Originality does not have to mean going out on a limb. Where research confirms earlier findings, whether or not (one might say especially when it is not) this was the subject of a formal hypothesis, it must be considered to improve their validity. Competing or ideologically opposed researchers who reach identical conclusions will convince in a way that no single body of work can hope to achieve. The process of introducing new ideas and principles or refuting established ones is, by contrast, a rather thankless task. People like certainty, get attached to ideas and often will meet new ones with scepticism and incredulity. They may even try to discredit the source. You need to be pretty sure of your ground if you want to try this route. Findings that 'break the mould' generally indicate that further work is yet to be completed.

9.4 Software tools for data analysis

What tools are available to assist the analyst in the task? Let us look at what is available. Traditionally, social scientists have tended to use SPSS (introduced in 1968 as the Statistical Package for the Social Sciences) or another veteran product known as SAS (Statistical Analysis for the Sciences). Both incorporate all of the techniques discussed in this chapter and both can be supplemented by additional software for data entry (see Chapter 7). These are certainly the products favoured by professional analysts but price, complexity and some shortcomings in terms of ease of learning make them less than ideal for the less experienced analyst. Over the years these products have encountered increasing competition from lower-priced, less comprehensive products that were designed specifically to meet demand from PC-based 'desk-top' research projects. Perhaps the best known of these is SNAP. This was originally very limited in terms of its functions but is now capable of carrying out the full range of statistical analysis discussed in this chapter.

As research becomes less specialized, there is increasing demand for all-in-one solutions that combine data entry, data analysis and report writing in an easy to use format. Logotron's Pinpoint is the most well-known example of the latter type of software. Again, all the basic techniques are included.

Some projects do not need analysis software as such. If all you need are frequency counts, medians, means and standard deviations then a spreadsheet is quite adequate. You can also carry out tests for significance (although you need to known how to write the formulae yourself). The big advantage here is that the chances are you already have this software installed on your computer. Best known in this category are Microsoft's Excel (part of Office 97) and IBM's Lotus 1-2-3. Less well known (and cheaper) brands such as Ability Spreadsheet are also available.

9.4.1 How much do these packages cost?

The SPSS Base package costs £795 with a renewal fee of £125 per annum (which includes upgrades). As an alternative, a licence may be purchased for the one-off cost of £920 including vat. SNAP costs £950. Excel is only available as part of Office 97 which costs £385; Lotus 1-2-3 costs £304; Ability Spreadsheet costs £19.98.

9.4.2. Where can you buy these packages?

If you want specialized statistical analysis software the chances are that your local computer or software supplier will not be able to help – that is our experience anyway. The simplest approach is probably to purchase over the Internet directly from the publishers. This means paying full list price, of course.

For spreadsheets, your local retailer probably is the best source. At present this market is highly competitive. The prices we have quoted are published prices from a national retailer, but further discounts appeared possible from talking to sales personnel.

9.5 Conclusions

The most important consideration for anyone who is thinking of carrying out statistical analysis of survey data is to be sure that you know what you are doing. This is not difficult. Many analyses will confine themselves to intuitive and easy-to-grasp concepts such as frequency counts, means and medians. This may be all that is required for reports or presentations made to non-statistical audiences.

Analysts should not allow their enthusiasm to rush them into testing hypotheses before a thorough assessment of the data has been completed. This avoids duplication of effort and the disappointment and the frustration that may occur when some interesting or controversial findings turn out to be wrong.

It is important to make a distinction between conclusions relating to the sample and those relating to the wider population from which the sample was drawn. You can make positive statements about the former ('34 per cent expressed concern') but not about the latter. Conclusions about the sample should never be based on trivialities.

Drawing conclusions about the wider population beyond the sample is a risky business indeed. The apparently precise nature of inferential statistics should never be allowed to obscure this. If you base your conclusions on conventional levels of statistical significance, five times out of 100 you can expect to be wrong.

Finally, its worth pointing out that if you make allowances for the less than completely random nature of your sampling, for the fact that people do not always answer truthfully, for interviewer effects, for errors in coding and keying-in, and for the in-built uncertainty when you try to generalize your results from the sample, then the whole thing starts to look like a minefield.

That is why you need to know what you are doing and where you are trying to go!

Example 1: Are you eating properly?

The survey of healthy eating has got as far as the analysis stage. Comparison of results between interviewers reveals big differences in the frequency with which cake is consumed. Significance tests indicate that the sample of respondents interviewed by interviewer 3 is unlikely to have been drawn from the same population as those for the other interviewers as far as their cake-eating habits are concerned. Cake-eating frequency is much lower for this group. Further investigation is made and it is discovered from tape recordings that interviewer 3 (a trained dietician) adopted a very scathing tone of voice when asking about certain kinds of cake.

The researchers want to test a regression model derived from half the respondents which indicates that consumption of certain foods has a very specific effect on the height/weight ratio. The procedure adopted is to compare the mean squares for the two studies with values of the F distribution. The F value is calculated as follows:

$$F(DF1, DF2) = (SS2/DF2)/(SS1/DF1)$$

Where DF1 and DF2 are the degrees of freedom for the source and test data, SS1 and SS2 are the sum of the squares of the deviation from the regression line and the expected values, respectively.

The F value given by this formula is looked up in standard tables and is found to exceed the value given for $F(DF1, DF2)$ at the 0.05 confidence level. The variation from expected values in the test sample is too great to be due to chance and the null hypothesis is therefore disproved. The regression model does not adequately describe this relationship as found in two subsamples.

Example 2: Community nursing

A large-scale questionnaire survey of 4,000 district nurses, practice nurses and health visitors reveals that district nurses and health visitors (employed by NHS Trusts) are evenly divided on whether their training is adequate (50 per cent expressed concern about this). For practice nurses (employed by GP) slightly less (nearly 48 per cent) express concern. For practice nurses, opportunities are found to be entirely dependent on the attitude of the GP. Several say they pay for training themselves.

In the final report for this project it is concluded that GP employees are significantly more satisfied with their training than Trust employees. This is because the sample size is sufficiently large even though the difference does not, at face value, seem likely to be important.

What tests would be used to reach this conclusion? If the sample size is much smaller could the same conclusion be drawn?

Example 3: West Birmingham

The senior research supervisor asks the analyst to produce 'statistics' relating to some of the medical findings of the study for inclusion in a paper he is writing for a leading journal. The analyst points out that the sample is only random in the sense of its being drawn from the lists of certain GPs (chosen for the large proportion of ethnic minorities among their patients). The supervisor points out that referees for the journal concerned do not consider the paper to be sufficiently scientific without these data.

How should this criticism be countered?

Further reading

Sapsford, R. and Jupp, V. (eds) (1996) *Data Collection and Analysis*, London: Sage Publications and Open University.

Chapter 10

Interactive methods in public service design in Austria

Günther Botschen and Martina Botschen

In this chapter readers will develop an understanding of:

- the key elements to consider when integrating users in the development of public services
- the characteristics of three user participation methods
- the public service context in Austria with respect to adult education and health services
- how to apply the three user participation methods demonstrated by short case studies.

10.1 Introduction

This chapter is concerned with the integration of users in the development and modification of public services. A common problem in profit as well as non-profit organizations is the understanding and acceptance of newly developed services by the relevant user group. The results of recent empirical studies indicate that users interacting during certain stages of the new service development process have a positive impact on the success of a new service. However, existing new service development processes, which have been mainly transferred from the new product development of consumer goods, lack the integration of advice of customers or user participation.

In this chapter we introduce a conceptual framework for the development of a user-oriented service. The framework is based on user characteristics, the type of user interaction, stages of the new service development process and the contribution to the degree of service innovation. To enhance the possibilities of integrating users in the new service development process three direct participation techniques are introduced. Their appropriateness for different stages in the service design are evaluated and their potential contribution to different types of innovation are discussed. The methods are: sequence-oriented problem identification, lead-users and planning cell. These methods have been chosen because they are characterised by an interactive user participation approach. The Austrian context for adult education and health services is described and the potential of each method is demonstrated in three case studies in Austria.

10.2 User participation in new service development

There is little disagreement in the literature that listening to the voice of the market is important for product and service development. A rich body of literature exists which underlines the potential advantages of using information from customers in product development (Foxall and Johnston, 1987; von Hippel, 1988; Johne, 1994). In total quality management the development of products based on the voice of the customers has become a key criterion. The first concept in the Baldrige Award criteria is that 'quality' is based on the customer (Juran, 1989; Griffin and Hauser, 1993). Blattberg and Deighton (1993) emphasize that the often required dimension 'always closer, my customer, with you' can hardly be achieved by marketing people alone. According to McKenna (1991) the whole company should continuously search and become involved in dialogue with customers. He calls this customer orientation based on close feed-back loops.

Similarly to the product innovation literature, the fundamental importance of users in the new service development design is noted (Groenroos, 1982, 1983; Cina, 1990). Edvardsson and Olson (1996) argue that to understand users' needs and wishes properly, it is appropriate and often necessary to involve them in the different stages of developing new services. Attractive and user-friendly services emerge from a dialogue with competent and demanding users. Therefore users should be included in service development projects, to set up a meaningful dialogue and to make it easier for them to articulate their needs, requirements and wishes. Through interaction, users can be integrated into an organization, made part of the service planning and development process. Talking with users and customers is one of the most important sources of new product ideas and the single best factor distinguishing successful from unsuccessful companies in new product development (Soderberg and O'Halloran, 1992; Meyer and Bluemelhuber, 1998). However, research analysing differences between developing services and products has shown that customer participation and the use of customer information is more common in product development than in service development (Martin and Horne, 1992; Martin, 1994; Edvardsson *et al.*, 1995).

10.3 A framework for user interactive service design

An analysis of recent empirical studies concerning the development of new services (Edvardsson *et al.*, 1995; Martin and Horne, 1995; Tabrizi and Walleigh, 1997; Gruner and Homburg, 1998) confirms that user participation plays a crucial role at different stages of the development of new services and products. Edvardsson *et al.* (1995) investigated in their two studies the development of seven new services in different companies of the Swedish service industries and two large development projects within the communications industry. They report a very low level of participation of customers in the stages of idea generation, business analysis, process, system design and testing as well as in marketing programme, design and personnel training. Although in this study no explicit link between the extent of customer participation and service innovations' success is explored, some problem areas due to very low direct customer participation are highlighted:

> This resulted in technical and marketing problems that had to be solved parallel to the launching of the services . . . There was a general lack of market information during the development processes. Including demanding customers as members of service development teams is one way to get closer to customers and their needs.
>
> (Edvardsson *et al.*, 1995)

From the discussion of the published conceptual and empirical studies some elements seem to be important to consider when integrating users in a new service development:

- in which stage(s) of the new service development process users are to be integrated
- which characteristics of users are to be considered
- which type of interaction takes place
- the extent of innovation which is desired.

10.3.1 Stages of new service development

For the purpose of developing a framework which sets the agenda for integration users in the new service design we have chosen a new service development approach consisting of nine stages built on the model proposed by Scheuing and Johnson (1989) and de Brentani and Riesen (1997) because it integrates existing new services models (Donnelly *et al.*, 1985; Bowers, 1986, 1987; Johnson *et al.*, 1986) and provides a balance between complexity and detail. We distinguish the following phases:

1 New service strategy.
2 Idea generation.
3 Idea screening.
4 Concept development.
5 Business analysis.
6 Process and system design and testing.
7 Marketing programme design.
8 Market testing.
9 Full-scale launch and then review.

(Zaltman *et al.*, 1973; Booz, Allen, and Hamilton, 1982; Cooper and Kleinschmidt, 1986; Scheuing and Johnson, 1989; Jallat, 1994; Johne, 1994; de Brentani and Riesen, 1997.)

10.3.2 Characteristics of users

From von Hippel's studies (1986, 1988) and the Gruner and Homburg study (1998) the following list of user characteristics can be derived: existing or potential users, the degree of knowledge and experience, involvement, creativity, reputation for the segment (opinion leaders), representativeness and extent of benefit through a new or modified service.

10.3.3 Types of interaction

The results of the four studies indicate different ways of interaction. Four main types of interaction can be identified:

- a short, feedback type based on specific questions users try to answer on certain stages of service design
- an open dialogue between users
- an open ongoing dialogue between customers and employees during selected stages, and
- an open dialogue which is preceded by specific information inputs to widen users' knowledge and assessment capabilities.

10.3.4 *Extent of innovation*

The extent of service innovation can be distinguished between service breakthroughs or major innovations (e.g. book orders via Internet), service line extensions (e.g. an airline offering new routes), service process changes (e.g. extended opening hours of a food retailer) and style changes (e.g. revising the logo of a business school) (Heany, 1983; Zeithaml and Bitner 1996).

Based on these four components and their described characteristics we propose a framework for user-integrated new service design, shown in Figure 10.1. In this framework user characteristics and type of interaction during one or more certain stages determine a specific user-integrated approach which ought to lead to service innovation.

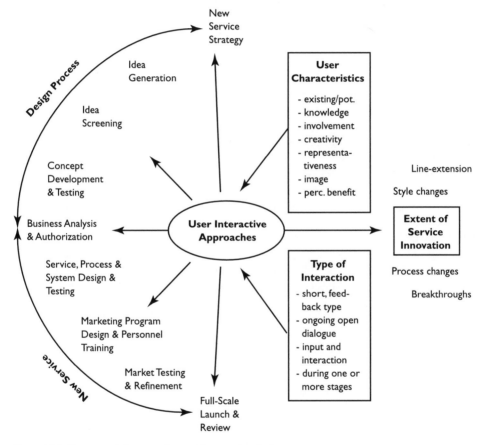

Figure 10.1 Framework for user-interactive service design.

10.4 The adult education system and the health system in Austria

This section provides background information on the public sector context in Austria for adult education and for the health system. This information is needed in order to understand the case studies that follow.

10.4.1 Adult education

In Austria there are three nation-wide adult education organizations that are offering services for the general public: WIFI (Wirtschaftsförderungsinstitut der Wirtschaftskammer), bfi (Berufsförderungsinstitut der Arbeiterkammer) and Volkshochschule (www.wifi.at, 1999; www.bfi-tirol.or.at, 1999; www.vhs.at, 1999).

The *WIFI* is organized by the Austrian Chamber of Commerce. Each of the nine regions in Austria have their own learning centre with its branches in the major cities. The main focus is on increasing the skills and qualifications of the Austrian workforce to enhance the competitiveness of Austrian companies. The course programme involves any sort of courses which contribute to professional skills. This includes intensive programmes over several years for skilled trades qualifications (e.g. hairdresser, builder, plumber, jeweller), communication training, management development and language courses. In addition, the WIFI offers consulting and support for Austrian companies in areas like innovation, environmental considerations, European law and export activities in general.

The *bfi* is a service organization of the Austrian chamber of labour and the Austrian Union. It has similar programmes to the WIFI, but traditionally has more focus on the employee than on the management level. The bfi works together with the unemployment office and offers courses for qualifying unemployed persons in other job areas. Companies who support the participation of their employees in courses that increase their qualifications get generous funding from the European Social Fund and members of the Austrian Union get individual funding from it.

The *Volkshochschule* is organized like a club independently in each region. There are approximately 300 Volkshochschulen offering courses for half a million people per year. The course programme of the Volkshochschule differs from the WIFI and bfi programme in its strong focus on non-professional related topics. The Volkshochschule offers courses to increase the general education of people (courses range from psychology to mathematics, a wide range of language courses), programmes for creativity, art and leisure, health and well-being, and society and culture. The Volkshochschule is supported by regional communes, state governments and the ministry for education and cultural affairs, the chamber of labour and the Austrian Union.

Despite the different origins of the above-described organizations, all courses are open to the general public and no membership is necessary. The course fees are generally low, as all the organizations are supported by either their respective chambers and or by tax money.

10.4.2 The Austrian health system

The Austrian health system is part of the social security system and is based on a compulsory insurance coverage. Contributions are related to income up to a specified income ceiling. All individuals (Austria has a population of 8 million) are insured with universal access to care on every level of provision. Although the GDP share of public expenditure is below the OECD average, the performance of the health system is comparatively very good. The number of hospital beds available ranges from 10.5 to 10.9 beds per 100 inhabitants depending on the region and the ratio of doctors per inhabitant is 126 GPs, 151 specialists and 47 dentists per 100,000 inhabitants in 1996 (www.bmag.gv.at, 1999; www.sozvers.at, 1999).

In general, the Austrian public health insurance organizations run hospitals only to a limited extent, the major part is owned by the state governments and the communes. The financing follows a duality principal. Roughly, capital costs, including maintenance and renovation of hospitals, have been purchased by the hospital owner, whereas current operating costs are covered by social insurers, patient co-payments and private insurers. To give an overview of the ownership of hospitals see http: www.bmag.gv.at (1999) and www.sozvers.at (1999).

The Austrian health insurance principles have a big impact on the availability of medical treatments for the population and the service provided by doctors. They differ considerably from the UK system. The Austrian public health insurance is built around seven principles (Huber, 1999):

1   The health insurance system is organized according to different professions and regions. There are separate organizations for private employees, public-employed persons, self-employed persons, farmers. If someone is unemployed then the insurance organization for private employees, which is the biggest one, is relevant. There are slight differences in the refunding of the different organizations. In total there are twenty-eight public health insurance organizations.

2   It is obligatory to be insured by the appropriate health insurance.

3   The health insurance provides money and service, e.g. if an employee is ill for several weeks, the employer stops paying the salary, then the health insurance pays for every day of illness. Services mean the coverage of medical treatment and drugs.

4   There is a small self-funding requirement for each treatment from the patients.

5   Freedom of establishment of practices: Any doctor who fulfils the professional requirements can open a practice wherever he/she wants and operate as self-employed. The Austrian insurance organizations keep contracts for direct payment of medical treatments with a wide variety of general and specialist doctors. The decision on how many and which types of doctor get a contract is made by health insurance organizations together with the medical council. (Out of the 10,188 GPs 4,326 and out of the 12,176 specialist doctors 3,714 held contracts with the public health insurance in 1996.)

6   Freedom of choice of general and specialist doctors: Patients can choose any general or specialist doctor they perceive as appropriate. Patients can consult a specialist doctor directly and do not have to be transferred by a GP. Only the availability of hospital treatment in general requires the transfer from a specialist or a general doctor. When choosing a doctor with a contract with one of the health insurance organizations, the patient has no further cost than the self-funding part. The consultation of doctors

Table 10.1 Ownership of hospitals and hospital beds

Ownership	Number of hospitals	Number of beds
Federal government	12	688
State government	95	42,264
Communes	67	12,158
Social insurance funds	41	6,140
Religious orders	50	11,900
Associations	11	939
Private persons	49	3,438
Total	325	77,527

without health insurance contracts has to be paid directly by the patient, but can be submitted to the relevant health insurance organization for refunding. The amount of refunding is limited by the fixed rates of the health insurance organizations for specific treatments, which follow the rates of the direct transfer the health insurance would make for their contracted doctors.

7   The health insurance is independently organized for each region. On a higher level the different organizations work together, e.g. developing guidelines, but each regional organization can decide independently which treatment and to which extent to fund.

10.5 Direct participation techniques – evaluation and cases

In this section of the chapter we present three techniques which allow users to interact along various stages of new service design. After a brief description, each method is evaluated according to its appropriateness for different stages in public service design and the potential contribution to the degree of innovation is discussed. The following techniques have been chosen: sequence-oriented problem identification, lead-user and planning cell.

All these techniques have been used to some extent at various stages of innovation processes although so far they are used more frequently for consumer and industrial goods than for services in the public sector. The three methods demonstrate different levels of intensity of user integration into public service development processes.

10.5.1 Sequence-oriented problem identification (SOPI)

This is an attempt to combine and extend blue-printing (Shostack, 1982, 1987; Kingman-Brundage, 1989) of service encounters with assessing user perceptions of critical incidents occurring in service encounters (Botschen et al., 1996a; Stauss and Weinlich, 1997). Each customer participating in a study on service quality is guided and asked to respond to each step appearing in the service blue-print, so the technique will result in greater completeness in detecting problems compared to the critical incident technique (CIT). The fact that CIT is limited to identifying particular user satisfying and dissatisfying activities in a service encounter, not minor incidents that also may affect customer evaluations, then intuitively a method designed to gain customer evaluations for all steps in the service encounter will result in a greater number of evaluations. Consequently, SOPI is used to learn the small, as well as the big, things that customers notice and evaluate in service encounters (Botschen et al., 1996a). The resulting list of problems may include interesting ideas for service modifications and provide a good starting point for the creation and evaluation of new ideas.

The method is characterized by the following steps:

1   Identify which steps in the process a user experiences with the service. This is the development of the blue-print. For the blue-print, service personnel and users will be interviewed.
2   Ask the user about critical incidents for each of the identified process steps. Critical incidents are strongly positive or negative experiences.

SOPI case

In a study to examine user perceptions of elements of the augmented service offering both facilitating and supporting services in an adult education centre, fifty-four users reported eighty-six critical or minor incidents along the specified phases of the blue-print. Some of the problems identified ranged from no parking space, uncomfortable and cold entrance atmosphere and small or hidden black-boards in the entrance and orientation phase, over-stressed encounter personnel and transaction failures during and after booking in the reception and booking phase to no discounts offered in the paying phase. For some of the identified negative incidents, ideas for potential avoidance were already generated at this stage.

The list of problems and ideas were used in further discussions by employees and management to generate and screen additional ideas. As a consequence fifty specific changes and improvements were designed into the service encounter based on the results of the SOPI data. Both human and non-human elements experienced by the customer were changed. The earlier mentioned problem examples led to the implementation of the following redesigns:

- five car parking spaces were contracted for daytime use by customers visiting the centre to register for evening courses
- warm lighting was added and heating was increased in the entrance and reception areas
- the bulletin boards were tripled in size and presented as a series leading from the front door to the service provider station
- two-person teams during most hours of course registration were started to reduce service provider stress and increase attention to the customer during human interactions
- an on-line backup computer software program was designed as a fail-safe system to customer experiences with transaction failures
- discounts for senior citizens and club enrolments were offered (Botschen et al., 1996a).

During the development and implementation of the specific changes no further direct customer participation took place although continuous feedback of customer contact personnel was given.

Method evaluation

- In which stage(s) of the new service development process users are integrated: the results from SOPI applications may be helpful particularly in identifying details that can be improved to help keep relationships with user. We consider SOPI especially appropriate to transfer directly customers' perceptions of critical and minor problems as a basis for the stage of idea generation.

• Which characteristics of users are to be considered: existing users with considerable experience with the service will be necessary for the application of this method. Users must have experienced critical incidents by themselves, to be able to describe problems in detail.

• Which type of interaction takes place: the method represents a rather short and feed-back type of interaction. Users are not more involved than by any other qualitative method.

• The extent of innovation, which is to be expected: as SOPI concentrates on the experi-ence with an existing service the degree of innovative ideas coming as a result will be rather low. Hence, we hypothesize that SOPI contributes most to the style changes and service improvements.

Figure 10.2 summarizes customer characteristics, type of interaction along stages of the SOPI method and its contribution to the degree of service design.

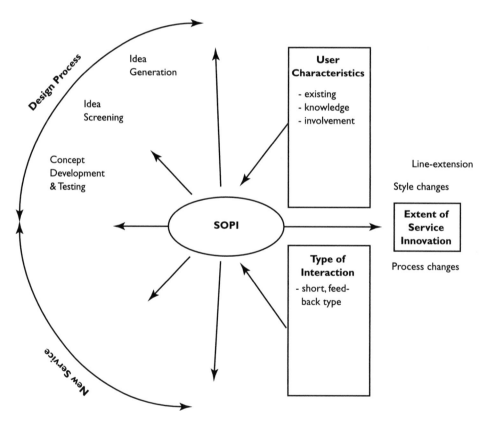

Figure 10.2 SOPI evaluation.

10.5.2 Lead-users

Lead-users are people who face needs that will become general in a market place, but they face them months or years before the bulk of that marketplace encounters them. Lead-users are positioned to benefit significantly by obtaining a solution to those needs (Urban and von Hippel, 1988). For example, customers of an insurance company with a strong need for a content or process innovation (e.g. cancellation of existing insurance contracts at any time or prevention and avoidance of potential risks and damages as a future new service strategy) which thousands of users will need in two years' time would match the definition of lead-users.

Users with real world experience of a need are in the best position to provide a team in charge of new service design with accurate data regarding it. Users at the front of new service trends have expectations and ideas which service companies should analyse to understand the needs which the bulk of the market will have tomorrow. The utility of the second lead-user characteristic is that users who expect high benefits from a solution to a need can provide the richest need and solution data for new service design (Urban and von Hippel 1988). According to von Hippel (1978) lead-users' requests include some functional specifications and standards for a product or service and do provide the new service idea. Lead-users by definition are highly involved and creative. Ideally they bring some opinion leader attributes as well.

A four-step methodology for concept development and testing is generally recommended (for a detailed discussion see von Hippel, 1986, 1988; Urban and von Hippel, 1988). We have slightly modified these steps for services.

1   *Specify lead-user indicators* by finding market or technological trends and related measures and defining measures of potential benefits.
2   *Identify lead-user group*, e.g. by analysing data of negative customer experiences and derived recommendations from customer panels.
3   *Generate service concept* by integrating lead-users in an active dialogue with cross-functional new service team members. Creative group sessions can be used to pool user solution content and develop new product concept. In some cases the user solution may represent not only a concept but a fully implemented service.
4   *Test lead user-concept* by assessing how lead-user data are evaluated by more typical users in the target segment.

Lead-user case

To demonstrate the application of the lead-user technique an application for preventive health care in one Austrian county is given and described along the four steps of the method.

I Specify lead-user indicators

To identify important trends in preventive health care a telephone survey with doctors, medical-related professionals, fitness gurus, nutrition consultants etc. is conducted. These 'experts' are asked about their perception of important future indicators in health care prevention. For this type of interview six to twelve experts are sufficient to develop a picture about major trends in the area of investigation. Important indicators within preventive health care might come from regular health checks, alternative medical advice and treatment, eating habits, leisure, fitness activities etc.

2 Identify lead-user group

This can be done by conducting a further telephone survey whereby a market research organization identifies, based on the evolved indicators, a group of eight to twelve people who are highly involved in health care prevention activities. Another way to determine a group of lead-users is to concentrate on people who are seeking alternative medical advice, participants of medical or well-being courses, who show a high involvement or have been known as active and self-motivated when it comes to preventive treatment. Another source for finding potential lead-users is their reading behaviour, e.g. subscribers of health-related magazines and journals.

3 Generate a health care prevention concept

Once a group of eight to twelve lead-users have been generated, these persons are contacted and invited to participate in a lead-user session, which might last up to two days. Due to the high involvement of the lead-users, full coverage of any costs and expenses plus incentives (financial or in-kind donations) only few refusals can be expected. The willingness of lead-users to co-operate is additionally high, because it lies in their interest to create such a service.

Under the guidance of an external facilitator, managers who are from different areas and are responsible for health care in the future in the specific city council or county work out in group discussions with the lead-users possible ideas and activities within the major trends. The presence of managers from planning, finance, human resource, legal matters etc. permits an *ad hoc* evaluation of proposed activities, their required resources and barriers to implementation. Ideas and activities which are considered as beneficial and show a high degree of successful implementation are integrated into a concept of health care prevention. The time horizon of the planned activities varies from:

*   *short-term* (within two months), e.g. the presentation and discussion of the results of the lead-user session in regional/national TV channels to inform the public, to raise awareness and to stimulate reactions to the concept from the population
*   over *mid-term* (within one year), e.g. the establishment of nutrition advising centres in the outlets of interested food retailers or community centres
*   to *long-term* approaches (within two or three years), e.g. yearly general health checks run by the local GPs.

4 Test lead-user concept

An evaluation with general users is recommended in order to make sure that the health care prevention concept developed together with the lead-users will be accepted on a broader base. As indicated under point 3, under short-term horizons one way to assess the overall interest and acceptance of the specific contents of the concept is to establish a kind of qualitative feedback mechanism. For a representative evaluation of the planned preventive health care activities a county-wide quantitative telephone, postal or face-to-face survey might be appropriate. In our case, a qualitative TV platform feedback or group discussion of the concept in selected cities and villages seemed sufficient.

Method evaluation

In sum, the lead-users can serve as a need-forecasting laboratory, where lead-users and members of a new service design team meet and perform open-ended dialogues.

- In which stage(s) of the new service development process users are integrated: Via the lead-user technique mainly the stages of idea generation, idea screening and concept development and testing will be covered. In specific cases lead-users might contribute to the phase of new service strategy and the stages of full development, market testing, implementation and review of the new service.
- Which characteristics of users are to be considered: Lead-users by definition are involved above average and interested in the topic under consideration. It is particularly important to invest some effort in identifying lead-user characteristics to get the benefits out of the method.
- Which type of interaction takes place: The method represents an intense form of interaction. Lead-users are not mere informants, but become co-workers for a short period.
- The extent of innovation which is to be expected: Concerning the degree of innovation we hypothesize that lead-users seem to be mainly suitable for process changes and line extensions, in rare cases leading to service breakthroughs.

10.5.3 The planning cell

Planning cells are groups of approximately twenty-five participants working on a decision problem for a limited period of time (normally 3 to 5 days). The participants are randomly drawn, because they should represent the population which is affected by the underlying problem. They get paid for their work, which lends to their participation a semi-employed status and indicates the value of their work.

To enable lay-people to work on specific tasks, experts provide basic knowledge about technical or social contingencies and 'process moderators' help in organizing issues. The goal of planning cells is to involve people in the decision-making process in respect of relevant public issues. The method was developed as an alternative democratic means for solving local problems in addition to the decision making by elected representatives.

The results of the work carried out in planning cells can be interpreted as political advice,

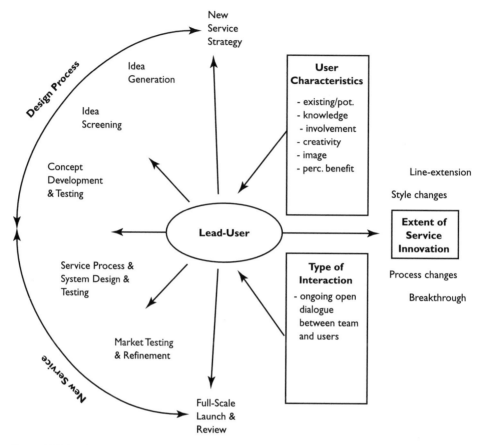

Figure 10.3 Lead-user evaluation.

exploring how 'the will of the people' is constituted (Reinert, 1988; Dienel, 1992; Garbe and Hoffmann, 1992). Most planning cells so far have been undertaken for the public service sector or for non-profit services (e.g. evaluation of alternative motorways, assessment of future telephone systems, elaboration of test criteria for consumer rights associations, planning inner-city areas; for further examples see Dienel, 1994). However, this does not mean that the usefulness of the planning cell is limited to those sectors. The identification of the people's will and the potential increase in the acceptance of new designed or redesigned services due to the involvement of existing and potential users could be beneficial to all types of service providers.

The planning cell case

For the development of a future study programme of a public learning institution in the city of Vienna, two parallel planning cells were undertaken (see detailed documentation of this planning cell in Botschen *et al.*, 1996b). It was the goal of this public learning institution to offer a study programme which addresses relevant social topics in a way that would attract existing and potential customers for and after the year 2000. A random sample of 400 people in the relevant parts of town was drawn and invited to participate in the planning cell. From the interested citizens forty-one were chosen to form the two planning cells (twenty participants per group). The final sample represented the population in terms of age, gender, education and profession of the relevant parts of the town.

The planning cells worked for three whole days. Experts provided general information about the following pre-defined topics: urbanization and city development of Vienna (researcher from DATINFORM-Büro für Sozialforschung), mobility and its impact on the environment (traffic and environmental psychologist), inter-generations conflict, pension and health systems (political consultant), north–south imbalance in its various forms (speaker from the 'Österreichischer Informationsdienst für Entwicklungshilfe-politik), attitudes/attitudinal change and roles in society (speaker from IFES market and opinion research) and methods of knowledge transfer (department of education, University of Graz).

Participants worked in groups of five people on the relevance of those topics for the city of Vienna, on how those topics were manifested in their environment and on concrete examples of how some of the identified negative effects could be overcome. Results of these group processes were a list of issues which the participants considered to be most important for Vienna: planning of the development of the city, traffic, education, the housing situation, the health system, the social integration of immigrants, citizen participation and crime. In order to work on a study programme which would inform and sensitize potential customers of the public learning institution to the identified problem areas, experts provided input and advice on methods and instruments of knowledge transfer.

Based on the availability and limitations of financial and personnel resources provided by the managers of the public learning institution, the planning cell participants developed study programmes for five topics: integration of immigrants, new initiatives for the reduction of unemployment, new initiatives to combat the isolation of elder people, health – self-help through prevention, caring and information, and reducing the level of individual transport. The study programmes were developed in terms of what content should be covered, which didactic elements should be incorporated and how long/intense the programme should be.

The planning cell described above demonstrated a means for addressing general problems and for relating them to concrete steps which would be understandable and accepted by the people involved. Some of the topics were already offered by the public learning institution, but the results of the planning cell provided the learning institution with a series of new ideas both in terms of specific contents to consider as well as ways to promote their programme.

Method evaluation

- In which stage(s) of the new service development process users are integrated: The remit for a planning cell incorporates all stages of the service innovation process with some restrictions concerning the stages of new service strategy, business analysis/ authorization and full-scale launch/review.

- Which characteristics of users are to be considered: Participants of a planning cell are randomly drawn. They should represent the population which is effected by the new service.
- Which type of interaction takes place: The planning cell demonstrates the most intense involvement of citizens in the design and redesign of services. For the duration of the planning cell the participants become employees of the organization and take responsibility for their decisions made in the project.
- The extent of innovation, which is to be expected: We consider the application of planning cells as especially beneficial for major service improvements, service line extensions, new services for existing markets, start-up businesses and, in rare cases, for breakthroughs in services.

Figure 10.4 shows the approximate position of the planning cell within the nine stages in new service design and types of new services.

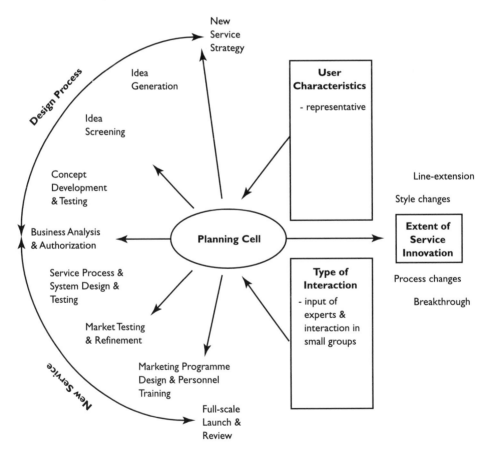

Figure 10.4 Planning cell evaluation.

10.6 Conclusions

From the preceding description and discussion of typical applications we conclude that the interactive approaches of planning cell and lead-users might contribute to almost all stages of the process of new service design.

We rate the planning cell slightly higher in its impact on the service strategy, business analysis, design of the marketing mix and full-scale launch/review.

Lead-users seem more promising when it comes to the innovation types of start-up business and service breakthroughs.

The SOPI method demonstrates the lowest extent of interactive user participation. Due to its nature we perceive SOPI as more appropriate for style changes, service improvements and possibly line extensions in the stages of idea generation, mainly based on identified problems, and idea screening.

However, specific applications of the user-integrating methods or modifications of them might cover additional or different stages and types of service innovations. We have shown that the application areas of the described techniques are partly overlapping. In practice this might result in the application of two or more techniques for the same service design project. By applying one or more techniques in the design or redesign of services, in the described or modified way, organizations could overcome one of the psychological barriers that prevents them from really listening and dialoguing, the attitude that users have little or nothing valid to say. Those organizations with a user-integrating perspective are sensitive to the interface complexity that people must deal with when interacting with them (Duncan and Moriarty, 1997) to innovate in services successfully.

Based on three cases, we have demonstrated and emphasized the importance of user integration along the different innovation stages. In this way mismatching of user expectations and standards of new services will be decreased or avoided.

Further reading

Edvardsson, B. and Olsson, J. (1996), 'Key concepts for new service development', *The Service Industries Journal* 16(2): 140–164.

Parasuraman, A., Zeithaml, V.A. and Berry, L. (1988) 'SERVQUAL: a multiple-item scale for measuring consumer perceptions of service quality', *Journal of Retailing* 64: 12–37.

Zeithaml, V.A. and Bitner, M.J. (1996) *Services Marketing*, New York: The McGraw-Hill Companies.

Part 3

Applications of market research

Part 3 consists of eight chapters each of which describes a case study. These case studies emphasize the importance of understanding the organizational context, how the survey methods were chosen, how the results were disseminated and what happened as a result. The case studies can be used by readers to stimulate thinking about potential applications of market research in health and social care organizations. They can also be used to illustrate the application of the methods described in Part 2.

The cases cover a wider range of applications including home care (Chapter 11), residential and nursing home care (Chapter 14), measuring quality in a hospital laboratory (Chapter 16) and patient and staff views of an appointment system (Chapter 17). Six of the eight are located in Britain, with one in Thailand (Chapter 13) and one in South Africa (Chapter 17). Because of commercial confidentiality, the real case study in Thailand (Chapter 13) has had to be disguised as a hypothetical proposal for market research.

The market research was carried out by external consultants in four cases (Chapters 11, 12, 13 and 17); in two by part-time MBA students who were managers in the organization (Chapters 14 and 15); in one by a full-time MBA student from outside the organization (Chapter 16); in one by a PhD student who had been a senior manager in the service (Chapter 18). The manager who carried out the case study in Thailand (Chapter 13) has remained anonymous. Because of this variety, the style of the chapters varies considerably, but this reflects the different balance required in dissemination between consultancy and academic criteria.

Chapter 11

Non-residential care charging policy in Southwark London Borough

Rob Pocock

In this chapter the reader will understand:

- how to balance central and local government objectives in social care research
- when the market research team has to take the initiative in developing a partnership model with a complex client group
- how to set up the project so that the findings are seen to be independent in order to ensure credibility
- how to carry out a literature search and a comparative exploration of policy
- how to develop and use a 'charging matrix' for research on charging for services.

11.1 Introduction

This chapter contains the description of a market research project carried out in Southwark, a local authority borough in London, which was concerned with exploring the charging policy for non-residential care services.

Charging for non-residential care services has been introduced within the framework of the previous government's NHS and Community Care Act 1990 which had as its main purpose to:

- meet that government's objectives for implementation of community care
- ensure local authorities meet their statutory obligations
- ensure Social Service Department (SSD) budgets are managed efficiently and effectively.

The allocation of central government funding for social services is determined through the local authority Standard Spending Assessment (SSA) and Special Transitional Grant. The allocation presumes that 9 per cent of the costs of non-residential care are raised from service users through charges. The decision to levy charges, and the determination of an appropriate charging policy, is a local one however, and has proved controversial with both service users and care providers.

In recognition of the difficulties, Southwark Community Care Forum, in collaboration with the SSD, commissioned M.E.L. Research to undertake a review of charges for non-residential care services and to identify evidence from service users in Southwark on the impact of charging on service uptake.

11.2 How the project was set up

The project was an unusual one in a number of respects. In particular, the construction of the 'client' was complex and reflected the politically sensitive nature of the study. The work was funded by the Southwark SSD but commissioned jointly by the SSD and the Southwark Community Care Forum (SCCF), a voluntary body established to resource the various voluntary service providers and service users. In the execution of the day-to-day management of the project the SCCF took on a more or less autonomous role with very little reference to the SSD.

The intention of this arrangement was to ensure that the findings of the study were felt to be genuinely independent and not influenced by the professional or political outlook of the SSD, which had taken the decision to impose a specific charging regime and formula. In particular, the SSD and SCCF shared a concern that the findings should hold credibility with service users and the local bodies advocating on behalf of issues such as poverty and disability rights.

In the event, this proved a highly successful formula but much of this can be attributed to the approach and working methods of the key individuals leading the various parties. From the perspective of this book the case study highlights the way in which both structural and behavioural aspects of the contracting relationship influence the way consumer market research is carried out in practice.

It was also noteworthy, but unusual in commissioned market research, that examples of other SSDs' charging policies were gathered as a preliminary to the primary fieldwork. This was not in the original invitation to tender nor the proposal submitted by M.E.L. Research. The idea emerged during the selection interview and was 're-worked' into the bid from M.E.L. Research by removing a previous commitment to undertaking preliminary focus groups prior to questionnaire design. A lot of commercially commissioned research suffers from the lack of reference to contextual material and literature review, which can seem an expensive luxury to clients who want to maximize the volume of primary data collected per unit of expenditure. The procurement practices of clients can often lead to this perspective. The priority given in this case to the more qualitative value of contextual material may stem from the particular structure of the client commissioning 'group'.

11.2.1 Aims and objectives

The specific objectives of this study were to:

- examine ways in which other SSDs have been dealing with the introduction of charging policy and procedures
- identify how service users in Southwark feel about the current policy and procedures
- examine the impact on equalities of the policy
- search for any evidence of a drop out, and
- highlight any areas for potential change.

Several methods were employed in the achievement of these objectives. In the first stage all SSDs in England and Wales were sent a questionnaire by fax and a literature review was undertaken. Based on the results from the first stage, the second stage consisted of face-to-face interviews with current service users in Southwark and, for comparison, interviews with service users in Lewisham, Camden and Croydon.

11.3 Literature review

11.3.1 Method

A review was carried out of professional and wider media coverage of community care charging issues between 1995 and 1997. The method involved library search and the Internet. This was supplemented by reports published by national bodies such as Mencap, Rowntree etc. and local authority reports regarding policies and recommended changes to the policy. Local authority reports were obtained through a written request to all SSDs in England and Wales which accompanied a 'fax-back' questionnaire on current policies, discussed below. Information was extracted on:

- what non-residential charging policies contain
- how charging policies are applied
- issues arising in the implementation of charging policies.

11.3.2 Findings

The literature review highlighted a number of issues. In many cases the problems associated with squaring up a community care charging policy with the local authority anti-poverty strategy resulted in a means tested charging policy rather than application of a flat rate.

Where charging policies included a financial assessment there were a number of concerns regarding various methods used.

1   The National Consumer Council and the Coalition against Charging suggest that neither the Disability Living Allowance nor Attendance Allowance should be incorporated in the financial assessment as they firstly are to cover the additional costs of being disabled and secondly are themselves means tested. In a survey by the Labour Research Department (1996) it was found that twenty-six SSDs (18 per cent) expect clients to put the care component of their Disability Living Allowance/Attendance Allowance towards the cost of their care.
2   In many policies, personal capital is not taken into account in the financial assessment.
3   The Citizen's Advice Bureau carried out a review of the experience of home care service users and found that many charging policies did not take into account outgoings in the assessment. Southwark does allow for outgoings to be included in the assessment.

Other concerns that were identified from the literature included:

- the majority of charging policies rely on the client to request a review of charges if they feel the charges are onerous – this is particularly important where SSDs have reviewed and changed the charging policy
- the charges appear to have had a detrimental impact on the social interaction between the service provider and client
- the charges are affecting the mental and physical well-being of the clients
- concern expressed regarding the mechanisms for ensuring clients are receiving all the benefits to which they are entitled.

11.4 Review of charging policies across England and Wales

11.4.1 Method

During the summer of 1997, a simple fax-back questionnaire was designed and sent to all 153 SSDs across England and Wales. The objective of the review was to place the work to be undertaken in Southwark within a national policy context. By the cut-off date forty-two responses had been received providing an overall response rate of 32 per cent. Over half (51 per cent) requested that their replies be kept confidential. This illustrates the sensitive nature of the subject under investigation and may also explain why some departments did not return their questionnaire.

11.4.2 Findings

The review reveals a variety of approaches to community care charging. In a number of cases respondents stated that they were about to introduce a policy or were going to review their policy suggesting that charging policies are still evolving.

Over three-quarters (76 per cent) of the councils were applying a variable charging rate. In seven cases there was not one rate applied across the board but different rates applied for different services, for example one council mentioned that they had a flat rate charge for day care services and transport but a variable rate for home care.

The responses received indicate that the policies appear to be based on the two main principles: cost of care package, and income or disposable income.

There is often concern that residents do not claim the welfare benefits they are entitled to and this may provide additional problems when seeking to charge for community care services. It was found in this study that a wide range and variety of personnel are providing welfare advice to clients, mainly benefits staff but also care management staff, Citizen's Advice Bureau, finance staff, voluntary sector staff and charging team staff (see Figure 11.1).

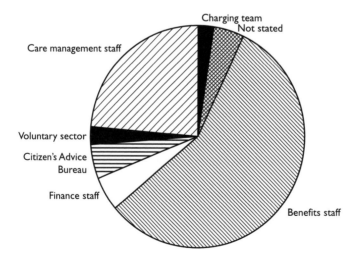

Figure 11.1 Who provides welfare benefits advice?

This variety suggests that there needs to be a mechanism developed for ensuring that clients receive appropriate welfare benefits advice.

Provision of alternative methods of payment for community care services is an important issue, when clients may be house-bound or have other difficulties in paying bills. The majority of councils provided a variety of methods of payment for services, allowing flexibility for users (see Figure 11.2). Particularly useful was the use of swipe cards or charge cards and savings stamps. These methods were used by 13 per cent and 17 per cent of councils, respectively.

Respondents reported a variety of policies for people who will not pay. Some councils reported more than one method. The first method stated was generally a soft approach, such as a personal visit or reminder letter; the second method mentioned was more often tougher, such as court action or debt collection.

A key area of concern is the impact on service use by clients when they are charged for the services that they need. The questionnaire asked whether there was any evidence of a fall-off in service use. Of concern, 48 per cent of councils stated that there was evidence of a fall-off in service use. The majority of councils who reported this drop in service use said that they had analysed statistics 'before and after' the introduction of a charging policy (70 per cent). In other councils, more anecdotal evidence was cited such as note taken of clients cancelling services and staff monitoring and feedback.

To conclude, this case study of a postal survey 'agency audit' shows how effective a simple one-page 'fax-back' survey instrument can prove to be, to gather general contextual information about organization policy and practice.

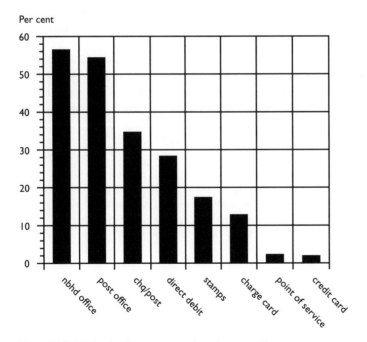

Figure 11.2 Methods of payment employed at councils.

11.5 Southwark service users' survey

11.5.1 Method

Charges had been introduced by Southwark SSD for a variety of non-residential care services run as domicilary care, day centre attendance and alarm systems. A questionnaire designed and piloted by M.E.L. Research for a similar project in another authority was amended for use in this study in agreement with the client to test the perceived impact of the new charging regime. This was used as the basis for a face-to-face interview with 200 service users from Southwark. Questions covered such issues as awareness of the level of charges clients receive, levels of information clients feel they have had, the concept and administration of the financial assessment, the appeals procedure and welfare benefits.

Specifications within the client's brief indicated that there were several client groups of particular interest to this study. These were older people (defined as those over 65 years of age), those people living with disabilities, and people from black and minority ethnic communities.

Southwark SSD drew the sample of clients to be interviewed from their database. Unfortunately, due to the nature of the information kept on record, ethnicity could not be used as a condition for sampling. A total of 400 names and addresses were drawn randomly from the database, 200 of older people and 200 of those living with disabilities. The target was to achieve 100 interviews with older service users and 100 interviews with those living with disabilities.

A letter was sent out to all potential interviewees prior to interviewing, informing them of the purpose of the study, what they would be asked to do, and how to decline to participate should they wish. Interviews were held with clients in their own homes. The interview took, on average, between 20 and 30 minutes to complete.

Some problems were encountered in achieving the 100 interviews with older people, mainly due to them not being at home or answering the door after three call backs by the interviewer. Due to this a further 100 names were provided by the social services in order to obtain the full quota of 100 interviews with older people. In general however, we did not encounter the degree of difficulty sometimes imputed to interview surveys of special needs population groups. Although particular care was taken to recruit and train highly skilled interviewers, our concerns about the possible problems proved largely unfounded.

A comparative study was undertaken in three other London boroughs with demographic and political similarities – Lewisham, Camden and Croydon. A total of seventy service users were interviewed using the same survey instrument as employed in Southwark.

11.5.2 Findings

Services received

Of the Southwark sample interviewed 92 per cent indicated that they were currently receiving non-residential services. Of those no longer receiving services ($n = 17$), financial reasons were given by four of the elderly respondents, two of the disabled respondents and none of the black and minority ethnic respondents.

Figure 11.3 illustrates the combinations of services received by the respondents. Over half

	Number	Per cent
Home care (HC)	113	56.5
Day centre (DC)	51	25.5
HC and DC	21	10.5
Sitting service	3	1.5
HC and sitting	2	1.0
Alarm	1	0.5
DC and sitting	1	0.5
Not stated	8	4.0
TOTAL	200	100.0

Figure 11.3 Combinations of services received.

(57 per cent) of respondents were receiving just home care, over a quarter (26 per cent) attend a day centre and just over a tenth (11 per cent) use both home care and attend a day centre.

It can be seen that a high percentage of respondents are receiving home care services, however, those in the older respondents group are significantly less likely to be receiving this service than either disabled or black and minority ethnic respondents.

Services no longer received

There were a small number of clients interviewed who were no longer in receipt of non-residential services. In total, 9 per cent ($n = 17$) of the sample indicated they were no longer receiving services. Of this group one-third stated that the reason was because they could not afford the charges.

Financial management

Half of the Southwark sample indicated that they deal with their own finances and half that they have help or someone else does it for them.

Those receiving help or having someone else deal with their finances had support from relatives (17 per cent), friends (14 per cent), formal care workers (9 per cent), professional financial workers (6 per cent) and social workers (5 per cent) (see Figure 11.4).

It is interesting to note that the potential personal sensitivity of the financial question did not in the event prove to be a barrier to response. We were keen to emphasize to respondents the ways in which participating in the survey would potentially help the service user gain a 'voice'.

Charges for services

Less than two-thirds (60 per cent) of respondents from Southwark indicated that they made a payment for their services, although the whole sample was drawn from the current data-base of those being charged. Over a quarter (28 per cent) did not know whether or not they were charged for the services they receive and 13 per cent indicated that they did not make a

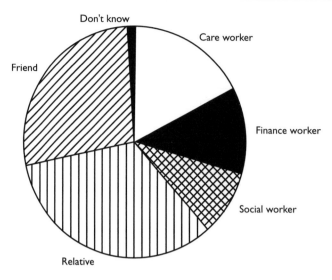

Figure 11.4 Who helps clients with their finances?

payment. Particularly noticeable are the older sample where over a third (36 per cent) indicated that they did not know whether or not they paid for their services, although their responses are not statistically significantly different from the disabled or black and minority ethnic samples.

Of those who knew that they paid, one-third (33 per cent) did not know how much the charges were.

This finding is largely replicated in the other three boroughs surveyed where 56 per cent indicated making a payment, 25 per cent did not know and 19 per cent believed that they made no payment. Not surprisingly, therefore, no significant differences were found between the Southwark and comparative samples.

Nearly two-thirds (60 per cent) of the sample pay their charges weekly at a post office, 18 per cent pay monthly at a post office when they receive notification of the charge, and 15 per cent pay monthly by post. Significant differences are seen between the three groups of Southwark respondents and their methods of paying for their non-residential services. Of the disability sample 82 per cent pay weekly compared to 68 per cent of the minority ethnic sample and just 45 per cent of the elderly sample.

The comparative study in the other three boroughs yields similar results to those found in Southwark with paying at a post office each week being the most common option.

Information

One-third (33 per cent) of the Southwark respondents indicated that they had not received information from Social Services about the charges that are made although we know that many letters were sent out to all clients (see Figure 11.5). This compares favourably with the comparative three-borough study where 54 per cent of the respondents indicated that they had not received any information. The differences between Southwark and the comparative samples are statistically significant.

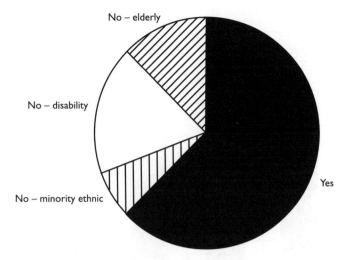

Figure 11.5 Recognition of having received information from Social Services Department.

The Southwark black and minority ethnic sample were the most likely to indicate that they had received no information. Of this group almost half (48 per cent) indicated that they had not received any information, compared to 39 per cent of the disabled clients and 27 per cent of the elderly clients. These differences are statistically significant.

It is also interesting to note that those respondents who indicate that they did receive information from the Social Services regarding the charges were significantly more likely to pay monthly than those respondents who indicated that they had not received any information.

Of those who acknowledged receiving some information 8 per cent found it very useful, 50 per cent found it quite useful, 35 per cent found it not very useful and 5 per cent found the information not at all useful.

No significant differences were observed between the three groups of respondents but there are significant age differences. The younger the respondent the more useful they found the information; of those aged under 50 years almost 90 per cent found it quite or very useful while less than half (48 per cent) of those over 80 years found the information very or quite useful (see Figure 11.6).

Financial assessment

Significantly more of the elderly sample were able to complete the financial assessment forms themselves and similarly, the older the respondent the more likely they were to have completed the form themselves, as Figure 11.7 shows.

Respondents who completed a financial assessment form themselves were asked how easy they found the form to understand: 59 per cent indicated that it was either very or quite easy, most of these coming from the disabled sample (65 per cent) and the smallest group coming from the elderly sample (52 per cent).

No significant differences were observed between respondents from Southwark and those from the comparative study regarding how easy they found the assessment form to understand.

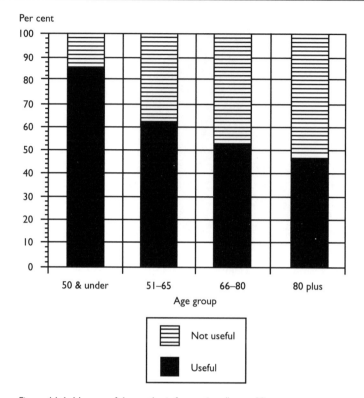

Figure 11.6 How useful was the information (by age)?

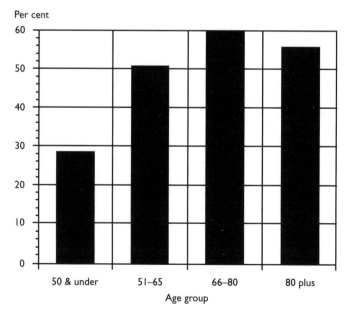

Figure 11.7 Completed form without help (by age).

The Southwark respondents who received help in completing their financial assessment forms were asked to indicate who helped them. Over a third (34 per cent) had help from social workers/care managers, just under a third from relatives (32 per cent), 13 per cent from friends and 12 per cent received help from home/day care staff. This compares with half (50 per cent) of those from the comparative study who received help in completing their financial assessment from a relative, a third (33 per cent) who received help from a social worker/care manager and 17 per cent who had help from a friend.

Over half (59 per cent) of the Southwark sample indicated the assessment form was very or quite easy to understand and two-thirds (66 per cent) found either all or most of the questions relevant. This compares to 60 per cent of the comparative sample who found the form very or quite easy to understand but only 45 per cent who found all or most of the questions relevant.

From the Southwark sample, those who acknowledged receiving information from Social Services and found that information useful were significantly more likely to view the questions on the assessment form as relevant. This suggests it is important for clients to receive information in a format that they remember and find useful.

Level of charges

Two-thirds (66 per cent) of the sample felt that the financial assessment was carried out fairly and accurately and no significant differences were seen between the older, disabled and minority ethnic samples in their responses. No significant differences were seen between the Southwark and comparative samples either.

Despite the relatively large proportion of Southwark respondents indicating that they thought the assessment was fair and accurate, over a quarter (28 per cent) were not happy with the result of the assessment (see Figure 11.8).

Elderly (63 per cent) and ethnic minority (67 per cent) clients had similar views where around two-thirds were unhappy because they felt that the services should be free. Disabled clients were more inclined to indicate that they were unhappy because the charges were too high (56 per cent).

Despite the large proportion of clients not happy with the charges, less than half actually appealed against the charges set for them. Only a very small percentage of the minority ethnic sample had appealed. Only two respondents from the comparative sample indicated that they had appealed about the charges that had been set for them. Perhaps, overall, this outlines the need for more information to be made available for clients on how to appeal and on how the appeal process works.

Reduction in service use

Just over a tenth (11 per cent) suggested that they had stopped receiving some services because of worries about the charges.

Most from Southwark had stopped receiving home care services (55 per cent) while others had stopped attending day centres (42 per cent). This is significantly different from the comparative sample where just one respondent indicated that they had stopped receiving services because of worries about paying for them.

In Southwark, the elderly respondents appeared significantly more likely to have reduced their services than people within either the disability or minority ethnic samples.

Figure 11.8 Satisfaction with the result.

The elderly respondents were also more likely to indicate that there are services that they would like to receive but have not asked for because of the charges, the disabled respondents were the least likely to indicate this. Most would like to attend a day centre or receive home care services.

Advice regarding welfare benefits

Although Southwark Social Services offers advice on welfare benefits and issues a separate benefits assessment form in addition to the financial assessment form, over two-thirds (69 per cent) of respondents expressed the view they were not given any advice on welfare benefits at the time of the financial assessment. As with other questions regarding information, the elderly sample were significantly more likely to indicate that they had received some information than the other respondents.

This may result from problems of communication, of recall, and also of the advice being given to an informal carer not the service user interviewed in this study. Whatever the source, however, the perception is important as it can influence the level of user dissatisfaction over the implementation of the charging policy.

A fifth of the total sample indicated that they had actually applied for some state benefit as a result of the financial assessment.

More respondents from the comparative study (79 per cent) indicated having received no benefits/welfare advice although a similar percentage (19 per cent) indicated having actually applied for benefit and no statistically significant differences were observed between the Southwark and comparative samples.

The study is an interesting one in the context of the wide approach to public health, in that it examines the instance of welfare benefit and anti-poverty advice as an integral part of a social care initiative.

Charging matrix

One of the key aspects of any charging policy is the extent to which service users are 'willing to pay' for the service. This has a lot of influence on the way service users feel about the fairness and reasonableness of the charges and in particular whether they will opt out of using a service if it becomes too expensive.

We asked service users to state the maximum they would be prepared to pay for three key services: home care, day centre attendance and the alarm system. The results enabled us to plot a 'price elasticity of demand' curve, showing the pricing levels at which increasing proportions of service users would opt out of receiving the service.

The results provide various findings:

- many people fix the maximum they would be prepared to pay at the level they are paying now
- less than one in six service users would be prepared to pay more than £10 a week for a care package
- less than one in ten would pay more than £5 for the alarm service.

The case study shows that valuable information can be obtained on this 'external market' aspect of health care provision. Future health care developments are likely to consolidate and even strengthen the external market, so it is noteworthy that the market research tools used in this study have been able to produce this kind of information.

11.6 Conclusions and recommendations

Most SSDs are applying non-residential community care charges but the policies and pricing systems vary considerably. A national forum for the development and exchange of 'good practice' on charging would be beneficial in helping SSDs reach an acceptable solution to this issue.

In Southwark, the survey of service users found that 3 per cent of users had withdrawn from one or more services 'because they cannot afford it', and overall, a little over 10 per cent stated that they had stopped receiving some services because of worries over the charges. The direct impact on service loss is small but measurable and significant to the users affected.

Most users do not believe they have been told enough about the service charges, despite the efforts expended to date in giving out information. This suggests other techniques, such as more direct face-to-face techniques, are needed to adequately inform service users. Minority ethnic users were particularly likely to believe they had received no information about the charges, and targeted efforts should be made to tackle the particular needs of this community.

Where users recall receiving information, most thought it was satisfactory. The problem therefore lies not in the effectiveness of the information *per se*, but in getting it over to certain service users.

Only 60 per cent of the users knew clearly that they were making a payment while over a quarter did not know and the remaining 14 per cent were adamant that they did not make a payment. A third of those who knew that they paid for their services did not know how much. This will be strongly influenced by the degree to which users have personal control of their financial affairs – half the sample have their affairs administered by others on their behalf.

Most of those who recall the financial assessment form found it easy to complete, and two-thirds felt the assessment was carried out accurately and fairly. From this viewpoint South-wark SSD would appear to have handled the technical assessment adequately. However, over a quarter of service users were not happy with the result of the financial assessment.

The appeal process was found difficult to follow and steps should be taken to simplify it and provide personal guidance for appellants through the process.

Two-thirds of respondents were not aware of receiving any welfare benefit advice in the financial assessment process. Steps need to be taken to convey more clearly the additional welfare benefit advice now offered through the process, both to improve customer satisfaction and to ensure there is maximum benefit uptake.

The level of charges would appear to be at the limit of what is acceptable without risking a further significant fall-off in service uptake.

11.7 Dissemination strategy

The findings of the investigation were presented and disseminated in a number of ways. First, a summary version was prepared by M.E.L. Research with assistance from SCCF, and circulated to elected members of the Social Services Committee on the 'public agenda'.

Second, the research team from M.E.L. Research gave a presentation personally to the joint Health Authority and Local Authority Community Care Liaison Group, which also contained patients' and users' representatives and the disability rights voluntary groups. This presentation was also given to the following committee meeting of the Social Services Committee.

There were no significant responses to the written consultation, but the Social Services Committee meeting produced a lively debate. The research proved to be a powerful catalyst for a political debate on whether the majority party had sensitively handled the issue of charges. The local MP had been centrally involved as a new Minister in a nationally contentious lone parent benefits debate, which helped to fuel the discussion. It is interesting to observe that market research of this kind is often integral to an underlying and highly charged party issue. In this book we have tended to present the techniques in a largely 'technocratic' managerial setting, but in reality there is frequently a hot political pot boiling underneath.

Third, SCCF was keen on national dissemination, both to promote its own profile within the field and also to stimulate the wider political and professional debate. SCCF therefore produced under their own 'covers' a copy of the report for sale at a nominal fee, and promoted its availability at local and London-wide conferences and events. Around fifty copies of this report were sold at a cover price of £10 within the first six months.

Here, therefore, is a client that has taken ownership of the results and sees the report itself as a device for pursuing its wider promotional objectives. This is unusual in commercial commissioned research where confidentiality is seen to be necessary in a competitive market. In all likelihood the desire for dissemination is a feature of the particular shape of the 'client' group.

11.8 Overview

This case study highlights a very wide range of issues relevant to the role and usefulness of consumer market research in the social care sector. Several key points stand out:

- consumer market research can play a useful role in conflict resolution in the highly politically and personally sensitive area of social care delivery
- most parties within that particular setting would term the process as 'service user research' even though the study itself has been very directly to do with the 'market' aspects of social care provision
- finding a successful role for consumer research depends a lot on the key stakeholders sharing a common view on the value of the research and the capability of the chosen instruments to deliver useful results
- the credibility of the research agency in the eyes of the stakeholders is critical to success and this includes service users and their representatives
- the ability to create a partnership model of working, involving the survey agency and the various stakeholders, is important
- a voluntary sector body can be just as effective at contract management as a professional or commercial client and can be just as keen to gain the benefits accruing from widespread dissemination of the findings.

Further reading

Labour Research Department (1996) *The Prospective Impact of Community Care Charging*, London: LRD Research Report.

Chapter 12

Healthy Living Centres: urban regeneration in Stoke

Rob Pocock

In this chapter the reader will gain an understanding of:

- how a genuine multi-agency partnership was formed prior to the preparation of the Single Regeneration Budget (SRB) bid
- the commitment of the Health Authority and Health Care Trust to a community health development approach
- the existence of a residents' group that took a strong lead in setting a non-medical agenda to the health needs assessment
- the community-centred paradigm followed by M.E.L. Research who were commissioned to carry out the assessment
- the wide-ranging health, social and quality of life services that emerged as elements of the proposed Healthy Living Arcade.

12.1 Introduction

As we have described in Chapter 2, there is a long history to the health care concept which in the UK is now encapsulated in the term 'Healthy Living Centre'. The earlier chapter spelt out the various ways in which market research has played a role in this form of health care development.

Here we look at a practical example of an urban regeneration scheme in the Bentilee estate in Stoke-on-Trent. The programme of regeneration was a seven-year Single Regeneration Budget (SRB) project which contained a strong focus on the development of what we termed at that time a 'Healthy Living Arcade'. The chapter examines a number of features of the market research which supported this development.

The project framework has been drafted by M.E.L. Research following initial consultation with residents, Bentilee Volunteers and the commissioning sub-group of the Villages Initiative Health Focus Group. The framework and project specifications stem from the detailed survey findings reported in subsequent sections.

12.1.1 Core strategic goal

The framework consists of five key strategic themes. These themes together pursue the core Villages Initiative community health goal:

- to enhance the positive state of health and well-being of residents in the SRB area with a view to achieving the long-term goal not just of an absence of ill-health, but a state of complete physical, mental and social well-being of residents in the area.

This core goal is a local reflection of the international 'Health for All 2000' initiative and in line with the 'Alma Ata' declaration which is the equivalent of a global and internationally recognized declaration of human health rights.

12.1.2 Principles and values

Projects and initiatives funded under the SRB community and primary health care programme should respond to ten core principles and values that are to underlie the programme and are integral to meeting the core strategic goal.

These are that projects should:

- define health holistically and within a social, not medical framework
- take a positive view of promoting health and well-being, not focusing on illness
- take a preventive rather than curative orientation
- where necessary to meet the core goals, challenge and seek to influence established statutory service provision
- derive their mandate from the community users and beneficiaries, not providers
- adopt a collective and 'inclusive' approach, actively seeking to engage groups and individuals who tend to be excluded from traditional resource and service planning
- emphasize a participatory approach building local people's confidence in defining and tackling their own health needs
- be free from bureaucratic structures and unnecessary professional constraints
- seek new ways of working, across professional boundaries, bringing people and organizations together, and integrating across other SRB programme areas
- aim to reduce inequalities in health deriving from socio-demographic factors and unequal access to services.

These ten principles should be formally addressed as criteria by agencies bidding for projects under the framework. The extent to which bids meet these criteria should be assessed in the appraisal stage.

Within the bounds of these core criteria, projects should also address the existing health care strategic frameworks, in particular, first the national Health of the Nation target areas and the local public health plan in respect of:

- coronary heart disease and stroke
- cancers
- mental illness
- HIV/AIDS and sexual health
- accidents.

It should be noted, however, that the proposed SRB Health Strategy does not directly follow this 'disease-oriented' framework. Projects should therefore seek to reflect the national Health of the Nation priorities within the more innovative and socially oriented framework set out in the ten core principles.

Second, projects should reflect current NHS policy of moving towards a needs-based primary care-led health service. The approach taken in the SRB health projects should therefore contribute to the wider health policy goals of:

- a primary care-led NHS
- patient focused care
- preventive rather than curative strategies
- needs-based and evidence-based (effective) health care initiatives
- integrated 'seamless' care based on cross-boundary and inter-agency working.

These and other themes within the health authority's current strategic plan should be given consideration by agencies bidding for projects. The intention is to ensure where possible that the SRB provides a mechanism by which the health authority can meet its public health goals and primary care purchasing intentions. In this way the SRB offers 'additionality' within the existing health care policy and programme, and is in effect an innovative form of joint locality-based, community-based commissioning.

It is recognized, however, that the community health aims of the Villages Initiative as stated in the core strategic goal may extend beyond the scope of existing policy and statutory powers of the health authority. Projects may therefore be acceptable within the proposed SRB framework even if they are not wholly in line with the policy priorities of the health authority.

12.2 Survey methods

The aims of the survey were to carry out an audit of the existing position and the strengths and weaknesses of the existing range of health and community-related services, and to develop a vision of change for a better future based on community perceptions, satisfactions with the present and aspirations for the future.

Three different methods were used to collect the necessary data. First, group discussions were organized with four different community groups. Second, groups not involved in focus group discussions were invited to complete a health audit form. Third, a formal residents' survey of over 500 households was undertaken.

The report initially presents the project framework for community and primary health care projects that could be considered within the Villages Initiative SRB programme.

12.3 Focus groups

12.3.1 Method

To explore qualitatively, people's views on health, well-being and what could be done to improve their health, a series of focus discussion groups was held. Community groups in Bentilee were identified and a short-list drawn up of those who could potentially form the basis for the community health focus discussion groups. Originally, five groups were asked to participate because they ensured a coverage of Bentilee, Berry Hill and Eaton Park; and young people, parents, employed/middle-class people, and older/retired people.

The community groups who were not invited to take part in focus discussion groups were invited, instead, to complete a SWOT analysis. This ensured coverage of a wide range of community groups.

12.3.2 Findings

In total, thirty-seven people participated (twenty-seven females, ten males) in a series of informal group settings. The groups were facilitated by a M.E.L. researcher and all covered similar issues although the discussion topics varied according to the direction the participants of each group took. The discussion group schedule covered three broad themes:

* definitions of health and well-being
* factors affecting local people's health, and
* what could be done to help improve people's health.

The groups were probed on issues surrounding the connection/difference between health and well-being. One lady at the Parent Group commented: 'Health is physical, well-being is more general but they go hand-in-hand.'

There was agreement at the Neighbourhood Watch Group in that the two can be seen as different but are, 'closely associated'.

> If you feel good then you are usually healthy.
> Yes, that's right. You can be ill but still have a feeling of well-being.

All of the groups commented on the lack of entertainment facilities in Bentilee when discussing well-being, not necessarily sports facilities, although at two of the groups this was also mentioned. Suggestions for improvements included a cinema, bowling green/golf course, better park facilities for young children and more social groups run when the play-group is on to allow parents to get out of the house and socialize. A community centre that can be used by all ages would be appreciated by those young people spoken to, they felt the Clowes Centre is not used enough because it has a 'posh floor', and this is the reason that discos are not held there.

There was strong concern about the pollution from both 'the chimneys', and from cars and also about the standards of housing.

All of the groups mentioned issues connected to the lack of entertainment and sports facilities as being a negative factor that affected people's health in the Bentilee area: many of the comments were connected to the lack of things for the young people to do. It is the general feeling that if there were more things provided for the young then they would not be as likely to hang around the estate in large gangs and intimidate the older people, vandalize things and shoplift.

> There are enough open spaces here they could build something on for the young'uns to go to. Then you wouldn't have them playing in the streets.

The participants at the Parent Group, however, acknowledge that finding some initiatives that would appeal to the young people is not necessarily very easy.

> If you are going to provide something for the youth, you need to do something that attracts them. They will not be happy with sitting in a hall drinking cans of pop, they don't want to be forced to do things by youth leaders when they can go out on their own and take drugs.

The young people themselves agree that they have nowhere to go and this means they get bored and turn to drink and drugs. They get told to get off the grass outside people's houses when they are playing football but there is nowhere else for them to go.

The young people who were spoken to agree that drink and drugs are factors that affect their health. For most of them drinking to get drunk out of boredom is common and quite accepted among their peers and although they realize that it is bad for their health they still do it, 'everyone does'.

Smoking, also seen as a negative influence on people's health by members of the Youth Group, was less accepted within their age group. A few of the young people spoken to smoked themselves but were trying to give up and all hated their parents smoking and nagged them to stop.

The emphasis of the discussions at all four of the groups lay mainly on the negative factors that affect health. Even when pushed, it was hard for the residents to think of positive influences.

Those at the Parent and Toddler Group and at the Neighbourhood Watch Group spoke of their satisfaction with the health services in the area, in particular there were named doctors that they felt provided a good service.

The two older groups of residents, the Neighbourhood Watch Group and the older people, both mentioned how they felt that the surrounding areas of Bentilee were very nice and provided encouragement for people to go walking. One commented that it, 'doesn't feel like we live near a city here'. It was their concern, however, that while the natural environment was there for people to walk in, there was no encouragement to do this because of the state of the footpaths and fields.

Not all of the older people spoke negatively of the younger generation. Some spoke of the enjoyment that they get from watching the young people playing in the parks.

> We want to see people. Like to see children, it makes you feel alive.

All four groups addressed the question of what might improve people's health. More facilities for the young people in the area was the most common response seen as a big step towards improving the health of the Bentilee residents.

It seems that although there is strong disapproval of the activities of the young people in the area, there is also sympathy for them. It is appreciated that they only hang around on the streets because they have nowhere else to gather and meet with their friends. If a facility were provided for them then it would make them happier and it would make the other residents who feel intimidated by them happier too.

Another suggested improvement that could be made to the area would be to clean up the air. Asthma is a big problem as recognized by all the groups of residents contacted (there was at least one asthma sufferer attendant at all the groups) and it is the general consensus that if the quality of the air were improved, then this would ease the suffering of those with asthma. Although the air is seen as improving it is still felt that this is not a major consideration for the authorities when planning new projects. For example, the participants at the Neighbourhood Watch Group spoke of 'smoky Stoke' and of how they, living on the hill, are able to say that their air is better. When the Coal Board wanted to open an open cast on Berry Hill around five years ago, the residents 'fought tooth and nail' to prevent this and to protect their clean air. The cast was not built and the residents feel that they have done their bit to help save a few lives and improve the quality of living for the future generations of Bentilee.

Suggestions were made to the effect that if the drugs problem that is 'invading our streets' were tackled, this would vastly improve people's health as would providing sports facilities.

Already mentioned in the discussion groups was the issue of the safety in the area and the lack of police presence. Those young people contacted in the Outreach Group spoke of when the police do frequent the area, the word gets around and the trouble makers just move from one place to another to avoid contact. The residents themselves, it seems, are afraid to go out and tackle the young people for fear of the retribution it may encourage.

> I daren't go out to tell them out 'cause they will totally abuse my house or my car or whatever.

Finally, the residents at the Parent and Toddler Group spoke of the knock-on effect of improving people's well-being in the area. Health is seen as physical and well-being as more general, if things can be done to make people feel better about themselves then this will have a knock-on effect by improving their physical health.

12.4 SWOT analysis

Focus group respondents and the non-responding community contacts were asked to work through a SWOT analysis (strengths, weaknesses, opportunities and threats) on health improvement in Bentilee. Outlined below are the main findings that arose from all the SWOT analyses.

Why do you think Bentilee is a good place to live?

- community spirit/the people
- surrounding countryside/open spaces
- good health centre/facilities
- good schools
- safe, well lit at night
- reasonable shops
- good housing.

Why isn't Bentilee a good place to live?

- vandalism/graffiti
- gangs of youths hanging about
- drug use/syringes/people drinking
- depressed housing
- lack of facilities for young people
- rubbish/smell
- crime.

What could be done to make Bentilee a better place to live?

- more security/better policing
- more entertainment/sports facilities for young people
- remove the drugs

- improve street lighting
- improve housing
- traffic-calming schemes
- generally tidy up streets and gardens.

What is stopping Bentilee becoming a better place to live?

- lack of money/resources
- police
- council not pulling weight
- apathy/lack of respect for area
- lack of things to do
- vandalism, litter.

Which services in Bentilee do you think are good?

- GPs/nurses/health clinic
- good shops
- dentist
- police
- library
- education facilities for both adults and young people
- volunteers
- buses.

Which services provided in Bentilee could be better?

- leisure facilities/play areas
- shops
- housing (service)
- transport (buses)
- roads/pavements/lighting
- reduce waiting times (GPs, dentist, hospital).

What services do you think are needed in Bentilee?

- places for young people to go/leisure services/play areas
- hospital/Accident & Emergency
- clinics (chiropodist, optician)
- job centre/advice centre
- doctors/nurses
- services for older people/lone parents.

What do you think is stopping services being provided in Bentilee?

- lack of money/resources
- outside reputation of estate.

12.5 Residents survey

12.5.1 Survey methodology

During the survey design stage it was decided at the outset to conduct interviews with representatives from at least 500 households within the Bentilee survey area. This figure was used to cover 9.4 per cent of the households which was considered large enough to yield a valid sample of residents.

Furthermore, a sample of 500 residents would be large enough to allow a statistically valid interrogation of the data by a series of different socio-demographic variables, e.g. age, gender.

To ensure that the sample of residents interviewed was representative of all Bentilee residents in terms of age, gender and working status, a quota was specially designed.

12.5.2 Sampling procedure

As a consequence of the time constraints placed on the interviewing stage by the time-scale of the overall project, a sampling procedure was specially designed which would allow the quota sample to be achieved by interviewers and would be time-efficient in the field.

The survey area was broken down into sixteen areas to which an interviewer was assigned. Each interviewer was then given a list of road names which they solely were to cover. The quota was to ensure representativeness of the population of the area, thus each interviewer had to complete their own quota.

The interview took 30–40 minutes to complete.

12.5.3 The interviewing team

An integral part of the project was that most of the interviewing would be done by local residents recruited and trained to the professional standards of the Market Research Society (MRS). To provide support to the locally recruited interviewers, there was a back-up team of professional MRS interviewers.

There were two main reasons for using a blend of new local recruits and professional interviewers. First, that the training and experience provided to local people would remain after the research had been completed, and could be used for other research in the area. Second, it would mean that some of the project money would be returned to the local community.

Community interviewers were recruited via a leaflet that went to all the 5,400 households on the Bentilee estate. The leaflet invited residents to apply for training as local interviewers. This leaflet also invited residents to complete a preliminary health perceptions sheet, the results from which were used to draw up the guide for the group discussions.

Eleven residents were trained to MRS standards in interviewing techniques. The training consisted of MRS Code of Conduct, how to ask questions, interviewing techniques, using a sample, and what surveys are and why we use them. The training included a role-play session whereby delegates were required to interview each other to ensure they understood the training.

All of the delegates who took part in the training session said they enjoyed the training and all agreed to conduct interviews for the project. However, only five of the eleven delegates were able to conduct interviews and of those, only three were able to conduct all the interviews they agreed to complete. For this reason, we recruited local professional interviewers to ensure all the 500 interviews were completed.

Within each section of the report of survey results, statistical analysis was conducted to test whether any differences between two samples, i.e. men and women, is due to chance or whether men and women are genuinely different in their answers to the question being asked.

12.5.4 Findings

After the questions on use and views on improvements and additions to both health and community facilities, the questionnaire then looked at the location of possible new developments. Respondents were initially asked to think about all the health services and community facilities that could be available in Bentilee. They were asked which option they would prefer: one large centre housing both health and community facilities, or separate health and community centres.

Over one half (57 per cent) of respondents indicated they would like one large centre, two-fifths (40 per cent) said two separate health and community centres and 3 per cent expressed no preference (see Table 12.1). When respondents were asked why they would prefer one building the majority (79 per cent) said it would be 'easier/more convenient/ less time-consuming', one-tenth (11 per cent) said there is 'not enough room for two buildings'.

Respondents who said they wanted two separate centres were also asked why they prefer this idea. Table 12.2 presents the responses. Just under one-half (47 per cent) said health and community facilities are 'two different issues and should be kept separate' and one-tenth (10 per cent) said two buildings would be more discreet, be more private and avoid embarrassment.

Respondents who said they would like two separate centres were then asked 'Would you like the health and community centres near to each other, say within easy walking distance, or further apart than that, say in different parts of Bentilee?'

Over three-quarters (77 per cent) of respondents said they would like the separate buildings to be near to each other, 14 per cent wanted them to be in different parts of Bentilee and 9 per cent expressed no preference.

Table 12.1 Reasons why prefer one building

	n	%
Easier/more convenient/central/less time-consuming	229	79
Not enough room for two buildings/cheaper	33	11
More people together/can mix/get to know each other	9	3
Services/problems sorted out in one place	5	2
Other	4	2
Discretion/privacy/doesn't single people out	1	<1
Can have more services	1	<1
Don't know	18	6

Note: n = 291. Respondents may give more than one answer, therefore may not add up to 100%.

Table 12.2 Reasons why prefer two buildings

	n	%
Two different issues/should be kept separate	95	47
Discretion/privacy/avoid embarrassment	21	10
Less crowded	16	8
Easier for people to use	14	7
People using community centre would interfere with those using the health centre	14	7
Other	9	4
People may be put off community centre as don't like health centres	6	3
One large centre would be an eyesore	3	1
Each one could be larger	3	1
Less chance of catching colds etc.	2	1
Don't know	9	4

Note: *n* = 189. Respondents may give more than one answer, therefore may not add up to 100%.

The respondents who wanted separate buildings were asked where they would like the health centre to be built. Over one-third (37 per cent) said they would like the health centre somewhere 'central' and one-fifth (19 per cent) mentioned 'Berry Hill area'.

The same respondents were then asked where they would like the community centre to be built. Similar responses were given for this question: one-third (33 per cent) want it 'central or by the shops' and one-fifth (20 per cent) want it in Berry Hill. Similarly, the respondents who expressed a preference for one building to house both health and community facilities were asked where they think the centre should be built. Over two-fifths (45 per cent) said it should be built 'centrally, near the shops', only 8 per cent thought it should be in the Berry Hill area.

Analysis by gender and age group

There are no significant gender differences as the percentages of men and women wanting one large health centre are equal (59 per cent) and the percentages for wanting separate buildings are also similar (46 per cent men versus 37 per cent women).

The 33–44 age group are the least likely to say they want one large health centre along with the 16–24-year-olds (47 per cent and 52 per cent) compared with the 55–64-year-olds (68 per cent, $\chi^2 = 14.42$, df = 10, ns).

People who have used the health centre either for themselves or someone else during the last 12 months are more likely to say they would prefer the health and community centres to be near each other than those people who have not used the health centre (90 per cent versus 77 per cent; $\chi^2 = 6.06$, df = 2, $p < 0.04$).

Access to health and community facilities

A set of questions explored respondents' views on a series of 'access factors' related to the use of new health and community facilities. The factors investigated comprised: easy access by bus, availability of a crèche, location of the facilities by shops, use restricted to members only and the availability of yearly health check-ups:

- 93 per cent would like GPs to give full health check-ups on an annual basis
- 84 per cent would like the facilities to be easy to get to by bus
- 82 per cent would like a crèche available
- 82 per cent of respondents said the facilities should be near the shops
- 42 per cent said they would like to see the use of the facilities to be restricted to members only.

Analysis by gender and age group

The only significant differences between men and women with regard to the 'access factors' are that more women than men would like the facilities to be in a central place, near the shops ($\chi^2 = 5.48$, df = 1, $p < 0.01$).

There are no significant differences with regard to age group. Although it is interesting to note that 100 per cent of 65-year-olds and over would like GPs to give full health check-ups annually.

Finally, respondents were asked if there was anything else they would like to add about the health and community facilities in Bentilee.

Over three fifths (62 per cent) of respondents said there was nothing else. However, a small yet not insignificant percentage of respondents (5 per cent) said the policing should be improved and 3 per cent said there should be more chiropodist health services in Bentilee.

Not surprisingly, when asked an open-ended question concerning what 'other things' residents would like to see in Bentilee, the most frequent response received was for a sports centre/swimming pool (9 per cent). The same percentage of people were also concerned about crime and safety within the area and wanted to see more police presence or perhaps even a police post or station in Bentilee.

Respondents were presented with five statements about the community facilities within Bentilee and asked whether they thought they were 'true', 'false' or whether they didn't know.

Two-thirds of respondents (66 per cent) agreed with the statement: 'There's not enough information about the social activities and groups running in Bentilee'. When analysed by age, significantly more of the younger age groups agree with the statement than the older age groups ($\chi^2 = 20.86$, df = 10, $p < 0.05$) (see Figure 12.1). No significant gender differences were found.

Responses to the statement: 'Bentilee needs a big community centre where lots of different activities and groups can be run' showed that 82 per cent agreed that a large community centre was needed in Bentilee. No significant age or gender differences were found.

Of the respondents 31 per cent agreed that: 'I would never go to any groups or activities run in Bentilee'. No significant age or gender differences were found.

There was strong agreement, 82 per cent of respondents, in reply to the question: 'I would like to go to a community centre where young children, teenagers, adults and retired people can all mix together'. Again, the level of agreement varied significantly across the different age groups ($\chi^2 = 22.22$, df = 10, $p < 0.05$) (see Figure 12.2). The figure demonstrates clearly that those in the age band 65 years and over showed the largest degree of uncertainty in answering this question. Analysis by gender also showed significant differences with more women agreeing with the statement than men (73 per cent versus 60 per cent, $\chi^2 = 8.69$, df = 2, $p < 0.05$).

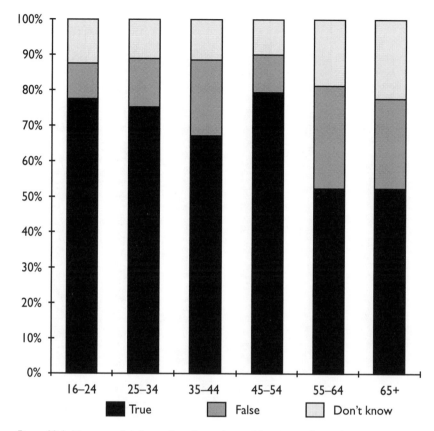

Figure 12.1 Not enough information about the social activities (by age).

12.6 Conclusions

In conclusion, the case study has shown how traditional forms of market research can be relatively simply adapted to quite radical community-led needs assessment processes, where committed lay members of the public, aided by a facilitating approach from the researchers, can produce challenging, high-quality research output.

As health care develops an ever stronger role of the public both as service users and in the wider democratic role as citizens, it will be important that market research develops from being a traditional weapon of power in the armoury of managers and professionals, to one more accessible to the wider public. This case study has shown that this can be practicable and does not necessarily erode the scientific validity of the process.

The questions that market researchers need to consider are:

1   How easy is it for managers to accept that the wider public can influence or even control the research agenda?
2   What needs to be done when commissioning market research for these wider purposes?
3   Technocratic aspects of research (such as statistical testing) still need to be delegated to professional researchers – does this undermine community-centred research?

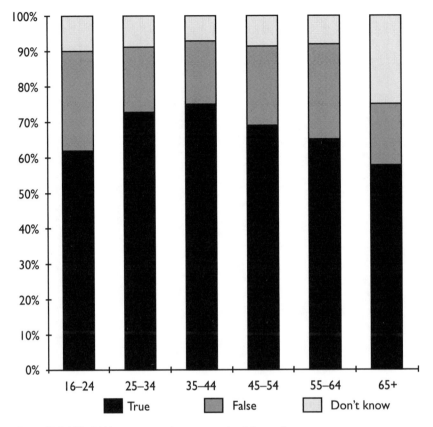

Figure 12.2 Would like a community centre mixed (by age).

4   How do we balance the inevitably ambitious aspirations of community researchers with the practical realities and boundaries set by managers?
5   Is community-led market research a device for co-opting, absorbing, professionalizing and dis-arming the radical and challenging role of the local community in health care planning?

12.7 Postscript

The work described here was carried out in the autumn of 1996, before the change of government in the UK and the formalization of Healthy Living Centres. Three years on, the SRB Board have completed the designs and are undertaking the reconstruction of the shopping centre on the Bentilee estate to incorporate the facility originally described in this case study as a Healthy Living Arcade.

Perhaps the most lasting change has, however, been the wider physical, environmental and social impact of the SRB. The sprawling estate has been consolidated into a patchwork of 'urban villages' each with a localized sense of place and focus. Housing improvements such as central heating, insulation and double-glazing have improved living conditions. Job creation and skill-building programmes have tackled long-term unemployment. It could be that these initiatives, rather than the Healthy Living Arcade, are the more significant contributors to future health gain. If so, this will endorse the findings of the very early parts of the community survey, where people were asked to say 'what really makes you sick'! The most common answers were poor housing, poverty, lack of employment and lack of recreational facilities. These answers are difficult to absorb within the clinical culture of the NHS but it could be in the long run that the people, not the clinicians, had the handle on the real issues. If so, there could not be a more positive endorsement of the value of community-centred survey research.

Further reading

Pearse, I. and Crocker, L. (1943) *The Peckham Experiment*, London: George Allen and Unwin.

Chapter 13

Entering the private health care market in Thailand

Jill Schofield

In this chapter the reader will gain an understanding of:

- why British private health care operators are looking to overseas markets
- how desk research can be carried out to explore investment opportunities using Thailand as a case study
- the political and legal context of health care in Thailand
- the private health care market in Thailand and the opportunities for investment
- how consumer surveys and country research can be undertaken to further evaluate these opportunities
- the main differences between the UK and Thai private health care markets and the implications for British companies.

13.1 Private health care in the UK

The private health care sector grew rapidly in the UK during the 1980s. To date, 11 per cent of the population have private medical insurance (PMI) and there are now 224 private hospitals with 11,000 beds. Of all hip replacements 25 per cent are now performed in the independent health care sector. However, since the beginning of the 1990s there has been a plateau in demand for PMI in Great Britain. In 1997 the number of subscribers for PMI grew by only 1.1 per cent, representing eight successive years of flat demand for PMI in Britain (Laing, 1998). Private hospitals have suffered accordingly and with the move from inpatient to outpatient treatment many of the hospitals have occupancies of 50 per cent or less.

The reasons for the levelling off of demand are well rehearsed elsewhere, but in summary it is sensitive to general economic cycles, particularly in respect of individual subscribers whose choice to enter and leave a PMI scheme appears to relate to levels of disposable income (Propper and Eastwood, 1989; Calnan *et al.*, 1993). The take up of PMI is also related to the actual and perceived quality and responsiveness of the state health care system, particularly in respect of waiting lists (Higgins, 1988; Yates, 1995; Bestey *et al.*, 1996). It is not totally clear whether PMI is price sensitive and whether there is a difference in attitude between individual and corporate payers. However, especially during an economic downturn there is a price at which, as a percentage of either a corporate reward package or individual disposable income, subscribers will no longer believe PMI is affordable (Propper and Maynard, 1989). Finally, the private health care sector is subject to state regulation in respect of how it impacts upon health care and upon financial services. Governments have the ability to levy insurance upon premium taxes as they have done in the UK, or on the other hand to provide regulatory encouragement to the industry by providing corporate and individual tax relief on subscriptions.

Given the levelling off in demand for PMI and the decline in private hospital operating margins in the UK domestic market, British independent health care companies need to develop new strategies for growth. One such strategy is to invest in emerging markets where demand for private health care has not yet been met. Thailand has been selected as the case study to determine whether there are opportunities for British companies to invest in that market.

13.2 Thailand: the country

Thailand has a population of 59 million people which is still growing at the rate of 1 per cent per year. The economy has traditionally been based on well-diversified agriculture but during the past decade its growth rate has been fuelled by a rapid increase in manufacturing and services businesses. The urban population is officially about 11 million of whom half live in Bangkok. Unofficially though, 10 million live in the capital city.

Politically, Thailand is a constitutional monarchy and the king, who is the world's longest reigning monarch, is well respected. Indeed he has provided stability during the country's turbulent political development which includes seventeen coups since the 1930s, the last of which was in 1992. However, the country is now moving towards greater democratization and the development of a new constitution is likely to bring greater freedoms and the eradication of corruption and political cronyism. Unlike its South-East Asian neighbours, the country has never been colonized and accordingly the Thais are very tolerant towards foreigners.

13.3 Private health care in Thailand

13.3.1 Desk research

Before embarking upon any financial investment appraisal or consumer research, it is important to understand the political and economic context in which the private health care market operates. Visiting the country can be expensive and therefore initial research can be conducted at home using publications and the Internet. One of the most helpful data sources for new entrants to the South-East Asian market is the Economist Intelligence Unit (EIU, 1998). The EIU publishes country forecasts based on a five-year forecast, updated quarterly and contextualized in terms of regional overviews. The EIU is one of the few global research-based organizations to provide such a service. The reports contain a political forecast, business outlook and commentary on economic prospects. However, such reports are expensive, with the Thai country forecast currently costing £465 and the Asian Regional forecast on CD Rom costing £6,550. A cheaper source of economic data is Tara Siam which is a locally-based research company. The Thai Embassy in London and the Commercial Section of the British Embassy in Bangkok will also provide political and economic reports. The two English language newspapers *Bangkok Post* and *The Nation* both have web sites on the Internet. Their business reporting tends to be accurate due to the freedom of the press.

With regard to understanding the private health care market itself, many insurance companies and hospitals also have web sites providing information about their products and services. Some of these companies are listed on the stock market and copies of their annual reports can be obtained directly or from the Ministry of Commerce. It is also possible to contact investment bankers, universities and the various government ministries who are happy to provide information by post. Unfortunately, there is very little accurate published census data covering health insurance penetration. There is nothing similar to the UK CACI information system that is based on the Acorn Lifestyle classifications (this organization provides geographically targeted financial research surveys which are designed to ascertain if targeted consumers already have or are in a position to buy PMI). However, the Department of Insurance in Thailand does report quarterly on the amount of premium sold by each insurance company.

As can be seen from the above, there is a wealth of information which can assist a British company in building up a picture of the private health care sector in Thailand before visiting the country.

13.3.2 Political and economic context

It is important to remember that publications can quickly become out of date. Even the venerable *Economist* is not always able to forecast catastrophic changes. Since 1960 the Thai economy had been growing at an average of 7.7 per cent per year and all the indications were that this growth would accelerate. The *Economist* therefore predicted with confidence in its 1997 Review of the World 'another year of stellar growth for Thailand'. However, in mid-1997 the Thai currency collapsed, the Prime Minister resigned and Thailand entered its worse recession this century.

If we accept the hypothesis that success in the private health care market is just as much a function of the national general economic system, then it is important to remember the consequences of volatile political and economic situations on foreign investment decisions. Indonesia also caught the Asian contagion and, as result of an unstable government and general intolerance amongst the different races and cultures, businesses were destroyed in riots and military intervention without reparation. Thailand itself was at risk of suffering yet another military coup but on this occasion there was a smooth transition in government with the election of a seven coalition government led by Democrat Party leader Chuan Leekpai. Chuan has succeeded in restoring foreign investor confidence by adhering to the conditions of the International Monetary Fund's loan awarded in August 1997. One of the consequences was the closure of fifty-six finance companies and regulations were introduced to ensure greater transparency in financial reporting. Bankruptcy laws are also being introduced for the first time. Nevertheless, the recession has been severe with a reduction in GDP of 8 per cent in 1998. The social consequences have been redundancies and a net outflow of people from the cities back to their families in the countryside. This has resulted in a drop in consumer spending with many people opting to save rather than use their disposable income. Accordingly, expenditure in the private health care market has also fallen, putting more pressure on the government sector. Private inpatient occupancies have declined by as much as 30–50 per cent whereas the government sector has witnessed a 20–30 per cent increase for both inpatient and outpatient services. This is at a time when the government has been under pressure to reduce spending on health care in order to reduce the public sector deficit. The World Bank is now assisting the Thai government in formulating a long-term health care strategy.

13.3.3 Public health policy

The government publishes every year a directory providing statistics on disease incidence and public health care provision including the number of facilities, doctors and nurses. The Ministry of Health requires all public hospitals to report on their activities. Private hospitals participating in the social security scheme are also expected to provide statistics. ICD 10 is used for disease coding and ICD-CM 9 for procedure coding.

In 1997, total health expenditure accounted for 7 per cent of GDP, with the state contributing only 30 per cent of the funding. This is the highest proportion of spending in Asia but Thailand has one of the lowest life expectancy rates. This is largely due to low investment in preventative medicine and the lack of enforcement of health and safety and environmental standards: 800,000 people suffer from food poisoning a year whilst 17,000 people died in road traffic accidents in 1996. Rapid economic development has resulted in 20 per cent of Thais suffering from stress with a suicide rate of three per 1,000 young males. Fifty per cent of children living in Bangkok suffer from a respiratory illness. It is also estimated that upwards of 10 per cent of the male population is HIV infected. In 1996, only 20 per cent of doctors graduated as general practitioners compared with 42 per cent in the UK. This can be attributed to the higher salaries paid in the private sector. As a result, 50 per cent of all graduates work in the private sector.

The government's declared health care policy is as follows:

- to accelerate the expansion of public health to the rural areas
- the creation of universal health coverage providing access to public health for all
- increase awareness and prevention of HIV and AIDS
- improve the environment and introduce public health standards
- eliminate infectious wastes and pollution in the water
- invest in modern technology in the public hospitals
- introduce and monitor food and drug safety standards
- improve the quality of medical and health personnel
- establish day care centres
- invest in health education and promotion.

To date though, a lack of central planning and legal vacuum has forged a profit-driven health network and only the higher income population has really benefited. The inadequacies of the health care system have shown up during the recent economic crisis and it is likely that government investment will move away from property such as hospitals and high technology medicine towards primary health care and disease management.

13.3.4 Health care funding

Aside from identifying the political and economic risks, before making any investment decisions it is also important to understand the model of health care funding in a foreign country.

Health insurance cover by household as of 1995 is shown in Table 13.1. However, before any company reaches the conclusion that there is a huge untapped market for PMI it is important to remember that the average GDP per head of population is just over $6,000 compared with more than $20,000 in the UK. At this time only 10 per cent of the population can afford access to private health care.

Table 13.1 Health insurance cover by household, 1995

Type of insurance	Percentage of households
Highest benefits	
Government/retired official, state enterprise	7.33
Social security	2.74
Workman's compensation	0.06
Private insurance	0.99
Private employer contracted with provider	0.23
Moderate benefits	
Health card	14.81
Low income welfare card	13.60
School health insurance	7.02
Children (under 12) and the elderly (over 60)	20.07
No benefits	33.15
Total	100.0

Government statistics also quickly get out of date. Since the above table was published, the most prestigious university in Thailand, the University of Chulalongkorn, estimated in 1997 that 9.73 per cent of Thais had some form of private health insurance cover. However, two independent surveys carried out in Bangkok in early 1999 reported that between 34 per cent and 40 per cent of respondents stated that they had health insurance cover.

Government health care funding

Since 1997 the public health care budget has been cut by 12 per cent in response to the economic crisis and it is not expected to return to 1996 levels until 2001. The government is currently reviewing the funding of health care with a view to saving money and reducing the complexity of funding arrangements. It would like to merge the various government insurance programmes and launch a nation-wide plan. However, little progress has been made on this front as the Ministry of Public Health would like the scheme funded from taxes whereas the Ministry of Finance prefers to involve the private sector with incentives for households to fund their own health insurance. In the meantime the government continues to support the following existing initiatives.

SOCIAL SECURITY SCHEME

Companies with ten employees or more can participate in the social security scheme. Both employer and employee contribute 1 per cent of the salary bill. The employee can then nominate one of the participating hospitals in which to receive their treatment. The participating hospital then receives an annual capitation fee of 800 baht a year for each person covered. With this amount they are expected to treat their social security members within the allocated budget. Additional payments are then made for treatment of major and critical illnesses such as transplants and dialysis. The capitation system has generated a surplus for the government and they have now added maternity and dental benefits to the scheme. To fill excess capacity 101 private hospitals are now participating in the scheme.

During the economic crisis many companies lapsed their private health insurance cover and relied on the social security scheme. The perception of those who have never used it is that it is adequate, whereas those who have used it feel that the scheme provides inferior treatment. Therefore as the economy improves companies may begin offering the additional benefit once more.

HEALTH CARD SCHEME

To provide additional cover for the self-employed and individuals, the government launched a health card scheme which offers unlimited treatment for a family of six for 12 months for 500 baht. The government claims that they have now in excess of one million card holders. But it is not supported by the hospitals which find it commercially non-viable as it only covers up to 15 per cent of the charges for an average hospital stay.

CIVIL SERVICE SCHEME

The civil service scheme covers 2 million employees and 5 million of their dependants. Claims have increased annually by 20 per cent a year and fraud is perceived by the government to be the main cause. The budget was accordingly cut by 30 per cent in 1997 and civil servants were no longer given access to private hospitals. As a result, many government agencies have been seeking additional private health insurance cover.

Private health care funding

SELF PAY MARKET

Many individuals and companies continue to have no health insurance cover but pay out of their own pockets. Hospitals have tried to attract and develop this market by offering hospital discount membership cards and fixed price packages. Companies often negotiate directly with one or two hospitals setting up preferred provider contracts. They then set benefit levels for their employees and arrange with the hospitals for the bills to be sent directly to the company for reimbursement. Claims administration is cheap because labour is cheap but these companies have little expertise in managing medical costs and in recent years have seen their health benefits bill increase significantly. Under these circumstances many are turning to health insurance companies.

PRIVATE HEALTH INSURANCE

Private health insurance is currently supplied by three different types of insurers: the specialist, the general insurer with a health portfolio, and the life insurer selling health insurance riders and health cash plans as an adjunct to life policies. Their market shares in 1998 by premium are shown in Table 13.2.

The dominant player remains AIA, an American life insurance company which has 62 per cent market share. AIA has operated in Thailand for sixty years and has developed a network of over 20,000 insurance agents.

Table 13.2 Market share by type of premium

Type of insurer	Premium in 1998 (thousand baht)	Market share (%)
Specialist insurer	534,019	9.2
Non-life insurer	207,415	3.4
Life insurer	5,356,096	87.5
Total	6,097,530	100.1

All the companies sell similar products reimbursing the cost of inpatient, outpatient, maternity and dental treatment. Some products also include health check-ups. The average annual premium is about £50 per person. Unlike the UK, the majority of claims are for doctor consultations and drug prescriptions as government funding of primary care is so under-developed. The other major difference is that persons are no longer covered after the age of 60 years. Accordingly, just when your health is failing you have to fall back on the state.

In order to control medical costs each benefit heading is sublimited. In recent years, however, new products have included full cover schemes linked to restricted provider networks and capitation schemes.

HEALTH INSURANCE AND THE REGULATORY FRAMEWORK

The private health insurance market is highly regulated, probably even more so than the UK. Regulation falls under the auspices of the Department of Insurance within the Ministry of Commerce. The life insurance companies are monitored by the life department and the specialists and general insurance companies by the non-life department. This can lead to a divergence in policy and unfair competition. For example, VAT was applied to all non-life policies at the beginning of 1999 but life insurance companies remained exempt. This meant that the specialist and general insurers were automatically 7 per cent more expensive. Medical riders are not supposed to be sold by the life companies on their own but the life insurance companies overcome this by charging a nominal premium for the life policy. Commission is also regulated differently. The life companies can pay up to 40 per cent by law whereas the non-life companies can only pay a maximum of 18 per cent. There is a separate pricing tariff but in this case the differences are not significant.

The Ministry of Commerce must license all insurance companies. In 1997, the market was deregulated with the creation of twenty-eight new licences, but only twelve new companies are currently operating and many of these have indicated that they cannot continue due to the requirements for financial liquidity and a tough competitive market. The Department of Insurance must also approve all new products and policy wording. This can take many months and inhibits innovation.

Ironically, until early 1999 the government has taken little interest in the financial solvency of the insurance companies. They are required to retain 20 million baht as a reserve but it is known that many are suffering cash-flow problems. In order to pay claims, companies have been pricing aggressively in order to win new business and keep the money flowing in. The government is now planning to increase the reserve requirement to 300 million baht for the non-life companies and 500 million baht for life companies. Many of the local companies will not be able to find the money and accordingly the government is also planning to allow foreign ownership to increase from 25 to 49 per cent.

13.3.5 Health care provision

Private health care provision

Following deregulation in 1989, the number of private hospitals increased by 89 per cent from 1990 to 1997. Encouraged by the Board of Investment's favourable policies and the absence of custom duties on imported medical equipment, an average of one hospital opened per month between 1989 and 1995. As a result, the private hospital industry today suffers from an estimated over-capacity of 300 per cent. The supply is particularly abundant in Bangkok and its environs where 40 per cent of beds are located. There are also more MRI scanners per head of population than anywhere else in the world with the exception of Japan.

The majority of hospitals tend to provide the full range of services including intensive and coronary care, trauma and maternity. Doctors will work in both the private and public sector. Full-time doctors in the private sector were employed on a salaried basis but recently the trend is more to fee reimbursement.

The regulations governing private hospitals are not onerous. They must be licensed by the Ministry of Public Health but after the initial inspection on opening there are no further checks. The standards of medical care are on the whole better than in neighbouring countries. There is very little clinical audit though and a hospital can undertake any type of procedure although this may be only once a year. Many of the hospitals now have ISO9002 as their quality standard and the Ministry of Public Health is developing accreditation based on the Canadian system. The government is also planning to regulate pricing for the first time.

Since the economic crisis began, private hospitals have seen a reduction in patient volumes of 30–50 per cent. Private ancillary facilities such as diagnostic and laboratories are running at half capacity or less and imported costs associated with pharmaceutical and medical supplies have increased by 20 per cent to 50 per cent due to the devaluation of the baht. Furthermore, the 50 per cent devaluation of the baht meant that the net working capital at most hospitals turned negative. Initially, the hospitals tried to pass on the additional costs to the consumers and funders but this manoeuvre has not been welcome. At the end of 1997, ten of the thirteen listed private hospitals on the stock market registered a combined loss of 6.05 billion baht. The outstanding debt for all the hospitals was 22.8 billion baht of which 61 per cent was denominated in foreign currency.

Historically, the private hospitals have had neither the incentive nor the knowledge to manage their costs. There are now the first signs of utilization reviews to determine the appropriate use of resources but few hospitals have the data or systems support to do this in a meaningful way.

During the next three years consolidation among the private hospital operators is inevitable but is currently being resisted. The majority of the hospital operators and owners are individual doctors with little or no management expertise. For reasons of pride they are reluctant to merge and achieve the required economies of scale. The ability to source capital will therefore ultimately determine whether providers acquire, become acquired, close or continue to have their losses subsidized by the original founders.

In the longer term, undeveloped areas of health care such as geriatric care, chronic care and sub-acute care, will be a necessary feature of Thailand's health care system. An ageing population will create more demand for such services. However, increasing co-operation and integration between the public and private sectors is unlikely.

Government health care provision

In spite of the private sector's rapid development it still accounts for only 30 per cent of the country's hospital beds. In addition to Thailand's 9,764 health stations and fifty-five community health centres there are 703 provincial hospitals and twenty-five regional hospitals offering secondary services. Aware that 40 per cent of its funds have been misdirected, the government aims to maximize its health care assets in a more cost-effective manner and focus on promoting preventative and primary care. A major initiative is the gradual privatization of the public hospitals. The University of Chulalongkorn Hospital will be the first to manage its own budget and set its own rates commencing November 1999.

13.4 Identifying investment opportunities

The desk market research summarized in the previous section indicates that, in spite of the economic crisis, opportunities still exist for investing in the private health care sector. There have been signs of recovery in the economy during the first half of 1999. Accordingly, the average wealth of the population and their disposable income will start growing again. More importantly, the research has identified some niche markets which are currently not being served.

Private health care *funding* offers opportunities including:

- companies who currently self-insure but are now seeking help in managing their medical costs either through insurance or third party administration
- management of government health funding schemes including the civil service scheme
- individuals who wish to buy health insurance on its own and not attached to a life policy
- self-employed individuals and families who are not covered by the social security scheme.

Health care *provision* offers different opportunities including:

- polyclinics offering primary care and minor procedures
- investment in and the rationalization of a group of hospitals to achieve economies of scale and improve profitability
- the employment of doctors and nurses to provide primary care
- home nursing service, geriatric care and rehabilitation.

The elderly care market has not been exploited at all. The family is very important in Thai culture and accordingly most of the elderly are looked after by their children at home. However, the population is getting older and at the same time more women are working. The elderly are therefore often left in the care of a maid or another relative who is not equipped or trained to look after somebody with geriatric problems, especially alzheimers. The last resort is to admit the elderly to hospital but this is often an inappropriate setting.

Over the next 10 years it can be anticipated that there will be an explosion in care for the elderly homes and home nursing.

Finally, for both funding and provision there are also opportunities for British companies to provide consultation and management services.

13.5 Consumer research in Thailand

Once the desk research has been completed and the opportunities identified it is then appropriate to carry out the market research in Thailand. This is necessary to validate your desk research to ensure that any information is up-to-date and it also helps to assess attitudes and future demands. Moreover, if a company is planning to invest through acquisition it is important to check out the reputation and financial security of any prospective partner. Country-based research also helps a foreign investor understand the operational consequences of their investment in the private health care market including, for example, doctor and nurse availability, skills levels, banking systems, distribution systems, technical support for medical equipment and computer systems.

13.5.1 Conducting surveys

The research can be undertaken by the company itself but language may prove to be a considerable barrier as English is not widely spoken or understood especially in the government. There are a couple of international market research agencies in Bangkok, Deemar and Asia Market Intelligence. However, their research tools for data preparation (see Chapter 7) and for data analysis (see Chapter 9) are not fully developed and quite often the survey or interview results have to be sent outside of Thailand for analysis. This makes such surveys very expensive and lengthy.

The design of such surveys has been explored elsewhere in the book (see Chapter 6). It is important to emphasize that some of the questions and answers may be distorted and lose their meaning when translating from English into Thai and *vice versa*. The other important factor to remember is that in Asian cultures people often give answers that they believe the interviewer wants to hear rather than what they actually believe. It is also important to understand the motives of the person being questioned. At present, many companies in Thailand are desperate for foreign capital and will paint a glowing picture of the private health care industry.

13.5.2 Surveying the stakeholders

It is important to identify who are the stakeholders in the private health care sector in order to gain their views. Indeed they are very similar to those in the UK. They are the individual and corporate consumers, the health insurance funders, intermediaries (agents and brokers) who purchase insurance on behalf of the consumer and the providers including the hospitals and doctors who deliver the medical services. The government also has a stake as developments in the private health care sector impact on the government purse. Professional bodies and trade representatives such as the Private Hospital Association can also be rich sources of information. Academics may have also carried out similar surveys which can be of use. Interviews with other British companies already operating in Thailand will give a perspective on how business is carried out there in general.

13.6 The differences in the private health care market between the UK and Thailand

One of the great mistakes many British companies make when considering investing in a foreign country is to assume that one model of health care and its operation can be applied to another. The purpose of the market research is to learn what can and what cannot be applied and to understand the risks associated with the differences. Below are just a few examples of those differences.

1 *Health care policy.* In Thailand health care is primarily funded from out-of-pocket payments rather than taxation. This means that it is far more sensitive to economic cycles and pricing than in the UK.

2 *Health care delivery.* The Thai health care delivery system is modelled along American lines without the litigation as medical practice is not challenged. Primary care is accordingly under-developed and most treatment takes place in expensive hospital settings. There is no gatekeeper and customers often self-refer to specialists. Thai doctors are also sometimes paid commission for diagnostic tests and inpatient admissions. This has implications for health insurers who are often paying claims for unnecessary or inappropriate expensive treatment. Private hospitals in Thailand also provide a full range of services similar to NHS District General Hospitals. UK private hospital operators will have little understanding of the commercial viability of emergency, maternity and intensive care services.

3 *Disease management.* Managed care is becoming well developed in the UK and many insurance companies are working in partnership with private hospitals to develop clinical protocols to ensure that treatment is carried out cost-effectively. The majority of treatment carried out in the private sector in the UK is cold surgery such as cataracts, hysterectomies and hip replacements. The disease profile in Thailand is very different and many UK insurers would have little experience of managing the costs of accidents and infectious diseases let alone AIDS.

4 *Distribution channels.* In the UK, health insurers will use brokers and agents to sell their products. In recent years though, telephone and e-commerce are playing a more key role. Agents and brokers are more common in Thailand although not as well structured. A Thai agent will normally sell to his family and friends only and it is not unusual for him to only sell one policy a year. Telephone sales and e-commerce is more difficult as 94 per cent of the population deal in cash only. The banks also find it difficult to support instalment payments through direct debit. Accordingly one of the agent's roles is to collect the premium from the customer's home.

5 *Labour market and skill levels.* Before the economic crisis it was extremely difficult to recruit well-educated and trained people. Salaries were accordingly sometimes higher than in the UK for the equivalent level of staff. However, the economic crisis brought with it redundancies and skilled labour is more plentiful.

6 *Language and culture.* English is not widely spoken or understood although this is beginning to change. This has repercussions for British companies as most correspondence and certainly government documents are all written in Thai.

Thai society is extremely hierarchical and this is reinforced by the education system. Learning is by rote and students are expected not to challenge their teachers or use their initiative. This carries on at work and accordingly a junior person will never question a senior person. This can lead to lack of involvement and bad decision making. For British companies it means that a higher level of supervision is expected than in the UK. Other cultural differences are conflict avoidance and the need to compromise even though it may be commercially non-viable.

7   *Fraud*. Fraud and corruption are still facets of operating in Thailand. Government officials expect to get paid for granting licenses or changes in documentation. Agents and customers often collude with hospitals and doctors to falsify claims and medical certificates. The situation is improving but it will take a couple of generations before it is eliminated altogether.

13.7 Conclusion

The purpose of this chapter is to demonstrate how market research could assist British private health care companies who are considering entering the Thai market. It has described what sources of information are available and how research can be carried out in the UK and in the country itself. It has also described how the private health care market operates in Thailand and what differences exist with the UK market.

For any company which does eventually enter a foreign market, it is important to evaluate the market research and determine how accurate was the information in hindsight. Lessons learned can then be applied to new foreign ventures.

Chapter 14

Evaluating the introduction of quality assurance in residential and nursing homes

Jackie Kimberley

In this chapter the reader will gain an understanding of:

- the background to the provision of residential and nursing care
- the rationale for undertaking the project and the factors which constrained and influenced the project
- how the methods were chosen and the importance of anticipating difficulties
- the need to understand and empathize with interviewees and the inhibitors and facilitators to effective communication
- the impact of quality assurance in homes for the elderly
- the importance of triangulation of research methods.

14.1 Context

14.1.1 National policy for community care

Between 1981 and 1985 the number of places in private and voluntary residential nursing homes rose by 138 per cent from 39,000 to 93,000 which conflicted with the Government's policy on community care to reduce institutional and increase community care. The cost to the public purse rose from £10 million in 1980 to £1 billion in 1989 (Challis and Hugman, 1993). The Government could not sustain this level of spending in areas which conflicted with its own policy objectives so a new financial and managerial structure was enshrined in statute by the 1990 NHS and Community Care Act. From April 1993 this enabled the Government to transfer resources to local authorities which would otherwise have been used to finance care through Social Security payments to people in residential and nursing homes. This money, referred to as the Special Transitional Grant (STG), is in addition to the Personal Social Services (PSS) expenditure. In the local authority the amount spent by Social Services increased from £62.7 million in 1991/92 to £96.2 million in 1995/96 (estimated turnout). If the STG (which is largely spent on residential and nursing home care in the independent sector) is combined with the spending on local authority residential care, a shift away from community care towards institutional care becomes apparent, contrary to both national and local policy objectives.

14.1.2 The Local Authority's search for quality

A key philosophy of the NHS and Community Care Act is the expectation that Social Services adopt a key enabling role by reducing the direct provision of residential services and promoting a mixed economy of care. Service providers are expected to be separate from assessors thereby encouraging this mixed economy of care and promoting greater choice for service users whilst achieving best value-for-money in the process. However, there is a perception, shared by staff, that private homes put profit before people. Many staff employed in Social Services genuinely believe that the interests of vulnerable elderly people are best promoted and safeguarded by the direct provision of care by Social Services. The Local Authority, however, is faced with some difficult decisions. Despite a continued improvement reported in occupancy levels since 1993, the current weekly cost for Social Services residential care is approximately £330 compared with an average of £229 for purchasing an external place. Though resources have been identified to refurbish some of the residential homes it would seem imprudent to spend money on local authority homes when residential care can be purchased more cheaply in the independent sector. Clearly, such a situation could only be justified on the basis of a quality differential. In the Local Authority there has been a definite shift in policy moving away from 'high-volume' to 'high-quality' services in residential care. This is evidenced by a real commitment in seeking continuous service improvements including the award of a Charter Mark in one residential home and the implementation of Quality Circles in two others. Innovative ways are also being sought to reduce the need for residential care with the introduction of the 'New Homes for Old' strategy which provides extra care sheltered housing.

The Local Authority's desire for high-quality, customer-focused services is possibly influenced by the realization that provision of care for the elderly is 'big business' and very competitive. Whilst services are demand-led there is a growing emphasis on service user empowerment promoted by Government initiatives such as the Citizen's Charter, the Community Care Charter and very recently 'Best Value'. This has led to increased public accountability coupled with a radical change in the philosophy of service provision moving away from a service-led organization (a 'take it or leave it' approach) to one which is designed to meet service users' needs and preferences ('customer-focused').

The demands on social care are set to increase dramatically over the next decade and in the Local Authority there has been an increase in the proportion of older people but a decline in the proportion of elderly people under 75 admitted to residential homes. The impact of this is an increasing degree of frailty and dementia among elderly people in residential homes. Central Government's wish to see care in the community extended means that more and more people are being discharged from institutional care with the expectation that agencies will work together in order to provide an appropriate package of care. The Local Authority has had to prioritize and rationalize services so that only those with the greatest needs are able to benefit. The resources for the service provided must be used to maximize quality and minimize cost, a key theme in the Government's latest initiative on Best Value.

14.2 How the research was set up

14.2.1 Commissioning the project

This project was commissioned by the Social Services Department (SSD) providing residential care for elderly people in thirty-five residential homes. The authority is also responsible for the contractual purchasing of residential and nursing care for the elderly from 216 homes in the independent sector involving £35 million per year (gross).

The commissioning of services is carried out by the Service Contracts Section who arrange tenders and operate an innovative pricing strategy linked to optional standards of care ('quality stars') in addition to the basic contractual standards. Concerns about *value-for-money* and *quality of care* resulted in homes being 'star rated' based on how many additional care standards they contract to provide. Whilst these star ratings are optional, a directory of homes is published by the Local Authority using the ratings to help prospective service users and carers identify 'quality' homes. At the time of this study, two star ratings were already in use and based on measurement of inputs. The care hours star was awarded on the basis of an agreed number of care hours per resident per week (19 hours for residential care and 29 hours for nursing care). The NVQ star related to the proportion of care staff qualified at NVQ Level 2 (35 per cent for residential care staff and 50 per cent for nursing care staff). The third (quality assurance, QA) star focuses on processes, outcomes and service users' views – in order for homes to be awarded this star their QA system has to comply with standards and criteria contained in the QA Specification. There is an assumption that homes with these 'quality stars' are more likely to deliver good-quality outcomes. Whilst this is supported by higher occupancy rates amongst homes with higher star ratings there is a desire to obtain more direct evidence by measuring the impact upon residents.

The purpose of this study, therefore, was to develop a tool for measuring the views of service users and, in doing so, to find out whether the introduction of a QA system makes any detectable difference from the residents' perspective. There is a substantial cost to the homes in implementing and sustaining a QA system and other costs accrue to the SSD in managing the QA process and paying the external verifiers' fees. Payment of the homes verification costs is intended as a further inducement in addition to that which accrues from the kudos of their accreditation and the perceived marketing advantage this affords them. The SSD was, and still is, keen to develop a tool to test out its assumptions that homes with quality stars provide better-quality outcomes for residents. This commitment to purchasing and providing high-quality care and value-for-money is in exercise of its financial accountability ensuring that limited resources are used to optimize quality outcomes.

14.2.2 Resource constraints

Resource constraints had an impact on the design and implementation of the project. Despite an investment of over £35 million on the purchasing of residential care for elderly people, no additional resources were available to support this project. Paying for interviewers was therefore not an option and even trying to obtain unpaid volunteers presented problems since a budget for expenses would have to be found and then appropriate training arranged to ensure consistency of approach. This would have created delays and from the SSD's experience of using volunteers there is the added risk of people withdrawing from the project. The author could not afford to take such risks within the time constraints imposed so she decided to interview all the residents herself. Help with inputting the questionnaire data was also considered but discounted because there was no one to delegate the task to and, even if there was, the time-scale for completion would have been more difficult to control. The author was also concerned about the consistency of the data input. Unfortunately, the database package at the author's workplace was not one she was familiar with so she decided to set up the database at home. Due to the implications of the Data Protection Act, however, anonymity for the interviewees had to be ensured by the use of codes, an index of which could not be kept in the same location as the database. The other major consideration, and constraint, was the author's job share situation. Although the author's line manager had been supportive in allowing her time within her work programme to undertake the study, job share commitments elsewhere, and the need to continue with her other duties within the two Local Authority departments, meant that the pressures were immense. When the work-load implications became clear, the original plan for the survey was amended on the suggestion of the academic supervisor who recognized that the aspirations of the author were unrealistic within the time-scale. Originally, it was intended to implement two phases of the project involving the interviewing (phase 1) and then re-interviewing (phase 2) of residents a few months later. It was decided that the MBA report would focus on phase 1 of the survey and that phase 2 could be carried out independently of the MBA requirements.

The survey involved five residential homes (four local authority homes, one voluntary sector home) and three nursing homes (two private and one voluntary). The number of residents interviewed was fifty-nine (forty-five females, fourteen males) ranging from 44 to 98 years of age but with a significant proportion between 81 and 90 years of age.

14.2.3 The stakeholders

The key players (stakeholders) were identified at the outset in preparation of the project brief; the author considered this an important and useful exercise. In this, like any other survey, there are numerous stakeholders who may try to influence the design, development and outcome in different and sometimes irreconcilable ways. Anticipating responses to the survey proposal and methodology is useful in crystallizing one's thoughts and developing a marketing strategy for selling the benefits of the project. Engagement of stakeholders provides an ideal opportunity for refining and strengthening the proposals whilst nurturing support and enthusiasm for the project. The stakeholders have varying degrees of influence or authority ranging from no executive authority to the power of veto. It is therefore in the interests of the researcher to take account of these views although ultimately the scope and nature of the project must be agreed with the client or commissioner. The stakeholders identified for this project included:

- the joint clients for the project (the commissioning officer and a quality adviser)
- the project supervisor (Social Services)
- the academic supervisor at the university
- the author's line manager
- the Service Manager, Elderly Resources (Social Services)
- the residents in residential/nursing homes
- Social Services team leaders
- local Social Services inspectors

- the heads of homes in local authority homes
- owners and managers of independent homes
- the care staff in local authority and independent homes
- the quality steering group.

The joint clients had slightly different views of the project and how it should be implemented. The commissioning officer who was promoting the use of Quality of Life Surveys was keen to have quantitative data. These are intended to give some measure of the feelings and perceptions of people and their state of mind, for example, how happy, sad or depressed they feel. However, from the literature search this appeared to be a controversial topic with much of the research having been carried out in clinical settings in the USA. After discussion with the quality steering group and in particular on the advice of the project supervisor (Social Services) and the academic supervisor at the university, the author decided not to pursue this line of research. Fascinating though it would have been, there was concern about the additional work-load (given the time-scale allowed to complete the survey) and the anticipated difficulty of interpreting the data. Since no additional resources had been allocated for the project all the administrative tasks, interviewing, analysis and general project management were entirely the author's responsibility and she had no one to delegate these tasks to.

Meanwhile, the quality adviser wanted external consultants commissioned to undertake the survey. Depending on the choice of consultants, this may have raised the profile of the survey and of the innovative work of the Contracting Section on the development of quality stars. Given the fees that private consultants charge, the study is likely to have been more adequately resourced and since the external consultant is perceived as being independent ('more objective') the findings would have been difficult to ignore (there is a tendency for external consultants to be afforded more credence than in-house consultants). External consultants often have useful experience and through their extensive networking facilities may know of similar studies they can readily refer to. In contrast, the main advantage of internal consultants is that their time is usually cheaper to purchase; they are more knowledgeable about the organizational values and protocols and they may have less difficulty in accessing the relevant people in the organization. It is impossible to generalize on issues of competence and expertise since some external consultants are extremely competent whilst others are less so and the same applies to in-house consultants.

14.2.4 The MBA project

In this study, the author's line manager was not convinced that the use of external consultants was a cost-effective exercise. As the relevant budget holder he decided to commission the author to undertake the survey and since she was actively seeking a project in completion of her MBA studies this arrangement was to their mutual satisfaction.

There was overall support for the project by managers and local authority staff because they were keen to find out if their commitment to quality assurance was improving life for residents in their care. Understandably, however, because the survey reflects on the behaviour and attitude of staff, there was some anxiety about the results of the survey and their potential use or misuse. The author, being very mindful of this, tried to develop and implement the survey sensitively and in way which she hoped would be non-threatening to staff. The author gave written assurance that individuals and homes would remain anonymous unless the author perceived that there was grave or serious risks to residents in which case she would have no option but to take appropriate action. This was a necessary caveat which was readily accepted by the care staff and fortunately did not require consideration in the course of the survey.

In any survey, it is imperative to identify and gain the support of the 'gatekeepers'. Gatekeepers are potentially powerful allies facilitating access and helping to ensure that the researcher's time is spent productively. The researcher is well advised to invest time and effort in obtaining the support of such crucial players. These are people who, due to their influence or position of authority, are able to facilitate access to the targeted interviewees. In this survey, the author identified the Service Manager (Elderly Services) with responsibility for all local authority homes for elderly people; via his team managers he was able to gain support from care staff. In the independent sector no overall gatekeeper was identified so each home had to be 'courted' individually which was resource intensive and not particularly effective based on the poor response elicited from the original invitations sent out.

For an undergraduate or postgraduate student, the choice of academic supervisor and project supervisor in the organization is crucial. This was not immediately apparent to the author and indeed she accepted her mentors without considering their suitability. Fortunately both mentors had considerable research experience and impeccable reputations which was somewhat daunting for an inexperienced, albeit keen, research student. Whilst there was an underlying fear of not being able to live up to their perceived expectations, the author recognized that this presented a golden opportunity and she was determined not to waste it. In her regular monthly meetings with the academic supervisor, the project supervisor and the quality steering group the author recorded the main issues of discussion or debate together with the agreed actions. The minutes proved to be a valuable tool as they provided a useful agenda for subsequent meetings and a record of progress which become invaluable in writing up the main project report. These notes also encouraged good time-management because they provided a catalyst for outstanding actions which might otherwise have been overlooked or delayed thereby jeopardizing the target completion date.

Learning points

- identify available resources and decide whether to employ internal or external consultants
- design the project taking into account resource constraints and any other constraints, including the characteristics of the interviewees, and be realistic within the available time-scale!
- identify the stakeholders and the gatekeepers and be prepared to defend the design, management and implementation of the project ('rehearse the script')
- learn about the lifestyle of the interviewees and establish a good rapport
- think of the relationship with the project or academic supervisor as an unspoken service level agreement with two-way responsibilities
- record the outcome of meetings. This provides crucial material for the project report and highlights outstanding actions which are essential for good project management.

14.2.5 Aims and objectives

This study focused on the feelings and perceptions of residents and was primarily concerned with qualitative data. The overall aim of the study was:

- to develop a tool to find out whether the introduction of QA actually makes a difference to the quality of life of residents and whether any differences are perceived negatively or positively.

The three main objectives associated with this were to establish:

- whether the hoped-for benefits of QA justified the human and financial resources
- whether a QA system ensures that quality of life (as defined in the Local Authority's specification for QA) is achieved
- whether quality assurance makes any noticeable difference to residents.

The overall aim belies the complexity of the task and in particular the difficulties in obtaining data which can be accurately interpreted. The author realized that her statement of intent would have to undergo further examination and clarification in order to proceed with the research. Numerous questions underpinned the overall objective:

- what tool is the most appropriate?
- how is quality of life defined?
- what measures should be used?
- how are any differences detected and measured?
- is there a direct causal relationship between the introduction of QA and improvements in the quality of life of residents?
- how does one isolate the QA variable?

The method of addressing these questions informed the methodology.

Key learning points

- reflect on the overall objectives
- break down statement of objectives into the constituent parts and analyse words, phrases and 'taken for granted' statements in order to clarify meanings.

14.3 Research methods

14.3.1 Choosing the methods

The choice of methodology depends on three main factors:

- the subject group and their characteristics and circumstances
- the researcher and his or her competencies/skills
- resource and time constraints.

The researcher must decide on the most effective methodology. What is effective in one scenario, however, will not necessarily work in another. Since robustness of methodology inevitably impacts upon the outcome it is clearly incumbent on the researcher to limit unwelcome distortions using whatever methods are the most effective in the given circumstances.

The information for this study was obtained from:

1   Primary sources including senior management colleagues, care staff in residential and nursing homes and principally residents in the homes.
2   Secondary sources which included a review of Local Authority Committee Reports, external library sources and social care organizations (e.g. Oral History Society).

The author chose to interview the elderly residents using a face-to-face questionnaire because she considered it more systematic in the evaluation of responses than would otherwise have been the case using unstructured interviews or focus groups. The quality of life principles, *privacy*, *dignity*, *independence*, *choice*, *rights* and *fulfilment*, formed the structure of the questionnaire upon which questions were focused. Participative or non-participative observation was discounted by the author because of the desire to listen to the views and perceptions of residents themselves. However, informal observation is an integral part of the researcher's role and in this survey it complemented, but sometimes conflicted with, residents' responses.

The difficulty with the questionnaire interviews is that they sometimes felt contrived. The responses of residents did not always lend themselves to 'yes' or 'no' answers and if an interviewer is determined to get ticks in boxes this may be at the expense of obtaining genuine feedback, especially if the interviewee feels bullied into responding. Whilst the author did rephrase questions in order to obtain a relevant response, with experience she became more confident in accepting inappropriate responses or no response at all rather than expose the resident to undue pressure. The author came to this view early on in the interviews when one resident was asked the same question in about three different ways and the resident finally retorted 'which would you like me to say, yes or no?' Sometimes the residents' reluctance to answer a particular question was evident from their demeanour or expression, and often it related to questions about staff behaviour or attitude. Clearly, the researcher has to be sensitive to the feelings of interviewees and respond appropriately even if that impacts adversely on the survey. To act otherwise would be unethical. Thorough design and testing of the survey questionnaire should reduce the likelihood of inappropriate terminology or methods but there is no guarantee that it will eliminate all the difficulties.

Although somewhat dated, a thorough examination of the advantages and disadvantages of the survey interview is provided by Dijkstra and van der Zouwen (1982). They describe the rules which interviewers should use in order to minimize distortion or inaccuracies in responses. Although these include common-sense directives some of them are difficult to adhere to and arguably unhelpful. For instance, the first rule is that questions must be read as they are worded in the questionnaire (that is, no deviations allowed). In the interviews carried out by the author, the residents had different levels of comprehension and where terminology or syntax was not understood she unpacked the questions and provided concrete examples they could relate to. It was reassuring to note that such a pragmatic approach was taken by Bury and Holmes (1990) when they interviewed elderly people over 90 years of age.

In an earlier study Oakley (1981) considered the traditional and impersonal style of interviewing people 'problematic and ultimately unhelpful'. She interviewed fifty-five women twice during pregnancy and twice afterwards. This was preceded by nine months of participant observation in hospitals. Her experience led her to question the paradigms of traditional interviewing techniques which suggest that interviewing is a one-way hierarchical process. She also rejects the view that interviews have no personal meaning in terms of social interactions and are restricted to statistical comparability with other interviews. During her interviews with women she found that interviewees did ask many questions and often this involved a two-way discussion. She also found professional detachment impossible (as did the author) and was not prepared to adopt a 'purely exploitative attitude to interviewees as sources of data'. She concludes that 'personal involvement is more than dangerous bias – it is the condition under which people come to know each other and to admit others into their lives'. The interviewer must therefore decide whether to follow the conventional paradigms of interviewing techniques or break with tradition by implementing alternative approaches.

14.3.2 The sample of respondents

The characteristics of the people under investigation and the environment in which they live are important factors for consideration in the design of a survey. In this project, the author hoped to interview five or six residents per day based on interviews lasting approximately one hour. Eager to commence the interviewing she arrived at the homes at about 9.00 a.m. but then found she had to wait whilst residents had their breakfasts and took medications. It was usually about 10.30 a.m. before interviews could begin only to stop again at about 12.30 p.m. whilst residents prepared for and ate their lunch. Interviews recommenced around 1.30 p.m. and continued until about 4.30 p.m. though these were sometimes interrupted for toileting, medication, nursing procedures or visitors. Clearly, the researcher has to plan her research to fit in with the lifestyle and routine of the interviewees but this means understanding what life is like for the interviewees. The project can then be managed to take account of these circumstances. Empathy with the interviewees enables the researcher to set realistic timescales for tasks based on an understanding of what life is really like for people in their situation. Spending time with interviewees before the project begins is a good way of building up relationships and fostering mutual understanding which the author believes is important to allow interviewees to develop trust and confidence in the researcher. By doing this, one hopes that the survey results will be more informative and reliable than might otherwise be the case.

Learning points

- know yourself and your subjects
- plan, and when you think you've done enough, plan a bit more!
- anticipate problems and try to deal with them beforehand
- meticulously record details and feedback (what is not important at the time may become significant in the future)
- learn from the mistakes of others (research thoroughly what others have done)

- test out the survey tools on a representative sample (if the sample is too small or unrepresentative, underlying problems might not emerge)
- be prepared to accept that your original plans may be unworkable or ineffective and take corrective action
- adopt the Deming philosophy of 'Plan-Do-Check-Act' (Walton, 1989) to ensure that mistakes are transformed into opportunities for improvement.

14.4 Findings

The findings of the survey tended to confirm previous studies carried out amongst elderly people in residential and nursing home care but also raised important issues for future studies.

The main findings were:

- some of the standards had no meaning, significance or relevance to residents (e.g. some of those relating to privacy) whilst others were important (e.g. those relating to activities within and outside the home) and those relating to interpersonal relationships
- when standards were not met residents often said they 'didn't mind'
- residents' interactions with staff were very important and provided much valued opportunities for conversation and friendship
- insensitive or rude comments by staff were remembered long after other things were forgotten
- 'staff know best' was a familiar theme amongst residents
- some residents obtained fulfilment by adopting a specific role or purpose in the home (e.g. cleaning or setting tables, running errands, etc.)
- very few residents noticed any changes as a result of QA. Any discernible differences related to staff shortages or staff turnover but there was a reluctance to say that these changes affected residents adversely.

14.5 Conclusions

It is difficult to detect change associated with the introduction of QA by relying exclusively on the views and perceptions of older people in residential and nursing home care.

- outcomes are difficult to measure and proxy indicators are a useful substitute which may suggest (but not confirm) quality of life outcomes
- the interviewer's direct observations sometimes contradicted the residents' responses
- triangulation is required to confirm service users' views and perceptions
- the likelihood of unreliable responses is increased due to residents' dependency, frailty, fear of reprisals and fear of 'not wishing to get anyone into trouble'
- there are inhibitors and facilitators to effective communication in interviews including:
  - residents' fears of hidden agendas
  - residents not wishing to bite the hand that feeds them (the 'gratitude factor')
  - personal characteristics and style of interviewer

- • personal characteristics of interviewee
- • language and method of interviewing.
- elderly people are not one homogeneous group – what is suitable for one person may be inappropriate for another (quality is an individual characteristic)
- the assessment of residents' mental and physical competencies would be a useful aid in the interpretation and understanding of residents' responses.

Further questions raised

- what importance do staff and managers attach to talking to residents. Is it considered a fundamental part of the job or perceived as 'skiving off'?
- to what extent is the physical environment a help or hindrance to a quality system?
- what processes or proxy indicators are measurable and most likely to suggest quality of life outcomes?
- what variety of tools should be used to measure indicators of change?

14.6 Recommendations

As a result of the findings from the first phase of the research, which formed the MBA project, it was recommended that the second phase of the survey should focus on:

- the level of physical and/or sensory disability or frailty and the extent to which it impacts upon freedom of choice for residents
- an assessment of residents for memory, communication and orientation based on a recognized behaviour rating scale (e.g. Barthel, Crichton, etc.)
- evaluating the importance attached by residents, managers and staff-to-staff inter-actions and conversations with residents
- the extent to which the physical environment impacts upon the quality of life of residents
- non-participant observation and interviews with managers, staff and relatives
- job satisfaction surveys with staff to evaluate the level of satisfaction and dissatisfaction amongst staff
- indicators or processes likely to achieve desired outcomes
- the expectations of residents as well as their perceptions.

14.7 Postscript

The Local Authority is one of the pilot authorities for Best Value which is a central government initiative intended as a replacement for white collar compulsory competitive tendering. Best Value focuses on the relationship between quality and price. If a local authority is unable to demonstrate value for money in the provision of in-house services, as perceived by service users, then it must be prepared to obtain services from the independent sector and enter into innovative partnerships with external organizations. Failure to ensure value for money will ultimately result in central government intervention.

The commissioning officer, now designated Market Development Manager, is confident that the quality stars system has the hallmark of Best Value. The higher occupancy rates of homes with the highest number of quality stars seems to suggest that service users are choosing on the basis of the relationship between quality and price. Furthermore, recent analysis appears to demonstrate that the duration of stay at homes with a higher number of quality stars is longer than at those with a lower number of stars. The requirements of Best Value include benchmarking and continuous service improvement; hence more detailed analysis is inevitable.

In the meantime the QA star system in residential and nursing homes is developing but there is also a commitment to obtaining more detailed information on service user outcomes and quality of life measures. Currently, the author is preparing a project brief for prospective tenderers to bid for the implementation of a pilot study to evaluate and measure quality of life indicators. This will include an evaluation of service users' frailty and mental capacity and it is also hoped to obtain some quantifiable data with the use of the Barthel score on the overall well-being of residents, that is, how happy, sad or depressed they feel. There is also an emphasis on service user expectations as well as perceptions so that some measure of the gap between the two is established. SERVQUAL (Parasuraman *et al.*, 1988) is the model normally associated with this type of assessment but it may be adapted, customized or simplified to suit the circumstances.

Further reading

Bury, M. and Holmes, A. (1990) 'Researching very old people', in S.M. Peace (ed.) *Researching Social Gerontology – Concepts, Methods and Issues*, London: Sage Publications.

Chapter 15

Assessing the need for family planning services in Coventry

Mary Parkes

In this chapter the reader will gain an understanding of:

- the important contribution of family planning services within the NHS
- why market research information is needed in this area
- the costs and benefits of a senior manager commissioning and undertaking research
- the methods and findings of the research
- what has happened to the services since the research was published.

15.1 Context

The importance of family planning and sexual health services within the National Health Services have been highlighted in many national documents, most notably the *Saving Lives: Our Healthier Nation* (Department of Health, 1999). However at the same time, the UK's poor performance on numbers of teenage pregnancies and unwanted pregnancies has also been highlighted (Social Exclusion Unit, 1999). The UK has the highest rate of teenage pregnancies in Europe and is the only western European country in which teenage conception rates have risen since 1980 (Babb, 1993).

Although some priority was given to family planning and sexual health services in the late 1980s with the emergence of HIV and AIDS, by the mid-1990s these services were under pressure as the financial constraints of health authorities grew. Family planning services were particularly vulnerable because of financial pressures but also because of changes in their provision and funding between 1970 and 1995.

Until the mid-1970s the Family Planning Association ran family planning clinics in the UK. Following the NHS re-organization act in 1974, services were to be run by health authorities and general practitioners also agreed to provide family planning services. Between 1975 and 1990 GP provision of these services increased dramatically and GPs are now the most common source of family planning services.

However, two sets of service providers offering family planning services brought with it a dilemma since there was no clear distinction as to whether they were providing different services, to different audiences, or to different quality. There was also little market research information to assess consumer views of the services they had received.

In addition, funding for the two types of family planning service (GP and clinic) came from different sources. Funding for family planning services clinics came from the health authorities' cash-limited budget for hospital and community services. In direct contrast, funding for family planning services provided by GPs came from the centrally funded and non-cash-limited general medical services.

Throughout the 1980s, when health authorities were under increasing financial constraints, they were tempted to cut family planning clinic sessions (which were funded locally) with a transfer of users to GP services (which were funded nationally). In 1993, a survey by the Family Planning Association revealed that some health authorities had actually reduced their provision of family planning clinic services on financial grounds, despite exhortations to reduce unwanted pregnancies.

Part of the justification for this was the assumption that the clinic and the GP services duplicated service provision. This view continued to exist despite several studies which showed that the two types of provision met the needs of different groups of women in terms of age parity and methods used.

Cutbacks in clinic services on financial grounds alone were temporarily halted when the government, as a result of pressure, restated its commitment to family planning clinics in order to provide 'an element of choice for women who did not wish to consult their general practitioner for family planning services'.

A gradual reduction in clinic provision has happened over the last twenty years not just because of financial pressures but because of the growth of family planning services provided by GPs. However, little was known about the range and quality of family planning services they provided nor whether they provided consumer choice.

The National Health Service Reforms of 1990 put more emphasis on health authorities to carry out needs assessment and purchase appropriate services to meet identified needs. In Coventry, as in many areas of the country, there was little local information about the population needs for these services or the quality of services being provided.

It was an ideal time in 1995 to conduct a review of family planning services since the Department of Health had asked for a review of services in 1992/3 which had not been actioned locally. The informal merger of Coventry Health Authority with Coventry Family Health Services Authority in 1994 had also made it easier to obtain information about services formerly provided by the two different organizations.

15.2 Health needs assessment for Coventry

This section provides a needs assessment for family planning services by highlighting relevant characteristics of the population such as births, ethnicity, fertility and abortions. It highlights areas where Coventry is different from national and regional averages and what would be expected for a population of its size.

15.2.1 Population

The mid-1993 population estimate for Coventry is 304,100 persons of whom 49 per cent are males and 51 per cent females. When fertility is analysed, the age groups from 15 to 44 are usually considered. There are 63,500 females and 67,600 males estimated to be in this age group in Coventry. This includes 7,500 students who are studying at either Coventry or Warwick University nearby.

15.2.2 Ethnicity

Approximately 12 per cent of the population of Coventry are from a black or minority ethnic group, the majority of whom are from the Indian subcontinent. However, approximately 16 per cent of births in Coventry are to mothers from black and minority ethnic groups since fertility rates in minority ethnic groups are higher.

15.2.3 Fertility

Coventry's total period fertility rate of 1.92 in 1992 was fairly high compared to the UK rate of 1.80. An analysis of wards within Coventry shows that there are significant variations between wards across the city.

15.2.4 Abortions

The abortion rate for Coventry at 16.9 is consistently higher than the England and Wales figure of 12.5. This varies by age group, ethnicity and geographical wards within Coventry. The total number of terminations has increased each year from 1988 to 1995. In particular, rates were rising in the 25–34 age range and the 35–44 age range. However, Coventry does not have a problem with late terminations.

15.3 How the research was set up

The research was initiated by the author, a senior manager within Coventry Health Authority, in partial fulfilment of an MBA which was being undertaken on a part-time basis. The topic was chosen because, as a senior manager with responsibility for purchasing family planning services, there was little information on local need or satisfaction with services currently provided. The project was supported by academic input from the University of Aston Business School and assistance from the Public Health Department at Coventry Health Authority.

The market research on consumer satisfaction was conducted jointly with the manager of the local family planning clinic who was anxious to learn about consumer perceptions of services being provided. The primary data collected by market research was supported by significant access to data from secondary sources. Although some of this was routinely produced and publicly available, other data, particularly on GP claims, was not collated and was only used within the health authority for payment purposes.

The fact that the research was initiated by someone from within the organization and much of it was undertaken internally meant that direct costs were low and consisted of printing, postage, coding of the survey and analysis. No one had to be seconded or employed for the project. However, this does not mean that the overall cost was reduced. The project consumed a considerable amount of time of both senior managers, and the resources of the health authority were used in terms of administration for sending out the postal survey, reminders and assistance with analysis.

There were obvious opportunity costs. Using the time of a relatively senior NHS manager on this research meant that she was not spending time on other important issues for which she was also responsible. It also meant the project was conducted over a slightly longer time-scale than if an outside agency was commissioned to undertake the work.

However, on the positive side, the fact that the research was initiated and partly conducted by a senior manager from within the organization which would have to act on the findings made it more likely that the recommendations would be implemented. It also guaranteed that the conclusions of the research, which had long-term implications, were built into the health authority's priorities and could legitimately be undertaken by a number of health authority employees and those responsible for managing service provision. The fact that the research was done in fulfilment of a masters degree also guaranteed that a full literature review was conducted before the market research was commissioned. In many cases health authorities would routinely commission market research without allocating time to conduct a full literature review.

Learning points

- before commissioning the research be very clear about the aims and objectives and get all the stakeholders to analyse them critically
- be realistic about what are the resources, skills, commitments, workload pressure and opportunity costs before deciding whether to employ an internal consultant
- conduct a literature review before outlining the broad aim and specific objectives. The outcome may affect both the content and methodology of your research.

15.3.1 Objectives

The objectives of the study at the outset were to:

1   Review the literature, trends in family planning and set the needs of Coventry people in context.
2   Establish the need for family planning services in Coventry and identify features particular to it.
3   Analyse the current services provided in terms of take up and see how effectively services are meeting needs in terms of appropriateness, accessibility, acceptability, equity, effectiveness and efficiency.
4   Establish whether there were balanced and complementary services being provided by GPs and family planning clinics within Coventry.
5   Assess whether current services provide value for money.
6   Make recommendations for improving these services.

In reality, so little comparative financial information was available in the period of the study that very little was included of objective 5. In addition, a much greater emphasis was given to objective 4 after this study was published, particularly in relation to GP claims. Very little comparative data on this area was included in the report as it was not routinely collated.

Learning points

- Ensure you can get access to the information which will meet your objectives. In this case objective 5 could not be met because comparable financial information was not available
- Ensure you can get access to information during the period in which the research has been commissioned. In this case objective 4 could not be fully met because the data had to be collated specifically for this purpose.

15.4 Research methods

A number of sources of information were used for this study:

1   Information from secondary sources routinely available.
2   Information from secondary sources, which were available but not routinely collated e.g. claim data by GPs for family planning.
3   Information from primary sources which was specifically commissioned for this study.

15.4.1 Secondary information routinely available

The majority of this data is routinely available within a health authority. The results are set out in Section 15.2 and formed the basis of the needs assessment highlighting areas where Coventry was different from the average district in terms of population, ethnicity, fertility, abortions etc. It also included first and total contacts with a family planning service in Coventry which highlighted the fact that Coventry had the third lowest rate of family planning first contacts in the West Midlands region. It also highlighted the fact that total contacts were decreasing year on year. Age, ethnicity and method of contraceptive used by those attending were also included.

15.4.2 Primary data collection

The market research specifically commissioned for this project was a postal survey of 500 recent users of family services in Coventry to obtain their views on the services they had received. Since it was not possible to obtain the views of all those who use the service in any year (some 9,000 people) efforts were made to be as representative as possible. The sampling method used was proportional stratified random sampling based on the age of users and ethnicity. The final response rate received was 60 per cent, although 5 per cent declined to answer the full questionnaire. This is reasonable for a postal survey and since the percentages of responses by age and ethnicity were close to the sample chosen we proceeded with the analysis.

The decision to undertake a postal questionnaire of consumer views was based on the following:

- its perceived versatility and cost effectiveness in collecting information
- high sample numbers could be handled relatively easily

- it is quick to complete
- the use of closed questions make coding relatively quick and easy so large numbers can be processed
- the method is recognized as satisfactory for quantitative information
- interviewer bias is eliminated and conformity response is therefore reduced
- the method is cheaper than personal interviews
- the method avoids the need for face-to-face contact which might be difficult for respondents because of the sensitivity of the topic.

Although the postal survey was selected as the most appropriate method for this study there have been a number of weaknesses identified with this method which had to be recognized. These were:

1   Sensitivity of the subject matter might reduce the response rate of the postal survey. This was recognized and women were given the opportunity of opting out of the questionnaire. The accompanying letter was also very sensitively worded to ensure that it did not state that the respondents had been chosen because they had visited a family planning clinic recently.
2   Lack of ability to explain questions with a self-completion questionnaire. Given that it was a self-response questionnaire the importance of ensuring that all the questions were unambiguous, relevant to the survey and non-judgemental were vitally import-ant in survey design. The questionnaire was piloted with fifty women and then reviewed.
3   Difficulties for those whose first language was not English. Again this was recognized as a difficulty and those respondents whose first language was not English were offered help in completing the questionnaire from a linkworker, or the provision of the ques-tionnaire in their first language. In the event this was not taken up.

Learning points

- no methodology is problem free. Assess the advantages and disadvantages of each carefully before deciding which is most appropriate to your objectives
- try to minimize any likely known disadvantages from the start
- pilot any method before the main survey starts and be prepared to amend the instrument.

Question areas focused on:

- knowledge and awareness of service provision
- service accessibility and acceptability
- appropriateness of service
- standards, e.g. choice, privacy, dignity, communication
- satisfaction with services
- future service developments
- personal details of user.

15.5 Findings

15.5.1 Awareness

Awareness of the services provided was high. The majority of respondents had been made aware of the service through family and friends. There were some interesting differences in awareness by age with 96 per cent of 16–19-year-olds being aware that the clinic offered emergency contraception as opposed to 64 per cent of 35–44-year-olds. The majority of those using the clinic were regular users.

15.5.2 Accessibility

Almost 80 per cent of respondents made an appointment to visit the clinic although this varied by age and ethnicity with only 60 per cent of 11–15-year-olds making an appointment and only 50 per cent of Pakistani women making an appointment. This may have indicated a problem in making an appointment such as low access to a telephone or family unhappy about them using the services. It may also have indicated that young women and women from minority ethnic groups are attending with a more urgent problem. The majority of appointments were non-urgent but 50 per cent of the 11–15-year-olds who attended had an urgent problem as did 42 per cent of black respondents. Overall 50 per cent of respondents with an urgent problem were seen the same day, 19 per cent the following day and 24 per cent within 48 hours. This again varied by age and ethnicity.

For those with a non-urgent problem, 30 per cent of consumers were seen within 3 days, 26 per cent within a week and 26 per cent within 2 weeks. User preferences for particular clinics and times seemed to be accommodated. Sixty per cent were seen at their appointment time, 36 per cent were not. The majority of these waited less than 30 minutes, but a small proportion (10 per cent) waited more than 30 minutes to be seen.

15.5.3 Acceptability

Less than 20 per cent of respondents were offered a choice as to whether they wanted to see a male or female doctor. Of those who expressed a preference for a female doctor 56 per cent were still not offered a choice. Only 27 per cent of respondents were aware of the names of the members of staff who they were seen by.

15.5.4 Appropriateness

The majority of respondents felt that they were appropriately consulted and involved in any of the decisions about their care and the majority felt they were given appropriate information to support what staff said to them. This varied by age and ethnicity with more black and minority ethnic women and older women saying they did not receive appropriate information.

15.5.5 Satisfaction with services

Overall, 75 per cent of respondents were satisfied with the services they received. This varied by age, ethnicity and member of staff seen. Almost 20 per cent of 11–15-year-olds were very dissatisfied with the reception staff and 15 per cent of 20–25-year-olds were dissatisfied with the doctor. Areas of dissatisfaction cited were attitude of staff, lack of information and lack of sensitivity.

15.5.6 Privacy and dignity

Levels of dissatisfaction with privacy at reception were high with 35 per cent of consumers feeling unhappy. This differed by age and ethnicity with 50 per cent of 11–15-year-olds feeling unhappy and 57 per cent of black women feeling unhappy. The majority of respondents were happy with privacy in the changing area.

15.5.7 Future development of services

The main services people requested if developments were planned were: Norplant (injectable contraceptive), better services for menopausal women, sterilization and more clinics in outlying areas.

15.6 Conclusions and recommendations

15.6.1 The postal survey

The main issues arising from the consumer survey were:

- the need to improve privacy and dignity for all users at clinic reception
- the need for members of staff to be clearly identified
- the need to enable women who particularly wanted to see a female doctor to exercise this choice
- the need for the service to be more appropriately targeted to meet the needs of younger women
- the need for the service to be more sensitive to the needs of women from black and minority ethnic groups.

15.6.2 The secondary data analysis

- high fertility rates
- high teenage pregnancy rates
- high abortion rates
- significant variations in fertility and abortion rates between wards within Coventry
- high rate of GP claims for contraceptive services
- significant variations between GP practices.

15.6.3 Recommendations

- the need for comparable data on users of GP-provided family planning clinics
- the need for more practice nurses to be family planning trained
- the need to increase the low level of first contacts at family planning clinics
- to review the future of family planning clinics in outlying areas with low take up

- to improve access to emergency contraception within the city at weekends
- to analyse the value for money of family planning services.

15.7 Dissemination strategy

After the MBA dissertation had been submitted, a short report was produced for internal circulation to planning groups, primary care teams and the commissioning group. A presentation was made to Aston students. A paper was presented at the Department of Health national conference on unwanted pregnancy.

15.8 Lessons learnt

1   For the MBA project topic it is important to choose an issue in which you are interested and committed.
2   The need for a thorough literature review to be undertaken first in order to define more precisely the area of study.
3   It is difficult to commission and manage research in terms of time-scale, resources and skills.
4   Select the survey methods carefully, all have weaknesses which should be weighed against the value of the information to be gained.
5   Being in-house does enable you to ensure recommendations are acted upon over a period of time.

15.9 Postscript

Looking back on the project after two years, there are three main issues where progress has been made.

15.9.1 Variation in GP claims

One of the most unexpected findings from this study was the variation in GP claims for contraceptive advice and services provided. Because this information is used for payment and has not been routinely analysed before, this variation had not been identified. Several very high and very low claims had been reviewed and the information on GP services across a locality has been provided to Primary Care Groups in order that they may look for gaps or duplication of services. Likewise, the information is collated at the health authority and may be used in the performance management of GPs and Primary Care Groups.

15.9.2 Family planning clinic quality of service

Funding was made available by the health authority and the local community trust to upgrade the reception at the main family planning clinic held at the Women's Health and Information Centre in Coventry. Several further improvements were made in terms of patient information and staff training, and in 1999 the centre was awarded the Charter Mark for quality services.

The clinics provided in the localities around Coventry are still under review. The setting up of Primary Care Groups this year may give an opportunity for family planning services to be planned as a whole service to a community, whether provided by a clinic or GP.

15.9.3 Access to emergency services at weekends

The contract held with our two local providers has been extended to provide a service on a Saturday and to improve information to patients, particularly young people. Under the Health of the Nation initiative, Coventry plans to target young people more effectively to reduce the rate of teenage pregnancies. This will be done in conjunction with local education and youth services.

Further reading

Social Exclusion Unit (1999) *Teenage Pregnancy*, London: The Stationery Office.

Chapter 16

Using **SERVQUAL** to measure service quality at an **NHS** specialist laboratory

Graham Flynn

In this chapter the reader will gain an understanding of:

- the emerging market for toxicology services
- how the market research was commissioned and carried out as an MBA project
- how SERVQUAL was used to analyse the customers' expectations
- the use of the market research information by the commissioner
- the success of the project two years later.

16.1 Introduction

This chapter describes how to measure service quality in a public sector laboratory. It is drawn from a larger project undertaken in 1996 that developed a strategy for the laboratory's survival and long-term development (Flynn, 1998a).

Service quality measurement was undertaken as a part of the process of determining the laboratory's degree of strategic drift and to suggest appropriate courses of action for its correction. The tool used for measuring service quality was the SERVQUAL instrument of Parasuraman *et al.* (1986).

The laboratory concerned is the Regional Laboratory for Toxicology (Toxicology), based at City Hospital NHS Teaching Trust (the Trust) in Birmingham. Toxicology is a specialist medical laboratory carrying out toxicology investigations on samples sent for analysis, mainly by the Trust and other hospitals within the West Midlands. Typical users of the service include: hospital pathology departments, drug treatment clinics, occupational health clinics, general practitioners and HM coroners. Toxicology was designated as a Regional Scientific Speciality in 1972 and has been part of the UK Supra-regional Assay Service for trace element analysis since 1974. It has close links with the University of Birmingham for which it provides specialist teaching and laboratory-based training to undergraduate and postgraduate students of biomedical sciences and medicine. It is also involved with the World Health Organization International Programme on Chemical Safety.

Toxicology applies chemical techniques to the analysis of body fluids and tissues for drugs and chemical poisons. Specialist investigations are performed in the areas listed below from a repertoire of over 100 different tests, many of which are available on a 24-hour basis every day of the year:

- general toxicology – the laboratory diagnosis of poisoning
- therapeutic drug monitoring (TDM)

- forensic toxicology (coroners and police)
- screening for drug and substance abuse (DoA)
- monitoring for essential and non-essential trace elements
- occupational and environmental toxicology.

Since 1991 the National Health Service (NHS) has been reorganized on business principles that have resulted in decisions over the supply and purchase of services being controlled by market forces, or as otherwise known – the NHS internal market. This, and the withdrawal of Regional Funding in 1994, forced Toxicology to reflect in its charges the true cost of investigations carried out for non-Trust patients. This caused a significant shift in the balance of services provided as buyers become more aware of the costs involved. For example, TDM business from other trust hospitals (a key source of work and revenue) decreased by 40 per cent with consequent effects on income. Toxicology became less able to provide cross-subsidies for complex or rarely requested investigations and surcharges were implemented for out-of-hours requests. The service balance moved towards the provision of more specialist toxicology investigations and it was hoped that access to these specialist services for new and existing customers inside and outside the region could be increased.

In 1996, the cost of individual investigations ranged from £10 to £400 per case depending on the clinical problem, and in the financial year ending 31 March 1996 contributions from the four key service areas were as follows:

- general toxicology/forensic – 26.1 per cent
- TDM – 20.0 per cent
- screening for DoA – 36.9 per cent
- monitoring for trace elements – 16.9 per cent.

Approximately 20 per cent of income was derived from the Trust, with the remainder coming from a large variety of users. Overall, 60 per cent of income arose from within the greater Birmingham area.

Against this background, what benefits arise through Toxicology providing a high level of service quality?

At the technical level, quality will ensure accurate and reliable results for assays which will help customers of the service make better decisions. At the functional level, quality should ensure that Toxicology is better meeting the needs of its customers. This is particularly important for a specialist service where most customers are unable to judge the technical aspects of one such service against another because they lack the specialist knowledge. The customer therefore judges the service at its functional level and will make comparisons between one specialist service and another on this basis (Berkowitz, 1995). There may even be occasions when the functional performance from a different, but similar service, e.g. haematology, may be used for comparison and judgement. Additionally, customers may not necessarily buy the highest quality service; convenience, price or availability may enhance satisfaction while not actually affecting customers' perceptions of service quality (Cronin and Taylor, 1992). Nevertheless, the management of quality is an important means of differentiation and has other benefits such as efficiency improvements and cost savings. The benefits of service quality would therefore seem to be generally advantageous.

When SERVQUAL was presented, evidence was also provided for the scale's factor structure, reliability and validity, which suggested its applicability among different service industries (Parasuraman *et al.*, 1988). However, this evidence came from empirical studies conducted on customers from service industries other than health care. Is SERVQUAL therefore suitable to measure the quality of service given by Toxicology?

With some adaptation of the basic approach, SERVQUAL certainly appears to be suitable and, furthermore, there are considerable benefits arising from its use that are related below, together with some of the disadvantages.

ADVANTAGES

- the relative importance of consumer expectations with respect to the different dimensions of service quality can be ascertained
- by running regular SERVQUAL investigations, service quality can be tracked over time
- an organization's customers can be segmented by perceived quality on the basis of their individual SERVQUAL scores
- SERVQUAL can be used to assess the performance of an organization relative to its principal competitors. SERVQUAL scores benchmarked against those of competitors are a real measure of competitive achievement – not a measure against an arbitrary target
- SERVQUAL is attributed with predictive qualities on the basis that there is a relationship between service quality and a range of basic consumer intentions (evidence for this is weak and the subject is open to much controversy).

DISADVANTAGES

- the apparent inability of the seven-point Likert scale to distinguish subtle differences in expectations and perceptions
- problems with the use of different scores to calculate a construct
- the construct of service quality presented by SERVQUAL may not be the most valid approach to defining the concept of service quality
- performance-based measures are believed to provide greater efficiency in obtaining scores.

16.2 Negotiating and undertaking the project

The SERVQUAL survey was part of a larger project which, for the author, formed the culmination of his MBA course and provided an opportunity to apply management theories and models from the taught part of the programme in solving a business problem. From Toxicology's point of view, the project was there to provide a marketing strategy that would enable them to expand their business.

The Trust's Public Relations Officer approached the Business School with the project at the suggestion of a consultant working for the Trust, who had completed an MBA himself. He was aware of Toxicology's need for assistance and recognized that it would make an ideal MBA/MSc project.

Following the fall off in TDM work, Toxicology's senior management were anxious to make up the deficit. It was felt that a marketing strategy was required to market and promote Toxicology's range of services to new and existing customers, in an attempt to develop new business that would make up and ultimately extend beyond that which had been lost.

However, after initial discussions with the Department Head of Toxicology it became evident that an even more fundamental approach was required. The lack of direction from the Trust had resulted in a period of short-term planning pending the new Trust strategy, which was in turn causing Toxicology to experience a considerable degree of strategic drift. Having identified this more fundamental problem, the author agreed with the Department Head that an overall strategy was required to provide the foundation and direction for marketing and operations etc.

The author undertook the project as an outsider with no previous connection to Toxicology, the NHS or the public sector. The author's background is principally in banking and financial services which, whilst providing a broad grounding in commercial practices, does not endow a contextual understanding of the issues and problems facing Toxicology or the NHS. This was certainly a disadvantage, but one that was overcome by involvement with Toxicology and other NHS staff and by researching and understanding their history and background. Doing this helped to provide a frame of reference for pre-understanding the issues and problems and a base from which to commence the hermeneutic spiral of further understanding as the project progressed. This approach proved successful although the major benefit was not realized until the later part of the project.

16.3 Modifying SERVQUAL to suit the laboratory

One of the key factors indicating the need to pursue a more fundamental strategy was the lack of direct interaction between Toxicology's staff and its customers. At best, this would be by telephone and at worst through a third party. Face-to-face contact was minimal.

Identifying customer expectations and perceptions of Toxicology's services was recognized as an essential starting point in analysing the external environment and SERVQUAL was suggested as being an appropriate tool for obtaining this information by the MBA project supervisor.

A significant literature review on SERVQUAL and particularly its application in medical situations was undertaken. Having done this the author considered the dimensions identified by Parasuraman *et al.* (1988) as being appropriate to Toxicology, whose services had many similar qualities to the original service categories.

This left the tailoring of the characteristic statements and the dimension definitions to reflect the service quality aspects of Toxicology. For example, because most customers have little direct contact with Toxicology or its staff, the tangibility characteristic statements focus on aspects of the service such as information material, telephone manner, etc. Likewise 'reliability characteristics' were focused on aspects for which customers were thought to have high expectations.

When developing the characteristic statements and dimension definitions, the author tried to view Toxicology's service from the customer's viewpoint, helping to stop the development of a biased survey reflecting the service provider's view. This issue was highlighted when the survey was piloted on Toxicology's staff, who challenged some of the statements that were not considered to be important or that they were constrained from meeting because of resources. The statements were left in, some highlighting previously unknown areas of concern – others not. However, the point serves to underline the importance of developing a survey that seeks the customer's views of the service, not those of the provider.

16.4 Research methods

The survey was mailed to 125 of Toxicology's customers accompanied by an explanatory letter and a stamped addressed envelope. Two styles of accompanying letter were used, one for clinical customers, e.g. drug rehabilitation clinics, and the other for customers using Toxicology as a business service, e.g. coroners.

The survey was piloted on internal customers from the Trust, the Trust's Clinical Audit department and staff from Toxicology. This produced a large number of recommendations for improvement. Most notable were a reduction in length, a simplification of the SERV-QUAL instructions and the 'de-Americanizing' of the original SERVQUAL phraseology. These changes were incorporated into the final version of the survey.

After two weeks a round of chase-up telephone calls were made, followed by a second and final chase in the third week after mailing. A total of sixty questionnaires were returned of which eight had been incorrectly completed and had to be excluded from the SERVQUAL assessment.

The survey was addressed to those people upon whose discretion Toxicology depends for its business and who also interact with Toxicology staff on matters concerning assay requests. The sample was compiled from a cross-section of the different types of customer and by use of the different categories of assay. The database and response profiles are shown in Table 16.1.

Low response levels from TDM, general toxicology, forensic/coroner and internal users, plus a similarity in their characteristics to other specific categories, meant that for reporting purposes the overall number of categories could be reduced to four. These were as follows:

1   Trace Metals.
2   Drugs of abuse and therapeutic drug monitoring (DoA/TDM).
3   General toxicology and forensic/coroners (Tox/Cor).
4   Mixed (those who use combinations from the full range of services/assays) and internal customers (the Trust) (Mix/Int).

Twenty-one statements were developed to reflect the five different SERVQUAL dimensions (see Table 16.2) and to suit the circumstances of Toxicology and its industry culture. Customers were asked to consider these and rate their expectation of them on a seven-point Likert scale, ranging from 'not at all essential' to 'essential'. They were then asked to weight the relative importance of each dimension by allocating 100 points across all five dimen-

Table 16.1 Response profile

	Quantity	Response	Percentage
Trace	45	15	33.3
Drugs of abuse	23	13	56.5
Therapeutic drug monitoring	8	1	12.5
General toxicology	9	5	55.6
Forensic (coroner)	6	4	66.7
Mixed users	27	20	74.1
Internal users	7	2	28.6
Total	125	60	48.0

sions. The greater the importance the greater the points allocated. Finally, users were asked to consider their perception of Toxicology's service quality as experienced customers, in terms of the twenty-one statements. Then, as for their expectations, customers were asked to rate their perceptions on a seven-point Likert scale, ranging from 'strongly disagree' to 'strongly agree'.

By collating the results of the individual SERVQUAL questionnaires, Toxicology's quality of service along each of the five dimensions was calculated by taking the following steps:

1   For each customer, the SERVQUAL scores (perception score and expectation score) on the statements pertaining to the dimensions were totalled and divided by the number of statements making up the dimension.
2   The results obtained in step 1 were totalled for all customers and divided by the number of respondents.

The unweighted SERVQUAL score for the service as a whole was then obtained by averaging across the five dimensions – giving an overall measure of service quality.

However, this does not take into account the relative importance that customers attach to the various dimensions. This was done by calculating the weighted SERVQUAL score as follows:

3   Step 1 above was undertaken to calculate unweighted scores.
4   For each customer, the SERVQUAL score for each dimension (obtained in step 3) was multiplied by the importance weight assigned by the customer to that dimension (the importance weight is simply the points the customer allocated to the dimension divided by 100).
5   For each customer, the weighted SERVQUAL scores (obtained in step 4) across all five dimensions were totalled to obtain a combined weighted SERVQUAL score.
6   The scores obtained in step 5 were totalled for all customers and divided by the number of respondents.

To calculate the weighted scores for the individual dimension:

7   The average weighting for each dimension was calculated.
8   The unweighted score for each dimension obtained in steps 1 and 2 was then multiplied by the respective average weighting calculated for the dimension in step 7 and divided by 20.

The various scores were then examined and a judgement made of the service quality as perceived by the customers.

16.4.1   Time, skills and resources

Undertaking the SERVQUAL survey proved to be a protracted process, probably taking about six weeks in all. Some of this was down to gaining the momentum necessary to drive the survey through to completion and the rest due to underestimating the time taken to complete each stage. For example, the process of agreeing the survey design with Toxicology took longer than expected (busy people often put reviewing something which might be used to judge their work low down on their priority list!) as did the piloting and the unforeseen need to gain approval from the Trust's Internal Audit Department.

Having developed the survey on a computer word-processing package, it was printed using Toxicology's own printer and sent out on their stationary with reply paid envelopes. An initial deadline for replies was set for two weeks after issue and this was communicated to the sample in a covering letter. After about ten days follow-up calls were made by the author using Toxicology's telephone and again by the Department Head during the third week. The survey was finally closed at the end of the third week.

Interestingly, some of the first responses were from customers who barely used Toxicology's services and the most difficult to obtain were from the largest contracted customers.

Analysis of the results was undertaken on a computer spreadsheet package using a simple programme developed by the author. This took about a day to design, write and test. Undertaking the analysis and writing up the results took approximately a further four days to complete.

16.5 Results and interpretation

Table 16.2 shows the expectation and perception scores of Toxicology customers, elicited by the twenty-one statements broken down into their respective dimensions. The service quality construct – 'discrepancy between customers' expectations and their perceptions' – (Gap 5) was calculated for each statement and is shown in the final column.

16.5.1 What the highest expectations indicate

1   A high proportion of all customer categories scored 7 on the Likert scale for the highest expectation statements.
2   Three of the highest expectations (statements 2, 12 and 17) were in the reliability dimension.
3   The highest expectation of the top five, statement 2 , was of particular importance to all customers except Trace Metals. Statement 2 states that 'Excellent laboratory services provide accurate results using validated and reliable analytical methods'. For a specialist laboratory this was not a surprising result, but as a technical aspect of the service it was one which customers were not well placed to measure. The judgement was therefore subjective and could have been affected by Toxicology better managing their expectations.
4   Statement 12 was particularly important to DoA/TDM.
5   Statement 17 was particularly important to DoA/TDM and Mix/Int customers.
6   The fourth and fifth highest expectations (statements 19 and 7) were both in the assurance dimension and concerned people's expectations of security and qualification. These were both scored 7 by a high proportion of DoA/TDM customers.

All of these expectations were concerned with the professional ability of Toxicology and by extension its staff. There was a clear expectation that the assay requests made to Toxicology would be performed to the appropriate quality standards by people with the right professional qualifications and training.

Table 16.2 Expectation and perception scores

	Expectation	Perception	Difference
Tangibility			
1 Have staff who promptly respond to customer's telephone calls	6.06	5.71	−0.35
3 Have clean and secure reception areas	5.38	5.15	−0.23
14 Issue information materials (service leaflets, price lists etc.) which are clear and free from jargon	6.00	5.63	−0.37
16 Have staff who are presentable in appearance	4.29	4.65	
			0.36
Reliability			
2 Provide accurate results using validated and reliable analytical methods	6.96	6.29	−0.67
4 Deliver results on time	6.50	5.65	−0.85
12 Always provide accurate and reliable advice	6.83	6.17	−0.66
17 Employ appropriate quality control procedures	6.92	6.35	−0.57
Responsiveness			
5 Offer their full service 24 hours a day	4.83	4.98	0.15
11 Are staffed to meet the needs of their customers	6.33	5.69	−0.64
18 Provide their customers with a named person to look after their needs	4.37	4.21	−0.16
20 Promptly respond to written correspondence from customers	6.12	5.73	−0.39
Assurance			
7 Have staff who are qualified to the correct professional standard	6.79	6.44	−0.35
8 Have staff who are always polite and helpful	6.06	6.04	−0.02
15 Have staff who are aware of and contribute to the latest developments in their field	6.04	5.81	−0.23
19 Ensure the security of their customer and patient records	6.83	6.12	−0.71
21 Have staff who instil confidence in their customers	6.38	6.08	−0.30
Empathy			
6 Issue result reports which are always easy to understand	6.52	6.29	−0.23
9 Have staff who can quickly understand my problems	6.17	6.08	−0.09
10 Provide reports which give the necessary information and interpretation	6.79	6.10	−0.69
13 Provide the full range of assays their customers need	6.12	6.08	−0.04

16.5.2 What the highest perceptions indicate

Four of the five highest perceptions (statements 7, 17, 2 and 12) also appeared as expectations in the highest expectations list.

The other highest perception (statement 6) concerns the understandable way in which result reports were presented and was of particular concern to Tox/Cor customers. This aspect as an expectation only just missed the highest five by one place.

Customers, despite having little against which to judge or confirm the reliability of the service, perceived it to be reasonably so (but see largest differences). The subjectivity of these judgements has been raised above, but what might have been the influences? These were probably factors such as the advice they received from Toxicology staff (statement 12) and the understandable result reports (statement 6) which were well received by Tox/Cor customers. The high perception of professional qualifications may also have been influenced by these factors and by media such as notepaper – which carries the Department Head's qualifications and guidance literature – which carries the names and qualifications of all the key staff.

16.5.3 What the lowest expectations indicate

1   All of the lowest expectations relate to tangibility and surprisingly responsiveness – where customers who had high technical expectations seem to have had much lower functional expectations.

2   As regards tangibility, customers had little interest in the appearance of staff, the state of the reception areas or the clarity of information material issued by Toxicology. With regard to the foremost two items this probably reflected the fact that very few customers actually came to the laboratory.

3   The two expectations relating to responsiveness (statements 18 and 5) were both features of the service which were perhaps unimportant to the majority of customers. Statement 18 concerned the provision of a named person to look after a customer's needs and was scored particularly low by a large proportion of the Mix/Int customers. For volume users of screening assays this aspect was perhaps less important, but for more complex requests involving a higher level of contact with Toxicology – something of greater value. Interestingly, the responding coroners rated this item either 6 or 7 on the Likert scale. The same reasoning applied to statement 5 which concerned the provision of service 24 hours a day. If a customer did not need it they gave it a low score, but to a customer running accident and emergency services it was an essential aspect of Toxicology's service. The degree of need and its correlation to high or low score was emphasized by the higher scores allocated to the other two reliability statements which were of more general concern.

16.5.4 What the lowest perceptions indicate

1   The five lowest perceptions all related to the five lowest expectations.

2   Statement 18 was scored very lowly by a high proportion of the Mix/Int customers, which was not surprising because Toxicology did not specifically name a member of staff appointed to look after the needs of a customer.

3   Perhaps of more concern was the low perception of Toxicology's 24-hour service,

particularly among the Mix/Int customers (the most likely users). This may have been because the service was not broadly promoted. Historically, it had been considered good practice to discourage the use of expensive out-of-hours services except in the case of clinical need. However, the assays which were available on a 24-hour basis could have been advertised more heavily to create awareness. Ultimately, the more customers who used this service, the more it would pay for itself. For non-urgent cases requested out of hours, a prompt to re-consider and save the surcharge would still have been in keeping with the spirit of promoting efficiency within the NHS, would have demonstrated professional integrity and could also have raised goodwill.

16.5.5 What the largest differences indicate

1   The largest difference (statement 4) was in the reliability dimension and concerned the on-time delivery of results. This was a serious matter and a deficiency across all customer groups, but especially Tox/Cor and Mix/Int. There were two aspects to this problem: one was operational within Toxicology and the other lay with customers' perceptions. Operationally, the process of undertaking a request could be regarded as having three stages. First, taking the sample and arranging for its delivery to Toxicology; second, undertaking the assay; and third, the delivery of the result to the requester. To cover problems within the first stage all result reports were marked with the date and time the sample was taken and the time it was received at Toxicology. The second stage was covered by marking the date on which the report was issued. But the process of completing the request did not stop when the assay result was dropped in the post box. This was recognized and steps to control stage 3 by the use of fax and e-mail alleviated delays caused by the delivery system.

2   Perceptions of the service could have been improved by setting and publishing target turn-round times and by emphasizing performance against these targets on the result sheet – assuming of course that the target was met or exceeded.

3   The second largest difference (statement 19) was also the fourth highest expectation and concerned the security of customer and patient records. This was of common concern, but particularly for DoA/TDM. Without further investigation explanations for this could only be made by conjecture. However, this aspect, whilst having been of great importance, was probably taken for granted. Raising the issue caused the customer to question it and, without knowing the measures taken by Toxicology, to mark the score down. An appropriate way to deal with this aspect would have been to form a focus group comprised of the respondents who gave the highest perception–expectation scores. This would have provided a forum for quickly identifying and addressing their concerns. The third largest difference (statement 10) was from the empathy dimension and covered the information and interpretation given in reports. It was of special interest to Mix/Int customers but not for Tox/Cor or most Trace Metals customers. This was another area that could have been dealt with by employing the use of a focus group. The remaining largest differences (statements 2 and 12) were concerns across all customer groups with the largest proportion of high scores belonging to the Mix/Int group. Both were from the reliability dimension.

16.5.6 What the smallest differences indicate

1 The smallest differences (statements 16 and 5) were both positive scores.
2 Statement 8, which concerned the politeness and helpfulness of staff, scored a very low difference most notably by the Mix/Int group.
3 The final two differences (statements 13 and 9) both related to empathy. Toxicology appeared to be providing the range of assays needed by its customers and its staff were able to understand customers' problems.

In summary, there was a very strong message being given by the customers of Toxicology. They rated reliability as highly essential to service quality. This was reflected in their expectations of the various statements, and whilst their perceptions were also high, the weighting leverages the shortcomings in their attitude towards Toxicology.

16.5.7 Dimension weightings

The final part of this analysis was to consider the relative importance attached to the five dimensions by Toxicology's customers. The definitive results are shown in Table 16.3, together with the PZB mean findings of Parasuraman *et al.* (1988) during their empirical research.

What is particularly noticeable is the large weighting given to the reliability dimension at 25 per cent more than the PZB mean findings. This dimension relates very strongly to the technical service whilst the others relate to the functional service. Assurance and responsiveness are similar in their weightings and close to the PZB mean findings. Empathy and tangibility are well below the PZB mean findings which, as stated before, probably reflect the lack of face-to-face contact and attendance at the laboratory. Whilst the weightings differ, the actual rankings of the dimensions are no different to the PZB findings, which adds weight to the suitability of the instrument for measuring Toxicology's service quality. However, this ranking is not in keeping with patient and physician-oriented SERVQUAL health care investigations where empathy has ranked ahead of assurance and responsiveness (Walbridge and Delene, 1993; Youssef *et al.*, 1996).

The unweighted SERVQUAL scores are shown in Figure 16.1. Two things are of particular importance: first, all of the scores were negative which indicated shortcomings across the

Table 16.3 Relative importance of SERVQUAL dimensions

Statements	Dimensions	Laboratory (%)	PZB (%)
1 The appearance of the facilities, staff and information material	Tangibility	9	11
2 The ability to perform the promised services dependably and accurately	Reliability	40	32
3 The willingness to help customers and provide a prompt service	Responsiveness	19	23
4 The knowledge and credibility of the staff	Assurance	22	19
5 The individual attention and understanding given to customers	Empathy	12	17

full range of service quality dimensions and second, the negative score for the reliability dimension was twice as large as its nearest co-determinant – assurance.

The weighted scores are also shown in Figure 16.1. The weighted score is a simple average of the scores of the five dimensions, but the weighted score takes into account the weightings allocated by customers to the five dimensions when completing the questionnaire. Again all the scores were negative although the weighting almost removed the tangibility dimension gap. Likewise the negative score for empathy was considerably reduced, but the reliability gap doubled! Toxicology was therefore under-performing in the aspects of service that were most important to its customers. However, this enabled Toxicology to leverage improvement activities by allocating its efforts and budget to the service quality areas identified as critical. Furthermore, Berry and Parasuraman (1991) found that whilst improving performance is undoubtedly important, managing expectations has largely been ignored by organizations. The opportunity presented by this assertion has already been highlighted.

The average SERVQUAL index for the five dimensions in the unweighted scores was −0.33, but was more negative in the weighted score of −0.41. This later score was the actual measure of service quality within Toxicology and could be used as an initial standard against which to rate future scores or scores measured for competitors. To put the score into perspective, the study by Youssef *et al.* (1996) which investigated service quality received by 174

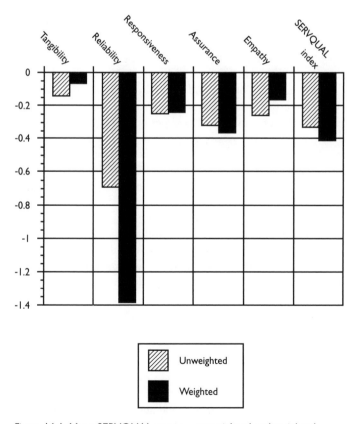

Figure 16.1 Mean SERVQUAL scores – unweighted and weighted.

patients who had received surgical, orthopaedic, spinal injury, medicinal, dental and other speciality treatment in the West Midlands region, scored the providers at −1.195.

Finally, given the importance of reliability, the construction of extra statements that reflect other reliability aspects of service quality should be worthwhile. To avoid increasing the SERVQUAL score because of the extra questions, allocate the weighting proportionately or raise the number of statements within the other dimensions. The longer-term benefits of having strengths and shortcomings highlighted in such a crucial area would be invaluable and worth the extra effort.

16.6 Conclusions

SERVQUAL has been identified as the most appropriate method to assess service quality within Toxicology. The results of the survey highlight the degree of importance which Toxicology's customers placed upon the reliability of the service. The unweighted score was considerably ahead of the other dimensions but when combined with the assigned weighting, the score indicated even greater shortcomings.

The gap scores for the remaining dimensions of assurance, responsiveness, empathy and tangibility, whilst all being negative, were low in comparison to other service industries and were a fraction of the reliability score. To improve the overall weighted SERVQUAL index score, the greatest return on investment would therefore have arisen by addressing the gaps attributable to the reliability aspects.

To monitor the effect of improvement programmes on service quality and for general improvement or deterioration, SERVQUAL-based surveys should be conducted on an annual basis. The format of the survey used here has shown itself to be lacking in some areas and further refinement of the instrument should increase the accuracy of measurement. At a basic level a large number of respondents failed to correctly complete the questionnaire. The section requesting respondents to allocate a weighting to each of the five dimensions was incorrectly completed on 13 (22 per cent) questionnaires. Of these, five could be recovered by converting the respondents' own weighting system to that of SERVQUAL. The simplification of instructions for this section appears to have been overdone and future questionnaires should contain an instruction to allocate a weighting to each dimension. The necessity for the sum of the scores to be 100 also needs to be emphasized.

The use of SERVQUAL has a secondary benefit: by seeking customers' expectations it is possible to determine the key facets of service quality which the organization should seek to satisfy. Equally, the perception scores tell the organization how well it is doing. What this provides is a strong idea of what the customer values and how well the organization is doing in providing that value through its service. In other words, the degree of strategic drift can be identified.

A number of suggestions have been made within this chapter as to how Toxicology could deal with its strategic drift, but to address this issue fully they must be considered against an internal analysis of Toxicology's strengths and weaknesses – in particular its value chain.

In the first instance the value chain asks 'What is value to the customer?' and second, 'How does the organization create that value for the customers through its product or service?' SERVQUAL can help to answer the first question and was used in this way for the wider strategic issues in the project.

16.7 Two years later

Two years later the Trust's strategy is still evolving. It is now supporting the pan-Birmingham plan for a health authority covering the city for the next 50 years. The Trust still envisages providing accident and emergency services and acute care, but concentrating on a core ambulatory care service which provides an 'all done in one day' outpatients' service and supporting care in the community.

If the ambulatory care plan was implemented then the prospects for Toxicology should be good because the Pathology directorate would need to be re-modelled to provide the degree of service required to support it.

However, these plans have yet to be approved and are subject to change. The Trust is still lacking direction and this is evidenced by problems within the finance department which has seen several finance directors come and go and the loss of key medical staff who have moved to pursue their careers at Trusts with a more defined future.

Against this background, Toxicology has prospered. In the last financial year (1997/8) income was up to £0.5 million and is expected to be up a further 10 per cent this year. The volume of requests continues to rise with 85 per cent of business now coming from outside the Trust. Three new members of staff have been recruited and plans have been drawn up to double the size of the facility by extending the existing accommodation at each end.

But how did the SERVQUAL survey contribute to this success? At face value, the survey informed Toxicology of its customers' expectations and perceptions and weighted these to show the areas of greatest importance. Indeed, simply reading the results reported earlier in this chapter provides the reader with a clear understanding of the areas that require attention and how efforts can be leveraged by focusing on those with the greatest weighting.

However, this information also tells Toxicology which aspects of the service provide the greatest value to the customer and enable an analysis of the activities that underpin the delivery of this value. Armed with this knowledge it should be possible to develop these activities and increase value and hence competitive advantage. This exercise was undertaken as part of the wider project and the conclusions drawn from the analysis were as follows:

1   Customers were not fully satisfied with the reliability, assurance and empathy aspects of the service offered by Toxicology, particularly the turn-round of results, their reliability and content.
2   Performance objectives designed to address these concerns and the means to monitor them needed to be developed to provide tighter management control.
3   Improvements to external communications for managing customer expectations, promoting achievements and raising the profile of Toxicology brand were also required, as were enhanced relationships with key customers to avoid switching. Finally, links with introductory sources of business needed strengthening and collaborative opportunities for developing markets should have been pursued.

These conclusions provided a summary of activities that Toxicology could undertake to address strategic drift.

We will now look at which of the actions recommended have been taken by Toxicology, how successful these have been and the reasons why other recommended actions have not been taken up and/or followed through to a successful conclusion.

16.7.1 Turn-round times

This is an area which has received considerable attention, with a number of changes made to speed up turn-round times:

- pre-addressed, Freepost sachets have been issued to customers to aid sample delivery to the laboratory
- all DoA and occupational health results are sent by fax (a new fax machine has been ordered that will work direct from the computer network)
- results in other areas can be faxed if required
- the number of Toxicology staff who can complete forensic reports has been increased to remove the bottle-neck that existed here.

Toxicology is driving towards 24-hour turn-round for DoA work and is currently the leader in the region, having acquired faster, more productive equipment. This competitive advantage is being used as a selling point to attract more custom.

16.7.2 Reliability

Concerns over reliability were primarily down to ineffectively communicating Toxicology's excellent reliability record. At the time the survey was undertaken Toxicology was already a member of a quality control group, although the results were not published outside the membership. It has since joined a quality circle undertaking benchmarking activities that is comprised of a number of laboratories in different fields.

A quality manager with executive powers has also been appointed within Toxicology to look at quality issues generally. However, Toxicology has still to achieve Clinical Pathology Accreditation. The process is nearing completion, but has been hampered by the daily operational burden.

16.7.3 Report content

Whilst there is flexibility to vary the reporting content of forensic reports, changing the format of results reports for the other areas of work is constrained by the Telepath system (the computerized assay monitoring and reporting system adopted by the Pathology directorate) which has a fixed reporting format. This was to have been replaced shortly after the SERVQUAL survey was undertaken, but these plans have yet to be put into effect.

16.7.4 Performance objectives

Efforts to develop a set of clear performance objectives have so far been limited to setting turn-round times for a number of different assay groups and investigating quality improvements. The most positive objective is the commitment to achieve 24-hour turn-round on DoA requests.

Failure to embrace fully the idea of performance objectives, suggests that there is still a lack of real direction within Toxicology's strategy. This is focused on expanding the customer base and reaching a critical mass (income of *circa* £1 million), which Toxicology's management believe will make it attractive to other medical sites should the Trust decide that it is not a core activity and divest it. Furthermore, they believe that reaching this critical mass will make Toxicology less vulnerable to competition.

This strategy is enabling Toxicology to expand, but taking note of the key performance areas identified by the survey and formally developing a set of customer-focused performance objectives to meet and ultimately exceed would do more to ensure competitive advantage than size alone.

16.7.5 External communication

Improvements in external communication have been made through a number of initiatives including expanding and improving the range of information material and the setting up of a website. However, the most effective means of setting and managing customer expectations, promoting successes and Toxicology brand has been the introduction of customer tutorials at the laboratory. These have been given initially to DoA customers, but when the laboratory extensions have been completed it is intended to expand this activity.

Additional success has been achieved by the Department Head who has made a concerted effort to network within the Trust and externally to promote Toxicology.

Unfortunately, improvements to report formats have been limited as described above and the planned newsletter has yet to get off the ground, although it is planned to give the job of writing and producing a newsletter to a new member of staff.

16.7.6 Customer relations

Improving the customer focus of staff at Toxicology has proved to be a difficult task. Resistance to change has generally come from the longer-serving members, although a few have embraced the opportunity. The greatest customer focus has been exhibited by new members of staff who have proved to be more open minded. With the introduction of new approaches and more new staff Toxicology's paradigm is likely to move further towards one of increasing customer focus, forcing compliance on those who are resisting.

No further loss of business has occurred since the original loss of TDM work (this has largely been replaced through the development of a number of new assays) and initiatives like the tutorials and the Department Head's networking will enhance relationships with customers. Introducing a formal customer management strategy could make this more effective.

Toxicology has also introduced regular customer surveys (not SERVQUAL) to evaluate customers' perceptions of the service and also new customer needs. This is a very positive step in developing stronger customer relations.

16.7.7 Links with introductory business sources

This issue is closely linked with customer relationships. The point was originally made to reflect the fact that the negotiator of a contract for the supply of Toxicology services was not the customer/initiator of assay requests. Success in this area will depend upon the Department Head's ability to manage relationships at a personal level.

16.7.8 Collaboration opportunities

Collaboration opportunities have not been developed as a result of political obstacles and a lack of will to really drive them forward. There have been elements of work-sharing and introductions, but larger projects such as the joint development of assays or the exploitation of new markets have failed to materialize.

Further reading

Berkowitz, E.N. (1995) 'Marketing the pathology practice', *Archives of Pathology & Laboratory Medicine*, 119, 655–658.

Flynn, G. (1998b) *Using SERVQUAL to Measure Service Quality at a NHS Specialist Laboratory RP918*, Birmingham: Aston Business School Research Institute.

Parasuraman, A., Zeithaml, V.A. and Berry, L. (1988) 'SERVQUAL: a multiple-item scale for measuring consumer perceptions of service quality', *Journal of Retailing* 64, 12–37.

Youssef, F.N., Nel, D. and Bovaird, T. (1996) 'Health care in NHS hospitals', *International Journal of Health Care Quality Assurance* January: 15–28.

Chapter 17

Patient and staff views of a new appointment system in a South African health centre

Max Bachmann and Hassan Mohamed

In this chapter the reader will gain an understanding of:

- post-apartheid reforms in urban primary care in South Africa
- issues and choices in designing a study to reduce waiting times in a health centre
- how the interviews and focus groups were carried out
- the responses of patients and staff in the interviews both before and after implementation of the appointment system
- how market research was integrated into change management.

17.1 Urban primary care in South Africa

Primary health care lies at the core of health service reforms in South Africa, as the post-apartheid government tries to rebuild the health service. This policy aims to fill the large gap in services lying between urban state hospitals and private care, that together consume almost all health care spending. The diseases that cause the most deaths and illness in the country could be treated effectively and inexpensively if basic primary care were more accessible. Respiratory infections, tuberculosis, diarrhoea and perinatal problems account for one in five deaths (Bradshaw, 1997). One in six people die without a diagnosis being made. Meanwhile diseases of ageing and urbanization are also increasing, with 19 per cent of deaths being due to cardiovascular disease. Acute infections require easy access to care so that effective treatment is started early. Chronic conditions like tuberculosis, AIDS, high blood pressure and heart failure also require good access to primary care so that patients continue to use them despite the need for regular visits. Although primary care is so important and potentially effective in preventing death and illness, under the apartheid government it only received about 10 per cent of all public health finance (McIntyre *et al.*, 1995). In recent years substantial resources have been allocated to building new clinics in areas of greatest need but it has been difficult to appoint and pay for suitably trained staff. Thus access to primary care is likely to remain a problem for years to come.

17.1.1 Access to primary care

Barriers to access can take many forms, including distance, cost and time. In rural areas long distances to clinics and hospitals are a serious obstacle. User fees deter poor patients from seeking care. One of the post-apartheid government's first actions was to abolish user fees for mothers and children using state health care. This has led to many more patients using the facilities, and has further increased waiting times. However, even in cities where government clinics are close to people's homes, and where fees are low or exempted, clinics' long waiting times make them inaccessible.

These problems are shared by public health facilities in many other parts of the developing world, whether in low- or middle-income countries. Rapid urbanization has led to large populations of poor people being reliant on relatively small numbers of clinics which are poorly organized to deal with them. Solutions seem impossible given the apparent overloading of services by large patient numbers. However, it is possible to make substantial improvements, with no extra resources, by applying simple techniques of operational management, change management and market research (Bachmann and Barron, 1997). This chapter reports on an attempt to reduce waiting times in a large health centre in Cape Town, South Africa. It focuses in particular on the ways in which staff and patients' views were elicited using simple qualitative research methods. Before describing the study, however, we will describe the health service context of the study.

17.1.2 The local health context

The best developed systems of urban primary care in South Africa have existed for some decades in two of its largest cities, Cape Town and Johannesburg. Large health centres are located in the poorest residential areas and provide a range of services including curative and preventive care, with some also providing emergency and obstetric care. The large scale of these health centres has made it feasible also to provide additional services such as X-ray facilities, laboratories, physiotherapy and psychiatric nursing, and to develop specialized clinics for conditions such as chronic diseases. Yet despite the proximity of these services to people's homes, many do not use them optimally, delaying seeking treatment for acute illnesses, not adhering to chronic disease management plans or bypassing local health centres to obtain primary care from teaching hospitals' outpatient departments (London and Bachmann, 1997).

The health centre described in this study was located in a deprived suburb of Cape Town, inhabited by people classified as 'coloured', that is, of mixed race. Primary care in Cape Town, as in all South African cities, is provided by both private and public sectors. Private care is provided mainly by single-handed general practitioners, but because most of the population cannot afford private fees and do not have health insurance, it is only used by a minority. Most people are reliant on state services, with the provincial government responsible for curative care and local government responsible for providing selective services such as for tuberculosis, sexually transmitted diseases and family planning. Under apartheid there were further administrative and service divisions along racial lines. However, at the time of the study there were substantial organizational obstacles to improving services.

The fragmentation of public health services at the time led to inefficient administration, and inequitable service provision. Management was highly centralized, with health centre managers powerless to make any changes and yet receiving minimal managerial support from the centre. The post-apartheid era has seen some rationalization of these problems (Barron, 1997). Racial barriers have been removed, health authorities have merged, subdistrict or facility-level management is being developed and local government is to take over responsibility for health centres from provincial government. This study took place at a time when enlightened senior managers in Cape Town were trying to democratize and decentralize their organizations, and to make services more responsive to patient and public demands.

17.1.3 Government bureaucracy and consumer responsiveness

The first part of the study took place in 1993 under the minority apartheid government, and the second part took place in 1995 under the new post-apartheid government which had come to power in 1994. Thus the small changes in this one health centre took place against a background of major national political transition. Under apartheid black people were regarded by the government as being second-class citizens, and it is thus not surprising that consumer views were generally not taken into account by managers or providers of health services. The authoritarian bureaucratic organizational environment, coupled with status hierarchies within and between health professions, as well as language and cultural barriers between staff and patients, meant that patients were often not treated with respect. A recent qualitative study attributed nurses' frequent humiliation of patients in South Africa to organizational pressures, professional incentives, a desire to gain control over stressful working environments, an ideology of patient inferiority and lack of accountability to local communities (Jewkes *et al.*, 1998). The fact that many patients are not formally employed also contributes to their time not being regarded as valuable. Thus market research has not thrived in South African health services.

It became apparent to health authorities, however, that critical diseases like tuberculosis and sexually transmitted diseases require a high degree of patient motivation and co-operation if services are to be effective. Without consumer satisfaction and acceptance, patients do not use available services, and continue to pose serious public health hazards to others. Thus research into patients' satisfaction with care, and service preferences, has slowly begun. Such research has usually been as a result of the interest of local managers and academics rather than as a result of government policy. For example, a survey instrument to measure patient satisfaction with tuberculosis care was developed (Westaway and Wolmarans, 1993). A survey of quality of care in Cape Town family planning clinics obtained high patient satisfaction scores but suggested that such surveys may be insensitive to patient dissatisfaction (Bachmann *et al.*, 1996). An investigation into why patients preferred to travel long distances to receive primary care from a Cape Town teaching hospital, rather than using the local clinic, revealed that many of such patients had previously used the clinic but had received poor quality care there (London and Bachmann, 1997). A key problem with perceived quality of care in all of these studies has been the long time spent waiting to be treated. A study in another Cape Town health centre found that most patients waited around three hours even for simple procedures like immunizations or collecting repeat prescriptions, neither of which required them to see a doctor. Modifications to the patient flow process reduced waiting times substantially (Bachmann and Barron, 1997).

17.2 Study design and qualitative methods

Health centres in Cape Town were instructed by senior management in 1993 to implement appointment systems so as to reduce waiting times. The authors, then based in a local university's Department of Community Health, were asked to evaluate the innovation in one health centre. The design of the appointment system was the responsibility of health centre staff, and the evaluation was designed by the authors of this report. External funding for the evaluation was obtained from the Health Systems Trust, an independent research funding organization, after submission and refereeing of the research protocol. The external funding was used mainly to employ additional research staff, while the salaries of the two authors were paid by the provincial health administration, independently of the study.

The design of the evaluation was a qualitative study combined with a quasi-experiment. Qualitative assessment of patient and staff views, and quantitative assessment of waiting times, were performed before introduction of the appointment system. These surveys were repeated eighteen months later, after the appointment system had been in place for some months. The aims of eliciting staff and patient views at baseline were to assess the desirability of appointments to both groups, and to inform the design of the intervention. The aims of eliciting their views eighteen months later were to assess whether service providers and users felt that appointments had improved the service, and to obtain ideas for further improvement.

The qualitative assessments included interviews with groups of patients and groups of staff, and interviews with individual key informants (as discussed in Chapter 5 this allows the respondents to identify what they consider to be the key issues rather than the researchers). At baseline we held discussions with one group of nurses, one group of pharmacy staff, two groups of doctors, one group of reception staff and three groups of patients with chronic illnesses. In the follow-up survey we interviewed two reception staff, two practice nurses, the nurse responsible for appointments, the senior nursing manager and fifteen individual patients, and held discussions with one group of doctors and with one group of pharmacy staff. Interviews and group discussions were tape recorded and selected quotes were transcribed from the recordings.

The quantitative assessment of waiting times has been reported elsewhere (Mohamed and Bachmann, 1998). We compared waiting times before and after the intervention, and after the intervention compared waiting times of patients with and without appointments. The baseline survey confirmed that waiting times were long. Half of patients waited more than three-and-a-half hours, and a quarter waited more than four-and-a-half hours. The follow-up survey found that waiting times in the clinic had decreased for patients attending chronic disease clinics, and for patients consulting with a doctor for acute illnesses, but they had not improved for patients who did not see a doctor.

17.3 Results of baseline interviews

The qualitative research conducted before implementation found that, in general, many patients were enthusiastic about the proposal, but clinic staff tended to be more sceptical.

For patients, long waiting times were a prominent problem. Several informants were highly aware of the time it took to be treated, which they estimated at between three and five hours. One regular clinic user detailed the timing of each step required to obtain care, from leaving home at about 5.30 a.m. until returning home at around 11.30 a.m. Another said that the long wait was frustrating because of the need to return to work that day. Another was frustrated by perceived unfairness: 'The patients who arrived with me this morning are already gone long ago'.

Staff tended to be indifferent to patients' long waits. A receptionist said, 'Patients are happy to wait'. Another said, 'If they come in at seven, they can't expect to be out by eight'.

One doctor said, 'Patients want to be here early', implying that early arrivals caused long waits rather than that long queues necessitated early arrivals. Another doctor minimized the waits, saying, 'At the larger hospitals, patients seldom wait shorter than four hours'. A nurse commented, 'The old patients – they are very patient', implying that waiting was less of a problem for the elderly.

Staff attributed the long waits to staff shortages, large patient numbers and inefficient organization. Several doctors felt that the method of retrieving patients' folders manually at reception created a bottle-neck in patient flows. One doctor said, 'Seldom is the hold-up at the doctor's door'.

Patients were almost unanimously in favour of appointments, with many saying that it was a good idea, that it would work or that it would be better than current arrangements. 'It's about time', said one. One patient specified that afternoon appointments would suit them better while another said they would prefer morning appointments. One said that having an appointment would make it easier to arrange child care. Several patients felt that 'patients would stick to their appointments because it's for their own benefit'. One said, 'I will feel more eager to come because I don't have to sit and wait for half a day'.

One patient acknowledged that patients did not always keep appointments, if they forgot their appointment dates or did not have money.

Staff varied widely in their attitude to the proposed appointment system, giving many different reasons why they felt it would or would not work. A receptionist complained that, 'They (senior management) didn't consult us'. They suspected that 'The appointment system was put there to prevent doctors from running away early'.

Another receptionist said, 'I'm not too happy about it. It might not be suitable because of the load'.

Several doctors were particularly hostile, saying 'It's going to cause chaos', 'Knowing our people, there will be bedlam', 'The authorities have done no research. It's a short-sighted way of dealing with the problems here' and 'How many general practitioners in this area have appointments or have tried it and it has not worked'. A receptionist also claimed to know patients' preferences: 'We know the hearts of the people. They are not going to accept it'. Staff were especially sceptical about whether patients would keep their appointments, saying, 'Most do not keep their current appointments', 'In a previous appointment system, only eight out of forty turned up', 'They can't keep their appointment date, what about time?' and 'If they don't have money, they don't come'. Staff anticipated specific problems: accommodation of patients at reception, motivating staff to change, confrontation between patients with and without appointments, unpredictability of patient numbers, complaints from patients while waiting at a doctor's door, incompatibility with public transport, the clinic pharmacy's early closing times and morning delays disrupting afternoon appointments.

Some nurses and doctors did however anticipate benefits for patients, saying, 'It will be good for patients to see the benefits of it' and 'Patients normally take a day off work to attend the day hospital. If they finish early, they can get to do other things that they need to do'. Some nurses anticipated that patients with chronic illnesses would benefit most: 'The new appointment system will reduce the wait for chronics' and 'It's going to work with chronic disease patients, not with general patients'.

Asked if they had any general comments, doctors and nurses spoke of the stress they felt at work: 'The people work hard here', 'The chronic disease patients are very demanding', 'It's stressful work. We are drained by 2 p.m. We are not able to take a break' and 'It's very taxing. It's frustrating working here'. This suggested that they did not have the extra energy to help reorganize the service but, on the other hand, that a more organized service could reduce stress on staff. As one doctor said, 'On the plus side, it would be nice. We could pace ourselves'.

17.4 Implementing the appointment system

The block appointment system was implemented as follows. Patients were given a choice as to whether or not to be given an appointment. Those who opted for an appointment were given a day and a time to attend. A nurse and a room were designated specifically to deal with appointments. Patients made their appointments by telephoning in or by approaching the appointments nurse in person. The allocated times were at hourly intervals, with about forty patients allocated to each hourly slot. Patients were asked to arrive one hour before the time of their appointment, to allow their folders to be located and to pay user fees. Several doctors were working at any time, and patients who needed to see a doctor were allocated to the next available one. After consulting with a doctor, appointment patients joined all other patients to collect their medication at the pharmacy. The system was advertised through local media and on an electronic notice board in the main waiting room. In the ensuing year, about 60 per cent of patients with appointments arrived at the appointed times.

Eighteen months after the baseline survey, patients' waiting times were again measured over six consecutive days. Appointments appeared to reduce waiting times for most kinds of patients (Mohamed and Bachmann, 1998). Among patients attending chronic disease clinics, who comprised about a quarter of all patients, the median waiting time for patients with appointments was 40 minutes shorter than for patients without appointments. Among patients with acute illnesses, who comprised about 60 per cent of all patients, patients with appointments waited an hour less. These differences were statistically significant. There was no advantage of appointments for patients who did not see a doctor. Total waiting time remained substantial even with appointments – about half of patients still waited over four hours. Compared to the baseline survey, waiting times in the health centre overall were not reduced, but they were slightly shorter for patients with acute illnesses.

17.5 Results of interviews and focus group discussions after implementation

Compared to the baseline survey, patients were in general less enthusiastic about the system, and staff were more enthusiastic, but there was a convergence towards accepting the system and thinking of ways of improving it.

Many patients were pleased with the system, but several others had complaints. 'The waiting time is better. If you come on time you get helped by the staff', said one, and another agreed, 'I think it's very nice. It shortens the waiting time'. Others were neutral or critical: 'I don't think it is working. I wait the same amount of time' and 'All the systems work in favour of the staff here. It's in favour of the nurses, not the patients. That's why it doesn't work'. One patient, half-jokingly, attributed long waits to staff having 'too much teatime and too much lunchtime' and added 'I hope there isn't a camera in the tape recorder, my brother', suggesting some fear of retribution by staff. Some patients felt that their appointments placed them at a disadvantage: 'People without appointments go home before those with appointments'. Some had criticism of specific details: 'What's the point of making an appointment if they only look for your folder once you get here?' Some patients showed themselves to be informed consumers, comparing appointment systems at the health centre and at the local teaching hospital: 'At Groote Schuur (hospital) the folder is prepared in advance. You see a specific doctor and it goes quicker there'. One patient suggested, 'Give a number as people arrive so that they may be helped in the order in which they have arrived'.

Staff members mentioned initial problems, which had largely been solved by the time of interview. There had initially been conflict between patients but this had settled, at times with the help of security staff and the social worker. Reception staff, doctors and nurses all felt that the system was working and had reduced waiting times. Reception staff perceived that 'The doctors and patients want the system to continue'. The chief nurse said 'There has been some improvement in staff and patient relations'. The doctors tended to be most positive, saying 'The discipline of the appointment system has improved patient compliance especially of chronics', 'It helps with follow-up care', 'It makes our jobs easier' and 'It has given order to the chaos that existed here before'. However staff also had criticisms. Reception staff complained that 'Patients either don't come or are late', 'The telephone lines are blocked by patients making appointments', 'Patients coming too early for their appointments expect to be helped early'. Several doctors and nurses also mentioned that many patients arrived late for their appointments. One doctor said 'We get abuse from patients who have not made appointments' and another said 'Generally there is staff resistance at all levels. It is difficult to educate the patients'.

A problem identified by a range of patients and staff was the queue that built up at the pharmacy, which meant that patients who had seen a doctor on time may still have had to wait a long time to collect their drugs. A pharmacist suggested that 'What we need is a bigger waiting room with TV etcetera, and make the benches more comfortable'. Suggestions made by doctors included the need to book more patients per hour to compensate for patients who did not arrive, the need to obtain patients' folders the day before their appointments and the need to ensure continuity of care: 'There's nothing worse than seeing someone else's patient two weeks later'.

In summary, the interviews and discussions with patients and staff revealed a variety of opinions, preferences, suggestions and objections. Eliciting these views beforehand helped to anticipate problems that might arise, or where there might be resistance by either patients or staff, and helped in the design of the system. By revealing a range of views it was possible to avoid the changes being obstructed by one particular group. It also indicated the need to proceed sensitively in implementing the changes. Whereas the baseline interviews and discussions were mainly hypothetical, based on people's expectations of what might happen, the later interviews and discussions elicited people's actual experiences. These too varied widely, but in general they showed that while there had been improvements in several areas, there were still serious problems, but there were also numerous suggestions for how these problems might be tackled.

The results of the study were reported back, as oral presentations and a written report, to health centre management and staff, and to patients and the public through the local Health Committee and the local forum of the Reconstruction and Development Programme. Results were also disseminated nationally through the newsletter of the Health Systems Trust that funded the study, and as a university working paper, and internationally through a journal (Mohamed and Bachmann, 1998). Several researchers from around the country requested details on the study design, to help them design their own similar studies.

17.6 Market research and change management

This example shows that it is possible to improve patient care and access even in overloaded health facilities in developing countries. Key problems may be lack of operational management and staff resistance to change, rather than scarcity of resources alone. Research can help clarify the issues. Differences of experiences or opinion between different patients, between different staff members and professional groups, and between patients and staff are potential sources of conflict, but they also provide a rich source of ideas from which health service developers can draw when designing new systems. The simple methods used in this study elicited many such ideas, as well as helping to identify possible sources of conflict or resistance.

The enthusiasm of front-line health workers is essential for service improvements to be effective. Aside from the information provided by the study, the process of speaking to staff probably increased their sense of ownership of, or identification with, the innovation. This was presumably less true of patients, as only a small proportion of the thousands of users could be interviewed. By initially showing patients' enthusiasm for the change, this research helped overcome staff resistance. By later showing that many patients were still not satisfied, staff were encouraged to continue to seek further improvements.

The qualitative research methods used were basic, which allowed rapid appraisal to be performed. More thorough analysis would have entailed transcribing all interviews and discussions, and exhaustively analysing the transcripts, in order to elicit nuanced feelings and subtle differences between subjects. Such analysis can be more costly and time consuming. That depth of analysis was not appropriate for several reasons. First, results were needed rapidly and at low cost. Second, the opinions and experiences were clearly stated, and differences between informants were readily apparent. If a more sensitive issue was being discussed – for example, if patients were asked about their feelings about notifying partners about their sexually transmitted diseases – then more sensitive methods would need to be used.

Finally, the role of the researchers should be considered. They were based in the Community Health Department of a local medical school, which had close links with local health service managers and a history of applied health services research. This helped the researchers and their research seem legitimate in the eyes of senior managers. In order to gain the confidence of staff at the health centre it was necessary to have the permission of senior management to do the survey so as to gain access, but it was also necessary to be seen to be objective and independent of management, and a conduit for expressing their views. It helped to have independent funding for the study so as not to place an additional load on staff. Local people were employed as research assistants, and so the project funding was channelled back into the local community. It is not clear how patients regarded the survey – only a small proportion of patients had contact with the researchers, whom they probably regarded as part of the health care system.

In summary, the researchers and their work contributed to the management of change by providing a channel for staff and patients to express their opinions, by drawing on their views to help design a better system and by applying their skills to a practical and important problem.

Chapter 18

Market research in the emerging market of forensic mental health

David Sallah

In this chapter the reader will develop an understanding of:

- how forensic mental health services are changing from a bureaucracy controlled by the Home Office to a planned market regulated by the Department of Health
- the emerging opportunities for market research and the importance of researchers who can obtain access
- how the focus group method was used to assess the views of patients about the effectiveness of service provision
- the origins of consensus conferences, their usefulness and limitations
- how a consensus-building conference was used to identify priorities for market research in forensic mental health
- the lessons learned from applying market research in the forensic mental health service.

In this chapter we describe two applications of market research in forensic mental health. These were both part of a coherent research programme carried out by the author. The first application, focus groups, adheres closely to the methodology described in Chapter 5 and, therefore, needs little introduction. The second application, a consensus-building conference, has not been described elsewhere in this book so it is necessary to give a review of the literature. The consensus-building conference can be seen to relate closely to the interactive methods described in Chapter 10. It is also an example of the relationship between market research and change management which is discussed in the final section of Chapter 17. Before describing the two applications it is necessary to explain the context and how the forensic mental health market has been changing and how this provides new opportunities for market research.

18.1 The emerging market of forensic mental health

18.1.1 Defining forensic mental health

Forensic mental health is that aspect of psychiatry whose field of operation is the overlap, interface and interaction with the law in all its aspects (criminal behaviour, civil litigation, family law) and the diagnosis, care and treatment of the mentally disordered patient (Bluglass and Bowen, 1990). It also involves the management of violence and the study of sexual deviance. Forensic mental health is therefore concerned mainly with the treatment, care and management of people who have committed or have the propensity to commit an offence but are judged to have behaved in such a manner as a result of suffering a mental disorder. Mental disorder is classified by the Mental Health Act 1983 which stipulates the reception, care and treatment of mentally disordered patients, the management of their property and other related matters.

The forensic mental health service provides the environment and the expertise for the care of mentally disordered offender patients and others requiring similar services. This latter group (others requiring similar services) are patients who, because of their disruptive behaviours, prevent the normal functioning of wards within local psychiatric hospitals. They may not be offenders in the conventional sense. The service is provided in diverse settings transcending health – public and private sectors, the criminal justice system, local authority and voluntary services. The NHS is the major service provider for high-, medium- and low-security services, and in the community; while the private or independent sector mainly provides services for those patients requiring medium- and low-security facilities. Table 18.1 shows the number of places available for the treatment and management of mentally disordered offenders in England and Wales.

It shows that in January 1999, 1,347 patients suffering from mental disorders were in high-security hospitals, 1,704 in medium security and 1,344 in low-security units in England and Wales. In the case of activity in the community, there are 130 court assessment schemes; fifty of which are directly funded by the Home Office, and many patients access the service as outpatients.

The service cares for some of the most notorious offenders in the country and because of this, policy makers and service providers are always concerned with the influence the media, the general public and relevant others can have on the effectiveness of the service. In recent times this media and public influence has been instrumental in government decisions to tighten service provider behaviour insofar as the quality and effectiveness of service provision and delivery is concerned (Blom-Cooper, 1992; Reed, 1992, 1994; Department of Health, 1996a; Fallon, 1998).

18.1.2 Becoming a market

Parts of the service (medium, minimum security and community) operate within the NHS and operate within the framework for commissioning and providing health care. However, the high-security services (commonly referred to as special hospitals due to the nature of their security) are not as yet fully accorded Trust status *but are on course to become fully integrated into the NHS*. Since 1 April 1995, these hospitals have been involved in a massive programme

Table 18.1 Mentally disordered offenders and service provision

	High security		Medium security		Low security		
	Hospitals	Places	Units	Places	Units	Places	Community
NHS	3	1,347	36	1,259	81	1,249	130 court assessment schemes
Private			7	445	4	95	
Total	3	1,347	43	1,704	85	1,344	

Sources: Department of Health and High Security Psychiatric Commissioning Board (unpublished).

of integration into the NHS (NHS Executive, 1995). Although they do not as yet achieve Trust status, they are allowed to set their own development agenda *and can negotiate directly with a nationally appointed health purchaser* (High Security Psychiatric Services Commissioning Board, HSPSCB) for finance and consequently for monitoring of the effectiveness of its contracts. This apparent slowness of approach in integrating the high-security hospitals into the NHS is due to the potential risk most of its patients pose to themselves and others and the Home Office's role in safeguarding public safety in so much as those patients who are restricted are concerned. The implication of this is that the discharge of patients, particularly from high-security hospitals, is not based on clinical outcomes only but also on the wider political consideration of the ability of the patient to be safely rehabilitated into the community. This aspect of care has been described as a problematic process as these judgements are often difficult to make by using objective arguments (Crighton, 1995).

18.1.3 A historical account of secure services

Institutions dedicated to the care of mentally disordered offenders (MDOs) in the UK have been in existence since the 1830s when the first high-security hospital (Broadmoor Hospital in Crowthorne, Berkshire) was opened. There are now three high security hospitals in England (Ashworth in Merseyside, Broadmoor and Rampton Hospital in Nottinghamshire) serving the whole of England and Wales. The State Hospital (Carstairs) in Scotland caters for patients in Scotland and Northern Ireland. In the past, patients have tended to spend long periods of time within these hospitals, in most cases over twenty years, often for minor offences; the average length of stay in these hospitals is now eight years.

In the 1970s, a major shift of emphasis in the way services are provided to mentally disordered offenders occurred (Glancy, 1974; Butler, 1975). New regional medium-security units were established (see Table 18.1). Their role was to maximize the rehabilitation of patients. These medium-secure units are intended for the treatment, care and management of people who are likely to respond to treatment within a maximum period of two years. The average length of stay within these units is between six and eight months. These units are now generally directorates within larger mental health trusts and are therefore much more integrated within the wider NHS and its related agencies; there are now 43 such units in England and Wales. They provided the foundations for what is now referred to as forensic psychiatry or mental health services in England and Wales. The establishment of these units increased the numbers of service users (see Table 18.1).

Effective management of the service has become crucial as the service has become more integrated in the environment within which it is situated. The policies and actions of various sections of the service have become more transparent and therefore open to critical review by policy makers, purchasers, the press and media, and users of the service.

18.1.4 Accessing the sector for research

An apparent over-sensitivity to how the service reacts in general to its outside, and indeed its inside, environment affects the way in which researchers are treated and welcome to conduct research within the service. In the course of conducting this study it was found that clinical practitioners and managers were sceptical of the reasons for undertaking this type of research and the subsequent use of data collected. A consultant forensic psychiatrist refused to allow any of *his* patients to be involved in the study even though approval by the research ethics committee had been granted and explanatory notes sent to all doctors and managers about the purpose of the research.

Patients expressed anxieties about participating in the study for fear of repercussions and could not believe that anything would change through their co-operation with the study:

> They never listen to us. It don't matter what I say. Why should I talk to you when nothing is going to change.

Other patients thought it unwise to talk about what their experiences and expectations were because they could not reassure themselves sufficiently that the 'authorities' would not take adverse actions against them.

These and many other examples provided the backdrop for the study in addition to the official hurdles that needed to be negotiated in the course of any research study. So why is this type of research within forensic mental health so contentious? Part of this question can be answered by examining the nature of the service's contribution to the health of the nation. The service caters for the most dangerous but vulnerable individuals within psychiatry. The public, the press, politicians and policy makers all have a stake in the way the service functions and each of these have a view, often very strong, on the way patients should be treated and cared for within the service. The therapy and security dimensions are sometimes at the very opposite ends of the same continuum and need to be considered at all times. These structural issues relating to access influence the way any research should be designed and data collection managed.

Consequently, a major aspect of conducting the focus group on eliciting patients' views and experiences of the service was the degree of co-operation in terms of gaining access to subjects and to services. Barnes (1977) argued that it is possible for social scientists to find that gaining access to the people they wish to study could be as difficult and lengthy a process as gaining financial support for the work. The argument for refusal of access to other researchers had been that the researcher may be an uninitiated member of the organization, who lacks the qualifications essential for access to 'the secrets' and, if qualified, cannot be trusted not to pass on the secrets to the world at large through publication.

In this study, the researcher found that access to subjects, patients and staff had been restricted by the nature of the research. Research into the effectiveness of a service which is regularly criticized for its poor responses to meeting patients' needs appropriately is bound to raise anxieties. The higher degree of attention attached to confidentiality of information and the media attention patients attract also places extra demands on researchers and the researched.

18.2 Applying the focus group in forensic mental health services

18.2.1 Introduction

The aim of the study reported here was to assess the views and experiences of patients in high- and medium-security mental health services with a view to assessing the effectiveness of service provision from their perspective. In total, four groups were conducted. The basic design and conduct of focus groups is described in Chapter 5.

18.2.2 Selecting the groups

Four 45-minute long focus groups were conducted so that the analysis of the results could look for patterns of themes across the groups.

- Group A consisted of a cross-section of patients in the community
- Group B consisted of mentally ill patients in a high-security hospital
- Group C consisted of mainly psychopathic disordered patients in a high-security hospital
- Group D consisted of a mixture of various diagnostic groupings in a medium-secure unit.

The groups were composed of five to ten people and their selection was conditioned by two factors: the groups must be small enough for everyone to have an opportunity to share insights and yet large enough to provide diversity. The rule of thumb that guided this selection process was that the more expertise participants have on the subject the lower the number of participants in the group. This degree of homogeneity was determined by the purpose of the study and was a basis for recruitment; and participants were informed of these common factors at the beginning of each discussion. Further, power differentials between participants were also minimized. For example, mixing patients from different diagnostic groups and various degrees of well-being was discouraged because of the tendency for intimidation, limitation of open communication and domination of discussions by any particular group of patients or individuals.

18.2.3 Running the groups

The role adopted by the facilitator in terms of moderating was neither that of a teacher providing instructions nor a participant in an engaging conversation, but more like a sponge soaking up the insights of participants. The approach was to guide the group discussion using questions, pauses, probes and eye contact to encourage participants to participate in the discussions.

The groups worked particularly well within the specific purpose of using this method which was to determine perceptions, feelings and thinking of patients to ideas, services or opportunities. Clearly questions at the beginning of the group meetings were typically more general and were designed to enable participants to gather their thoughts, reflect on their experiences and hear about the experiences of others. The process of one group is described below.

Group A comprised eight ex-users of the forensic services who had accessed inpatient services within the past year. Three were currently receiving aftercare from the service and the rest were no longer under the care of the service and were from different parts of the country and were invited to a national conference. The approach adopted here by the facilitator was less structured to allow for issues that were of interest to the participants to be aired. This flexibility was designed to allow all participants to feel that they too have bene-fited from participating in the group and to allow them to discuss what was important to them rather than merely fitting into the facilitator's research paradigm.

At one point during the Group A session, one of the participants who was consistently disrupting others walked out of the meeting in a fit of anger when other participants decided not to allow the interruptions any further. He returned to the group without prompting after a while and contributed effectively thereafter. This behaviour was important in understanding researching user characteristics in mental health. Within the context of this group, there were users who were at different levels of recovery and therefore likely to behave inconsistently.

18.2.4 Findings

Some of the key findings from the four focus groups are now given.

1   Managers failed to lessen the domination of white male psychopathic patients in established communications group forums such as the patient council. This excluded other diagnostic groups including women and patients from ethnic minorities.
2   Patients within the medium-security sector tended to report higher degrees of satisfaction with their care than those in high-security hospitals.
3   Patients complained about the lack of consultation and in some cases dialogue between them and staff on their living conditions and the quality of their care.

The conclusion to be drawn about this research is that, in general, mentally disordered offender patients have not benefited substantially from the opportunity to input into decisions relating to their care.

4   A point of concern to patients from the minority ethnic groups was that because they were thought to be too dangerous no one considered developing a care plan for them. They were thus excluded from the mainstream of care provision.
5   Group members observed that they were not taken seriously when they complain about their care. Practitioners believe that mentally ill patients who complain are either too mentally disturbed to be believed or malicious in intent.
6   Nearly all participants in the four focus groups complained about the lack of explanation and inadequacy of information that was given to them. They argued that the priority for staff was to ensure that they were taking prescribed medication, staff failed to tell them what the medication was for, how it would help them and what adverse reactions they would experience.

Empowerment of both staff and patients had not happened within the high-security hospitals, according to interviewees, sufficiently to enable the development of working in teams and in partnership. This lack of communication had resulted in suspicion of actions by managers, staff and patients and consequently allowed a culture of blame to evolve within the service.

18.2.5 Lessons learnt

Focus groups provide raw data that need skilled interpretation and analysis if they are to inform policy and practice. In this study, the method was helpful in obtaining general first-hand background information from participants, for seeking new ideas and concepts to develop and had helped in generating views of users on service quality, effectiveness and appropriateness. The data generated by the use of this method showed that there were gaps in the services on offer.

The groups provided data primarily in response to open-ended questions but also through observations of respondents in group discussions. A variety of recording methods were used: audio tapes, note taking and the help of an assistant with short-hand skills.

18.3 Consensus building in health care

18.3.1 Introduction

This section describes how consensus building was used in forensic mental health. Because this method has not been described elsewhere in the book it is necessary to give some background and a brief review of the literature.

The enterprise culture of the NHS, together with the competition introduced by the internal market, had brought the consensus that existed before the reforms of the 1980s a step nearer to extinction. Hewison (1995) observed that the Conservative government of 1979 failed to restore that consensus because they had entered office convinced that the failure of the effectiveness of the public sector could be linked with consensus management. This process of decision making had been prevalent in the NHS prior to managerial reforms of the service (Griffiths, 1983). Even though this approach has almost disappeared in the management of the service, its use for changing service provision has increased. Professional staff have continued to use this approach to set clinical standards and to agree how these standards could be implemented and measured. However, whilst clinical staff in the NHS continued to develop team working which was strongly based on consensus, intra Trust or hospital collaboration had waned considerably.

> The New Labour administration has pledged to reverse this trend and has made building partnerships and consensus the pillar of its health service policy (Department of Health, 1997, 1998a).

18.3.2 Defining the terms

The *Oxford English Dictionary* traces the origin of the word 'consensus' to the Latin 'consentire', meaning 'to feel together' as opposed to 'census' which indicates enumerative activity. However, this fundamental difference is often a source of conflict between expectations and realistic goals of consensus guidelines (Fallen 1995). Consensus development conferences originally began in the USA in the 1970s and are extensively practised in Britain, parts of Europe (Vang, 1986; King's Fund Forum, 1987) and widely used in health service research (Moscovice *et al.*, 1988; McGlynn *et al.*, 1990; Bellamy *et al.*, 1991; Crotty, 1993).

Consensus building can be defined as a process whereby a decision is reached through the participation and contribution of members of a team to resolve an organizational or clinical problem. Taking decisions in uncertain situations has led to high use of the consensus methods in the health service. Consensus-building conferences can provide clarification on key issues of interest and narrow the gap between existing knowledge and practice on topics with a sufficient base of scientific data to make expert scrutiny feasible. According to Goodman (1995), it is a variant of group judgement methods and can be used in dealing with conflicting scientific information (Gowan and McNichols, 1993; Jones and Hunter,

1995). The three most popular of the consensus-building methods used in health care are the Delphi Process, the Nominal Group Technique (also known as the Expert Panel) and the consensus development conference (CDC).

Delphi Process

The Delphi Process takes its name from the ancient Greek Delphic oracle's skills of interpretation and foresight. It is a highly specialized application of the nominal group technique for developing forecasts and trends based on the collective opinion of knowledgeable experts. The technique has been used widely in health research (Pill, 1971; Rowe *et al.*, 1991; Kitzinger, 1994), education and training (Elder and Andrew, 1992; Crotty, 1993), setting priorities and information (Moscovice *et al.*, 1988; Oranga and Nordberg, 1993) and in developing nursing and clinical practice (Mobily *et al.*, 1993). The Delphi Process enables a large group of experts to be contacted cheaply by mail and involves participants in resolving inconsistencies and ambiguities in wording of the questions.

Nominal Group Technique

The Nominal Group Technique uses a highly structured meeting to gather information on a given topic. It consists of two rounds in which small groups of experts rate and re-rate a series of items or questions (Jones and Hunter, 1995). An expert on the topic or a credible non-expert facilitates the group meeting. This method was developed in the 1960s, and had been applied to problems in social services, education, government and industry (Fink *et al.*, 1984). Within health, this technique has been used to examine the appropriateness of clinical interventions (Hunter *et al.*, 1993), education and training (Battles *et al.*, 1989), practice development (Justice and Jang, 1990) and for identifying measures for clinical trials (Felson, 1993).

18.3.3 Consensus development conference (CDC)

The CDC is often organized through defined programmes, for example the Kings Fund in Britain and the National Institutes of Health (NIH) in the USA, and requires a considerable array of resources (Stocking, 1985; Stocking *et al.*, 1991). Within it, discussions are held in public and led by experts in the field being investigated. The experts present their evidence to a consensus panel made up of practitioners from a broad range of backgrounds that listen to the evidence and prepare answers to a set of questions about the technology or procedure. There are two models within this approach; scientific peer review and the judicial model.

The scientific peer review model, which is the favoured method in the USA, comprises representation from users and experts who are known not to have any biases on the technology or procedure but are knowledgeable about the subject. The questions asked are restricted to scientific issues as well as the need for further research. The judicial model, as pioneered in the UK by the King's Fund, has a panel whose members are not experts and are not exclusively medical practitioners but have no user representatives. It also considers the economic impact and its implications for the wider service provision if that particular procedure is to be recommended. Stocking (1985) argued that, in spite of the apparent focus on finding economic implications for the procedure, the main task of the panel is to consider the procedure's scientific merits.

The key features of consensus conferences are that they help health care stakeholders to take a new technology and assess its applicability to various aspects of care provision. Basically, a panel from a broad range of backgrounds listens to evidence presented by experts and views from participants and prepares answers to a set of questions about the technology, practice or the procedure. The adoption of the consensus method enables an assessment of the extent of agreement (consensus measurement) and to resolve disagreement (consensus development) on a given health care issue, using a group approach to decision making.

Anonymity in developing consensus is achieved through different stages of the process with an opportunity for the individual to rank responses without any group pressure. This process is particularly helped when a questionnaire is used during the Delphi Process and by private ranking when the Nominal Group Technique is used. The next step in the process to ensure consensus is through a stage-by-stage approach to the development of statements. This is known as iteration, and can provide individuals with the opportunity of matching their responses against that from other respondents, in addition to changing their minds in view of what others have said. There is also a controlled feedback stage so that information that is given is relevant in enabling participants to make decisions on informed bases. The process is completed by applying to it a degree of statistical analysis, thus providing participants with more information than just that a consensus is reached.

Consensus methods allow a wider range of study types to be considered and are used to resolve differences and conflicts in scientific evidence. However, the usefulness of consensus development conferences has been questioned on the grounds of their reliability, ability to change practice and cost effectiveness (Durand-Zaleski *et al.*, 1992). Lomas (1991) reported that consensus statements have not influenced what he thought was its purpose, i.e. to effect change for the better in clinical practice during a review of its use in hypertension. He reported on a review of what he termed nineteen 'methodologically credible' studies of the impacts of consensus recommendations and found that the majority had no significant impact except for six studies which had contributed to changing behaviour moderately. He pointed out that only three amongst this group had contributed to changing clinical practice in a major way.

- consensus conferences should focus on those areas that truly need improvement
- follow-up is required at national and local level
- the greatest inducement to change is provided by local leadership.

The King's Fund ran a series of consensus development conferences in the 1980s and found the process useful in developing guidelines for practitioners in various aspects of health care (King's Fund Forum, 1987).

18.3.4 The need for consensus in forensic mental health

The specialty of forensic mental health is one of the most diverse sectors of the health service in terms of case-mix, although there are similar diagnostic groupings (see introduction to forensic mental health for further information). It is firmly rooted in the application of many aspects of the law within the practice of mental health. Patients as end-users of the service have a common denominator, which relates to their behaviour and mental disorder. The provision of the service at whatever level requires joint working with practitioners within relevant agencies. Consequently, there is a strong call by policy makers, users and other stakeholders that the service must develop effective measures of service provision as the medium-secure sector continues to grow. However, as more of these services become integrated within the NHS service-commissioning mechanisms, there is an increasing willingness to share good practice.

Another aspect to consider is the rapidly escalating knowledge in mental health services about mental disorder, which is based on the perspectives of various disciplines within the field. *There is therefore more knowledge available than any one profession, discipline or individual could understand, synthesize and use.* On this basis the individual practitioner is limited in scope and depth of knowledge needed to satisfy the needs of the patient effectively. The promotion of multi-disciplinary and inter-agency working is therefore necessary in developing effective interventions and services.

18.4 Applying the consensus-building method – a case study

A three-year study into outcomes measures identified key areas that were of concern to various stakeholders of forensic mental health care. The findings were presented to an expert panel who selected key areas to put to a consensus conference of health care providers, commissioners, policy makers, patients and educators. A combination of the Delphi Process and Nominal Group Technique was used to identify common areas to develop into outcomes measures of forensic mental health practice.

18.4.1 Method

Data for the conference were collected by reviewing the effectiveness literature, conducting organizational case studies, survey questionnaires and focus groups of the sample group referred to above, together with an assessment of current practice within the field in terms of measuring outcomes. A portfolio of descriptors of areas was compiled and sent to a panel of expert practitioners. They were asked to prioritize the areas and met three times to agree on common areas to put to a consensus conference for discussion and agreement. At the conference itself, 180 participants were put into nine mixed groups of stakeholders. A member of the Expert Group was nominated to lead each group so that further information necessary for decision making could be supplied and pertinent issues clarified should group members require them. Each group leader made a presentation on the group's conclusions to a plenary session of all delegates.

18.4.2 Analysis

Through the use of content analysis, data collected from the methods were coded by categories analysed and presented to the Expert Panel. Panel members individually further ranked the categories in order of priority. Their conclusions were then presented to conference participants in their respective groups. The groups were asked to agree that the particular category was a priority and what specific actions were needed to develop them into outcomes measures.

18.4.3 Outcome

The following priority areas were identified:

- define the objectives of the forensic mental health services
- developing seamless clinical services
- recruitment and retention of the best staff
- develop the Health of the Nation outcomes scales as a clinical outcomes measure
- multi-disciplinary and inter-agency working
- assessment of patients' needs
- involving patients and other users in care
- increased research, training and education for development.

Consensus was reached on all the selected categories and specific recommendations made for their development. These areas were selected as key priorities for further research, which the Department of Health is supporting in its research funding bids.

18.5 Lessons learnt

In this section the relevance and application of the focus group and the consensus-building method as market research tools are reviewed.

18.5.1 Focus groups

In this study the intention was to access the views and experiences of patients in high- and medium-security mental health services with a view to assessing the effectiveness of service provision from their perspective. The study identified various pertinent issues that should be considered by the researcher using such an approach within this environment.

Access to patients is a lot more restricted than in other areas of mental health practice. On the one hand, this is due to the need to safeguard confidentiality while on the other it could be due to the desire by these organizations to protect themselves from criticism. The researcher needs to develop alliances and partnerships amongst the multi-disciplinary staff for a project using this method.

It is also important that researchers take time to select the best mix of patients, taking into account their degree of recovery from their illness, the level of security within which they are being cared for and the diagnostic group to which they belong. The answers to these questions are best provided by clinicians, which is why it is imperative that the researcher develops an effective network of these professionals.

Another issue to consider is the probability of disruptive behaviour by participants. Conducting focus groups of patients within the mental health field is problematic, particularly if the moderating strategy is rigid. The groups would be more productive if accommodation is made for participants to be heard, even when what they are saying is not relevant to the information being sought. The skill is to allow these interruptions and at the same time ensuring that they do not become more important than the objectives of conducting the focus group.

18.5.2 Consensus-building conference

Consensus-building conferences can improve quality of care by issuing practice guidelines that are based on evidence and agreement, and are focused on a given evidence, practice or procedure. The experience from this conference was that the use of the consensus-building method was a valuable tool in clarifying diverse views and sharing information between practitioners of health care and those whose needs the service is designed to meet. The conference has helped to include the views of key stakeholders of forensic mental health practice, especially those of patients who are not able usually to articulate their views effectively.

The application of the consensus-building method shows that decisions can be reached amongst the many stakeholder groups. The main lesson learnt from applying this method was that consensus was achieved because the focus of the original study was of a particular interest to all stakeholders. In this way, the outcomes of the conference reflect and reinforce the changing nature of practice rather than promoting change. However, it is imperative that where the intention is to produce a substantial change in practice, the production of the statements needs to be developed as part of a more comprehensive programme. The study reported was used to set the research agenda for the forensic mental health service for improving the effectiveness of practice.

In applying the concept in the context of market research, the consensus-building conference is valuable in identifying, agreeing priority areas and setting the agenda for further research into the needs of the many stakeholders of the service. Therefore in this context it has contributed to keeping pace with the many changes and challenges within the forensic mental health services. As a market research tool, the consensus-building conference can provide the forum where the views of service users could be collated and included on agendas for service development, training and research. In this way the market researcher is a conveyer of such user views. The consensus method as a process was valuable as a medium for disseminating important research findings. Information provided prior to the conference helped in the development of discussions and arguments, and contributed in enabling decisions on an informed basis. A criticism of the process could be that patients receiving inpatient care were not included in the conference due to legal constraints.

Part 4

Prospects for market research

In this final Part there is a single chapter in which we first summarize the emerging developments of market research methods and of applications that we have carried out. Then we scan the trends in the political and organizational context of health and social care markets. Finally, we speculate on the relevance of these trends for the prospects for market research in health and social care.

Chapter 19

The prospects for market research in health and social care

Mike Luck and Rob Pocock

In this chapter the reader will gain an understanding of:

- the topic areas where market research has been applied and where it could be extended in the future
- the research methods which have been applied successfully and the trend towards interactive and participative methods
- the first steps towards a coherent theory of how the citizen's and consumer's voice can be influential in health and social care systems
- the political, economic, social and technological changes which influence the opportunities and challenges for market research in health and social care.

19.1 Purpose

This book has been written to systematize the experience of the three editors and fifteen contributors in applying market research in a variety of situations using a wide range of methods. We want to communicate this systematized knowledge to students, to managers and professionals in health and social care agencies, and to interested lay people. We think that by disseminating a greater understanding of what can and cannot be done with market research this will help to articulate the voice of the citizen and consumer more efficiently and effectively. In pluralistic democracies there is increasing public pressure for services to be responsive, but there is, on the other hand, the danger of unrealistic expectations.

For market research contractors, there is the need to develop comparative frameworks together with an understanding of what works and what does not work, and a body of theory that will enable us to synthesize diverse experience. It is probable that many of the same mistakes are being made because of lack of communication. We just do not know.

For potential commissioners of market research and for those who are going to be affected by the results, it is important to transmit theoretical and practicable understanding of the potential and limitations. This can best be done in education. This will help to avoid decisions being made without consumer views or inappropriate market research being commissioned that never gets used.

19.2 What we have learnt

In this section we first review the topics and contexts that have been covered in the case studies in Part 3; then examine critically the methods that have been explained in Part 2 and applied in Part 3; and finally begin the task of developing a conceptual framework.

19.2.1 Applications

The majority of the applications in this book are located in Britain. An important question is whether market research can be applied in the same way in other countries or will require substantial modification or perhaps not be applicable at all. The discussion of the contexts of health and welfare systems in western European countries in Chapter 2 together with the applications in Chapter 10 indicates that there do not seem to be any fundamental barriers.

Outside of western Europe the case study from South Africa described in Chapter 17 suggests that market research can be carried out successfully in a period of huge political change from the apartheid to post-apartheid regime. The case study from Thailand shows how valuable secondary research can be done from outside a Third World country and then followed up with primary research adapted for local cultural and material circumstances.

Applications have been carried out at the *national level*, Chapters 10, 13 and 18, at the *agency level* of local authority and health authority, Chapters 11 and 15, and at the *local level* of the estate, Chapter 12. Although the scale of logistical preparation differs depending on the level, this does not seem to pose particularly different methodological questions for design of the research.

Markets may be *well-established* such as for family planning services, Chapter 15, or *emerging* such as the forensic mental health service and toxicology, Chapters 18 and 16 respectively, or *innovative* such as the healthy living centre in Chapter 12. The main difference between these three situations seems to be in the ownership of the research. The more innovative the market, then it is more likely that the commissioner will consist of multiple stakeholders who are inexperienced in market research and so the contractor will have to take a stronger initiative in 'selling' the results and acting as a change agent (this is the case in the Home Care example in Chapter 4).

19.2.2 Methods

Our experience of applying market research in health and social care suggests that it is not the formal content of the methods which offers the main difficulties but rather choosing and fitting them into the organizational context and making them acceptable to the population being surveyed.

A thorough *literature review* is always important. In the Thailand case study, Chapter 13, this was carried out from England before setting up primary research in the country. In the study of non-residential care, Chapter 11, the commissioner had to be persuaded to add the literature review into the original project specification and costing.

Secondary research, in addition to the literature search, should always be considered before primary research. In Chapter 15, Mary Parkes used routine secondary information about family planning services in order to define the problem and focus her study. But the original part of her study was that she found the claim data from GPs which was used to pay them had never been analysed for the purposes of estimating demand.

Primary research increasingly includes focus groups because they allow exploration of 'why' questions which is needed to gain understanding beyond mere description. In Chapter 12, M.E.L. Research used focus groups which provided insights into the issues which mattered to people, and this was then used to design the residents interview survey. Qualitative interviews and focus groups with both patients and staff in the Cape Town health centre were more than sufficient in setting the agenda for change and evaluating the results afterwards. In Chapter 18, David Sallah describes how he, as an experienced worker in the forensic mental health service, was able to run the focus groups with patients who could be disruptive.

The use of questionnaires and interviews are described in several of the chapters. Particularly interesting are the questionnaire by fax, Chapter 11, and the SERVQUAL questionnaire, Chapter 16, where the adaptation of a standard questionnaire allowed comparison with service quality in sectors other than health and social care and set a benchmark.

The main innovations in methods are the use of the *interactive method* of the consensus development conference, Chapter 18, and the three versions of *user participation methods* used in Chapter 10. This trend is likely to continue with the pressure of rising consumer expectations and acceptance by politicians that professional judgement cannot go unchallenged in service design and evaluation. Developing a partnership model with community groups described in Chapter 11, is also an example of harnessing conventional market research methods in an unconventional framework.

19.2.3 Understanding and theory

Most of the applications described in this book started from the request to help solve problems or influence decisions about the design, management or evaluation of services. What we wanted to do by writing this book is to establish the first steps towards a coherent theory of how the consumer's voice can be influential in health and social care systems. At present, neither potential commissioners nor contractors of market research have a framework beyond their own experience which would help them to see where market research is likely to be effective and where it will not be suitable. Without some such framework or theory it is impossible to generalize from experience and to communicate to students other than in apprenticeship projects.

The framework presented in Figure 3.5 gives us a good start. It shows us how market research fits into the cycle of sensing, thinking, acting and reflecting, and where we have good examples and where we need to look for case studies or new applications. It also shows how other techniques and disciplines can be used. We do not want 'market research' to be constrained by hard boundaries or 'turf wars' with other specialisms.

We have also placed emphasis on the relationship between the commissioner and contractor and how this can be worked out in a process (Figure 4.1). In the case studies there are a wide variety of arrangements including that of MBA students making successful contributions to the organizations as well as attaining their academic objectives.

19.3 The future

Throughout this book we have sought to place market research within a 'business planning' approach to developments in health and social care services. It is appropriate for us therefore to draw on a business planning concept when looking ahead to the possible environments that might influence demand for market research in future. The 'PEST' method – reviewing in turn the political, economic, social and technological aspects of change – is applied in this section.

19.3.1 The political and policy environment

One of the changes most likely to influence the nature and function of market research in health and social care is the Best Value approach to service development. To date, this has progressed rapidly in local authorities and is starting to influence thinking in health care. Replacing the concept of 'lowest cost minimum standard tender' for determining the choice of contractor, Best Value has introduced a more all-embracing set of considerations aimed at achieving continuous improvement in services. The 'Four Cs' (challenge, compare, consult, compete) are used as the basis for undertaking fundamental reviews of existing services and alternative options.

Market research is evidently central to the requirement to 'consult' and it is applied to all key stakeholders in the decision – service users or potential users (the public), the people providing the service, as well as others such as partners and funders. Best Value in one sense marks the coming home of market research – from the days in the NHS of the early 1980s when, as our first book set out, the approach was innovative, the culture unfamiliar and the applications viewed with some suspicion – to a period now when the techniques of market research supply the bedrock to high-quality service development planning.

One by-product of the move towards Best Value in both local authority and NHS is the development of joint consultative initiatives. Many local authorities are setting up Citizens Panels – representative groups of usually about 1,000 residents – who are consulted regularly about key issues and strategic choices. In some cases, such as Barnsley, the local authority and health authority have co-funded the Panel and consultation surveys are being undertaken and the opportunity exists to take a multi-agency approach to issues concerning the public's health and to address key issues – poverty, housing, employment, healthy lifestyles – in the round.

Bringing health issues into the remit of the democratic local government system has also accentuated the increased politicization of the decision-making context. Health has become an issue not just for national elections but local council elections too. Trends towards 'political engagement' with NHS decision making have placed market research in a somewhat uncomfortable environment. The future of health care has become a 'mass public issue' with MPs and political parties embroiled in the midst of the lobbying process. Is market research relevant to this politicized decision making environment? Can the systematic scientific methods and rational analytical methods offer a paradigm that can survive the heat of the political furore? This is very much an unanswered question.

19.3.2 The economic environment

The 'economic' dimension of the health care services, which one might summarize as centring on the rational distribution of scarce resources, is also changing fast. The new NHS is one where management models have evolved into 'clinical governance' – based on the premise that clinicians should have sovereignty over the decision making or rationing process. The National Institute of Clinical Excellence (NICE) decides when specific drugs ought to be available through the NHS and which therapies are of proven benefit. Locally, primary health care professionals have the prevalent influence on the Primary Care Group/Trust Boards.

Here again, however, there is a tension between two paradigms, as with the political/technocratic tensions above. Within the health care economy, clinical governance has to wrestle with the challenge from 'consumer sovereignty'. Do we have clinical governance or patient-led care? Can these co-exist? Is market research a tool for clinicians or a voice for articulating patient involvement? During the early 1990s much use was made of the term 'Voices' in legitimizing the introduction of market research as a mechanism for creating a more 'listening NHS'. But market research is commissioned by agents of management. Might market research under clinical governance simply strengthen the medical profession's control over the market research process (i.e. what and who is researched)? Is this consistent with the competing notion of a consumer-centred NHS? What happens when the patient agenda is in conflict with the professional agenda?

19.3.3 The social environment

Family and lifestyle are changing. Increasingly people are less and less willing to 'do surveys'. The wholesale disengagement of people under 30 from many civic and communal dimensions of life is a matter of serious concern to politicians who see mass abstention from the democratic process within this sector. Anyone practising market research will equally have observed a significant and threatening trend for younger people to say 'no thanks' to the invitation to fill out a survey or take part in an interview.

This process is simply an extension to the so-called 'hard-to-reach' groups that have always beset market researchers. More often this is projected as a question of culture and ethos, and in particular around minority ethnic communities. Here again social change will accentuate the point – we will soon have ethnic majorities in many of the UK's major conurbations. Birmingham will probably be a 'Moslem city' by 2030. How will this affect the way the health and social care services approach market research? Once the views of the hard-to-reach groups have become majority views, there will be very serious questions asked of the validity and value of market research if it has not been able to develop ways of securing the engagement of such groups.

This problem also besets the growing emphasis on tackling inequality. The key mechanism for raising the standards of health of the population is going to be through raising the health of the least healthy fastest. This target sector of the 'market' is, however, the one least attuned to the workings of the conventional market research survey. How do we combat this problem?

19.3.4 The technological environment

Much has been said in Chapter 6 about the IT revolution and the potential impacts on market research. It is necessary to re-state only the very fundamental point, that IT will revolutionize market research and that we should already be planning for this. We are not just talking about interactive Internet-based communication. The technology already exists and is coming into application using virtual IT models of potential new facilities to test public attitudes to design features and potential uses. This offers a radically different way for people to be engaged in the development of new facilities.

But IT will also change people's relationships with health care providers. Telemedicine (where clinicians at a remote site make diagnoses of a patient's condition and recommend appropriate therapy) is on its way and the replacement of pharmacists by 'hole in the wall' medicine dispensing and mail order is a real option (mail order is already beginning to dominate pharmaceutical supply for some key high-user groups).

So it is important for market research not just to adapt its own tools and techniques. It will also have to adapt the fundamental concept and understanding of the 'service provider and service user' relationship. Much market research is about this human relationship, and one of the most valuable roles market research has to play in the future is in ensuring that the vast technological changes that have so much potential to improve health care do not let us lose sight of the irreplaceable value of the human relationship.

19.4 The challenges ahead

As a result of writing this book in which we have brought together some of our experiences in teaching (Part 2) and applying (Part 3) market research in health and social care, we have identified some challenges and ways forward. This has been helped by referring to the contextual analysis in Part 1 and by undertaking the reviews in this chapter (Sections 19.2 and 19.3).

We hope that the dissemination of this book will lead to more dialogue about the potential for market research between potential commissioners and contractors. We hope that the frameworks will lead to more comprehensive information collection and sharing about successes and failures. We hope that there will be better-informed students at both undergraduate and postgraduate levels who will be equipped to carry out their own research projects and to feed into management and research practice. Finally, we hope that the whole topic of the feasibility and limitations of citizen and consumer involvement in health and social care systems on an international comparative basis will be moved forward at the theoretical and practical levels.

Bibliography

Abbott, P. and Sapsford, R. (1994) 'Studying policy and practice: the use of vignettes', *Nurse Researcher* 1: 81–91.

Accounts Commission (1997) *Bulletin No.1, Expanding on contracting: health board contracting in Scotland*, Edinburgh: Accounts Commission for Scotland.

Acheson, D. (chair) (1998) *Independent Inquiry into Inequalities in Health*, London: The Stationery Office.

Allott, M. and Robb, M. (1998) *Understanding Health and Social Care*, London: Sage.

Audit Commission (1995a) *Quality Counts: A Standard Consumer Survey*, London, Audit Commission.

Audit Commission (1995b) *Setting the Record Straight: A Study of Hospital Medical Records*, London: Audit Commission.

Babb, P. (1993) 'Teenage conceptions and fertility in England and Wales 1971–1991', *Population Trends* 74: 12–17.

Bachmann, O.M. and Barron, P. (1997) 'Why wait so long for child care? An analysis of waits, queues and work in an urban health centre', *Tropical Doctor* 27: 34–38.

Bachmann, O.M., Mtwazi, L. and Barron, P. (1996) 'Quality of care in family planning clinics in a South African peri-urban settlement', *Journal of Comprehensive Health* 7: 34–40.

Bainbridge, D. and Pearce, G. (1996) 'EC Data Protection Law', *The Computer Law and Security Report* 12(3): 160–168.

Bainbridge, D. and Pearce, G. (1998a) 'Data protection: data controllers and the new Data Protection Law', *The Computer Law and Security Report* 14(3): 259–326.

Bainbridge, D. and Pearce, G. (1998b) 'Data protection: the UK Data Protection Act 1998: data subject's rights, *The Computer Law and Security Report*, 14(6): 401–405.

Bainbridge, D. and Pearce, G. (1999) 'Data protection: the new UK data protection in law and the transitional arrangements', *The Computer Law and Security Report* 15(4): 343–347.

Barnes, B. (1977) *Interests and the Growth of Knowledge*, London: Routledge.

Barron, P. (ed.) (1997) *South African Health Review*, Durban: Health Systems Trust.

Batchelor, C., Owens, D.J., Read, M. and Bloor, M. (1994) 'Patient satisfaction studies: methodology, management and consumer evaluation', *International Journal of Health Care Quality Assurance* 7(7): 22–30.

Battles, J.B., Kirk, L.M., Dowell, D.L. and Frnka, S. (1989) 'The health service communicator as faculty developer', *Journal of Biocommunity* 16: 2–8.

Becker, H.S., Geer, B., Hughes, E.C. and Strauss, A.L. (1961) *Boys in White: Student Culture in Medical School*, Chicago: University of Chicago Press.

Bellamy, N., Anastassiades, T.P. and Buchanan, W.W. *et al.* (1991) 'Rheumatoid arthritis anti-rheumatic trials. III. Setting the delta for clinical trials of anti-rheumatic drugs – results of a consensus development (delphi) exercise', *Journal of Rheumatology* 18: 1908–1915.

Berkowitz, E.N. (1995) 'Marketing the pathology practice', *Archives of Pathology & Laboratory Medicine* 119: 655–658.

Berry, L. and Parasuraman, A. (1991) *Marketing Services: Competing Through Quality*, New York: The Free Press.

Bestey, T., Hall, J. and Prestan, I. (1996) *The Demand for Private Health Insurance: Do Waiting Lists Matter?*, *Working Paper 96/7*, London: Institute for Fiscal Studies.

Birmingham HA (1995) *Closing the Gap. Ten Benchmarks for Equity and Quality in Health*, Birmingham: Birmingham Health Authority.

Blattberg, R. and Deighton, J. (1993) 'Interactive marketing: exploiting the age of addressability', *Harvard Business Manager* 15(1): 5–14 [reprinted from *Sloan Management Review* (1993) 33: 5–14].

Blaxter, M. (1990) *Health and Lifestyles*, London: Tavistock.

Blom-Cooper, L. (Chairman) (1992) *Report of the Committee of Inquiry into Complaints about Ashworth Hospital*, Vol. II. CM2028–11, London: HMSO.

Bluglass, R. and Bowen, P. (eds) (1990) *Principles and Practice of Forensic Psychiatry*, Edinburgh: Churchill Livingstone.

Boaz, A. and Ziebland, S. (1998) 'A 'five-a-day' fruit and vegetable pack for primary school children. Part 1: development and pre-testing', *Health Education Journal* 57: 97–104.

Bond, M. and Bywaters, P. (1998) 'Working it out for ourselves: women learning about hormone replacement therapy', *Women's Studies International Forum* 21(1): 75.

Booz, Allen and Hamilton (1982) *New Product Management for the 1980s*, New York: USA.

Borque, L.B. and Clark, V.A. (1994) 'Processing data: the survey example', in M.S. Lewis-Beck (ed.) *Research Practice*, Sage: London.

Botschen, G., Bstieler, L. and Woodside, A. (1996a), 'Sequence-oriented problem identification within service encounters', *Journal of Euromarketing*, 5(2): 19–52.

Botschen, G., Botschen, M., Gutmann, W. and Mairamhof, G. (1996b), *Zukunftsfaehiges Wien – die VHS Hietzing im Jahre 2005*, Wien: Volkshochschule Hietzing.

Bovaird, T. and Tricker, M. (1997) *Assessing Service Quality Through Market Research*, *Working Paper RP9724*, Birmingham, Aston Business School.

Bowers, M. (1986) 'New product development in service industries', Ph.D. dissertation, Texas A&M University, College Station.

Bowers, M. (1987) 'Developing new services for hospitals: a suggested model', *Journal of Health Care Marketing* 7(2): 35–44.

Bowling, A. (1997) *Research Methods in Health. Investigating Health and Health Services*, Buckingham: Open University Press.

Bradshaw, D. (1997) 'The broad picture: health status and determinants', in P. Barron (ed.) *South African Health Review 1997*, Durban: Health Systems Trust.

Bradshaw, J. (1972) 'A taxonomy of social need', in G. McLachlan (ed.) *Problems and Progress in Medical Care: Essays on Current Research*, Oxford: Oxford University Press.

Brinnington Community 2000 (1997) *Community Audit Action Plan*, Stockport Metropolitan Borough Council.

British Sociological Association (1996) *Guidance Notes. Statement of Ethical Practice*, Unit 3 F/G Mount Joy Research Centre, Stockton Road, Durham DH1 3U: British Sociological Association.

Bruner, J.S. (1991) 'The narrative construction of reality', *Critical Inquiry* 18(1): 1–21.

Buchanan, D., Boddy, D. and McCalman, J. (1988) 'Getting in, getting on, getting out, and getting back', Chapter 3 in A. Bryman (ed.) *Doing Research in Organizations*, London: Routledge.

Bury, M. and Holmes, A. (1990) 'Researching very old people', in S.M. Peace (ed.) *Researching Social Gerontology – Concepts, Methods and Issues*, London: Sage Publications.

Butler, Lord R. (1975) *Report of the Committee on Mentally Disordered Offenders*, Cmnd 5698. London: HMSO.

Cabinet Office (1998a) *Better Quality Services – Guidance for Managers*, London: Stationery Office.

Cabinet Office (1998b) *Service First: The New Charter Programme*, London: Stationery Office.

Calnan, M., Cant, S. and Gabe, J. (1993) *Going Private: Why People Pay for the Health Care*, Buckingham: Open University Press.

Cartwright, A. (1983) *Health Surveys in Practice and Potential*, London: King's Fund.

Challis, D. and Hugman, R. (1993) 'Editorial: Community care, social work and social care', *British Journal of Social Work*, 319–328.

Chisnall, P. (1986) *Marketing Research* (3rd edition), London: McGraw-Hill.

Cina, C. (1990), 'Five steps to service excellence', *The Journal of Services Marketing*, 4(2): 39–48.

Citizen's Charter Unit (1996) *Asking Your Users: How to Improve Services Through Consulting your Consumers*, London: HMSO.

Collins Concise Dictionary (1989) London: Collins.

Collins Thesaurus (1986) London: Collins.

Collins, M., Sykes, W., Wilson, P. and Blackshaw, N. (1988) 'Non response: the UK experience', in R. Groves, P. Bierner, L. Lyberg, J. Massey, W. Nicholls and J. Waksberg (eds) *Telephone Survey Methodology*, New York: John Wiley.

Cooper, R. and Kleinschmidt, J. (1986) 'An investigation into the new product process: steps, deficiencies and impact', *Journal of Product Innovation Management* 3(2), 71–85.

Cotterill, P. and Letherby, G. (1993) 'Personal auto/biographies in feminist research', *Sociology*, 27(1): 67–79.

Council of Europe (1981) *Convention for the Protection of Individuals with Regard to Automatic Processing of Personal Data* (Convention 109), Strasbourg.

Crighton, J. (1995) 'The prediction of psychiatric patient violence', Chapter 3 in *Psychiatric Patient Violence: Risk and Response*, London: Duckworth.

Cronin Jr, J.J. and Taylor, S.A. (1992) 'Measuring service quality: a re-examination and extension', *Journal of Marketing* 56: 55–68.

Crosier, K. (1975) 'What exactly is marketing?', *Quarterly Review of Marketing* Winter: 21–25.

Crotty, M. (1993) 'The emerging role of the British nurse teacher in Project 2000 programmes: Delphi survey', *Journal of Advanced Nursing* 18: 150–157.

Dahlgren, G. and Whitehead, M. (1991) *Policies and Strategies to Promote Social Equity in Health*, Stockholm: Institute for Futures Studies.

de Brentani, U. and Riesen, A. (1997) 'Developing new business services through provider–customer partnerships: a case-study', in Arnot *et al.* (eds) *Progress, Prospects, Perspectives*, EMAC-Conference Proceedings, I, Warwick: 342–361.

Department of Health (1989a) *Working for Patients*, London: HMSO.

Department of Health (1989b) *Caring for People*, London: HMSO.

Department of Health (1993) *Changing Childbirth. Report of the Expert Maternity Group*, London: Department of Health.

Department of Health (1994) *Draft EC Proposed Directive on Data Protection : Analysis of Costs*, London: HMSO.

Department of Health (1995) *Variations in Health. What Can the Department of Health and the NHS Do?*, London: Department of Health.

Department of Health (1996a) *Guidance on Supervised Discharge (Aftercare Under Supervision and Related Provisions)* HSG(96)11,15 February, London: HMSO.

Department of Health (1996b) *The Patients Charter and You*, London: HMSO.

Department of Health (1997) *The New NHS: Modern – Dependable*, CM 3807, Government White Paper, London: HMSO.

Department of Health (1998a) *A First Class Service: Quality in the New NHS*, London: The Stationery Office.

Department of Health (1998b) *Details Announced of First Ever Nationwide Survey of NHS Patients' and Users' Views*, London: Department of Health. Press Release 98/333.

Department of Health (1999) *Saving Lives: Our Healthier Nation*, Cm 4386, London: The Stationery Office.

Dienel, P.C. (1992) *Die Planungszelle. Der Buerger plant seine Umwelt. Eine Alternative zur Establishment-Demokratie*, Opladen: Westdeutscher Verlag.

Dienel, P.C. (1994) *Buergergutachten Rathaus/Guerzenich-Koeln*, Wuppertal: Forschungstelle Buerger-beteiligung & Planungsverfahren.

Dijkstra, W. and Zouwen, J. van der (eds) (1982) *Response Behaviour in the Survey Interview*, London: Academic Press.

Dingwall, R., Watson, P. and Aldridge, A. (1992) 'Covert research – poor ethics and bad science', Pharmaceutical Journal 249:182–183.

Donnelly, J.H. Jr, Leonard, B. and Thompson, T. (1985), *Marketing Financial Services*, Homewood, IL: Dow Jones-Irwin.

Doyle, P. (1994) *Marketing Management and Strategy*, London: Prentice Hall.

Duncan, T.R. and Moriarty, S. (1997) *Driving Brand Value Using Integrated Marketing to Manage Profitable Stakeholder Relationships*, New York: McGraw-Hill.

Durand-Zalenski, I., Bonnet, F. and Rochant, H. (1992) 'Usefulness of consensus conferences: the case of albumin', *The Lancet* 340: 1388–1390.

Economist Intelligence Unit (1998) *Country Forecast: Thailand*, London Economist Intelligence Unit, http://www.eivu.com.

Edvardsson, B. and Olsson, J. (1996), 'Key concepts for new service development', *The Service Industries Journal* 16: 140–164.

Edvardsson, B., Lars, H. and Mattson, J. (1995) 'Analysis, planning, improvisation and control in the development of new services', *International Journal of Service Industry Management* 6(2): 24–35.

Edwards, N., Ferguson, B., Munro, S., Piercy, J. and Ryder, S. (1993) *York Health Economics Consortium, Business Planning for Providers of Health Care Services*, Harlow: Longman.

Elder, O.C. Jr and Andrew, M.E. (1992) 'Important curriculum content for baccalaureate allied health programmes: a survey of deans', *Journal of Allied Health* 21: 105–115.

Esping-Andersen, G. (1990) *The Three Words of Welfare Capitalism*, Cambridge: Polity Press.

Esping-Andersen, G. (ed.) (1996) *Welfare States in Transition*, London: Sage.

European Union Council and the Parliament (1995) *Directive on the Protection of Individuals with Regard to the Processing of Personal Data and on the Free Movement of such Data*, COM 95/46/EC, OJ L281/31, Brussels: European Commission.

Ewles, L. and Simnett, I. (1992) *Promoting Health: A Practical Guide*, London: Scutari.

Fallen, E.L. (1995) 'The Consensus Report: is it ever the last word?' (Editorial), *Canadian Journal of Cardiology* 11(6): 338.

Fallon, P. (Chair) (1998) *Report of the Committee of Inquiry into the personality disorder unit, Ashworth Special Hospital*, CMND4194–11, London: The Stationery Office.

Felson, D.T. (1993) 'Choosing a core set of disease activity measures for rheumatoid arthritis clinical trials', *Journal of Rheumatology* 20: 531–534.

Fink, A., Kosecoff, J., Chassin, M. and Brook, R.H. (1984) 'Consensus methods, characteristics and guidelines for use', *American Journal of Public Health* 74: 979–983.

Fleming, B., Naylor, S. and Pajack, F. (1993) *Talking to Customers: An Assessment of a Consumer Feedback Exercise Using Focus Groups*, Birmingham: West Midlands RHA.

Flynn, G. (1998a) 'Using SERVQUAL to measure service quality. A re-examination and extension', *Journal of Marketing* 56: 55–68.

Flynn, G. (1998b) *Using SERVQUAL to Measure Service Quality at a NHS Specialist Laboratory RP918*, Birmingham: Aston Business School Research Institute.

Flynn, N. and Walsh, K. (1988) *Competitive Tendering*, Birmingham: ILGS.

Flynn, R., Williams, G. and Pickard, S. (1996) *Markets and Networks. Contracting in Community Health Services*, Buckingham: Open University.

Foxall, G. and Johnston, B. (1987) 'Strategies of user-initiated product innovation, *Technovation* 11(1): 77–102.

Frey, J. (1989) *Survey Research by Telephone* (2nd edition), Newbury Park, CA: Sage.

Garbe, D. and Hoffmann, M. (1992*)*, *Soziale Urteilsbildung und Einstellungsaenderung in Planungszellen*. 3. Aufl. Wuppertal: Forschungstelle Buergerbeteiligung & Planungsverfahren.

Glancy, J. (1974) *Revised Report of the Working Party on Security in NHS Psychiatric Hospitals*, London: DHSS.

Glyn, J.J. and Perkins, D. (1997) 'Control and accountability in the NHS market: proposition or logical impossibility?', *International Journal of Public Sector Management* 10(1/2): 62–75.

Goffman, E. (1961) *Asylums*, Harmondsworth: Penguin.

Goodman, G.R. (1995) 'Group processes of decision making for hospital based technology assessment committees', *Biomedical Instrument Technology*, 29(5): 410–417.

Gowan, J.A. and McNichols, C.W. (1993) 'The effects of alternative forms of knowledge representation on decision-making consensus', *International Journal of Man-Machine Studies* 38: 489–507.

Graham, H. (1984) 'Surveying through stories', in C. Bell, and H. Roberts (eds) *Social Researching Politics, Problems, Practice*, London: Routledge, Kegan Paul.

Gray, D.A. (1989) *Start and Run a Profitable Consultancy Business*, London: Kogan Page.

Greenfield, J. and Pearce, G. (1998) 'Managing personal data protection flows to third countries', *The Computer Law and Security Report* 14(3): 185–189.

Greenhalgh, T. and Hurwitz, B. (1999) 'Narrative based medicine: why study narrative?', *BMJ* 318(7175): 48–50.

Greenhalgh, T., Helman, C. and Chowdhury, A.M. (1998) 'Health beliefs and folk models of diabetes in British Bangaladeshis: a qualitative study', *BMJ* 316: 978–983.

Griffin, A. and Hauser, J.R. (1993) 'The voice of the customer', *Marketing Science* 12(1): 1–27.

Griffiths, R. [Chairman] (1983) *NHS Management Inquiry* [The Griffiths Report], London: Department of Health and Social Security.

Groenroos, C. (1982) 'An applied service marketing theory', *European Journal of Marketing* 16(7): 30–41.

Groenroos, C. (1983) 'Innovative marketing strategies and organization structure for service firms', in L.L. Berry, L. Shostack and G.D. Upha (eds) *Emerging Perspectives on Services Marketing*, Chicago, IL: AMA.

Gruner, K. and Homburg, C. (1998) *Customer Interaction as a Key to New Product Success, Scientific Working Paper Series*, Centre for Market Oriented Management, Koblenz: Germany.

Ham, C. (ed.) (1997) *Health Care Reform. Learning from International Experience*, Buckingham: Open University.

Hammersley, M. (1990) *Reading Ethnographic Research*, London: Longman

Hantrais, L. (1995) *Social Policy in the European Union*, Basingstoke: Macmillan.

Harrison, J.J.H. (1996a) *Southern Birmingham CHT: Survey of Birmingham and Solihull General Practitioners*, unpublished client report, Birmingham: Business Development Consultancy.

Harrison, J.J.H. (1996b) 'University Hospital Birmingham: staff expectation survey', unpublished client report, Birmingham, Business Development Consultancy.

Harrison, J.J.H. (1998) 'Corporate governance in the NHS – an assessment of boardroom practice', *Corporate Governance: An International Review* 6(3): 140–149.

Harrison, J.J.H., Roberts, W.R., Pinson, R. and Dorning, B. (1997) 'The application of marketing research in the Birmingham Dental Hospital', *Journal of Marketing Practice: Applied Marketing Science* 3(1): 31–42.

Hartley, J. (1997) 'Employee surveys: hand grenades for organisational change in local authorities', paper presented at the IRSPSM Conference, September, Birmingham: Aston University.

Hayward, A. (1996) 'Matching enterprise with public service', *British Journal of Health Care Management* 2(1): 5–7.

Heany, D.F. (1983) 'Degrees of product innovation', *Journal of Business Strategy* Spring: 3–14.

Herbert, M. (1997) *Planning Your Research Project*, London: Cassell.

Hewison, R. (1995) *Culture and Consensus: England, Art and Politics since 1940*, London: Methuen.

Higgins, J. (1988) *The Business of Medicine: Private Health Care in Britain*, London: Macmillan.

Hoinville, G. and Jowell, R. (1978) *Survey Research Practice*, London: Heinemann Educational.

Hood, C. (1991) 'A public management for all seasons', *Public Administration* 69(1): 3–19.

Hope, P. (1992) *Making the Best Use of Consultants*, Harlow: Longman.

Huber, A. (1999) 'Principles of the Austrian Health Insurance', Agricultural Social Insurance Fonds, Innsbruck, unpublished work.

Hudson, B. (1994) *Making Sense of Markets in Health and Social Care*, Sunderland, Business Education Publishers.

Humphrey, L (1970) *Tearoom Trade*, Chicago: Aldine.

Hunter, D.J.W., Mckee, C.M., Sanderson, C.F.B. and Black, N.A. (1993) 'Appropriateness of prostatectomy: a consensus panel approach', *Journal of Epidemiology and Community Health* 48: 58–64.

Hurst, J.W. (1991) 'Reforming health care in seven European nations', *Health Affairs*, 10(3): 7–21.

Hutton, W. (1996) *The State We're In*, London: Vintage.

Jallat, F. (1994) 'Innovation dans les services: les facteurs de succes', *Decisions Marketing* 2, 23–35.

Jepson, M., Jesson, J., Kendall, H. and Pocock, R. (1991a) *Consumers Expectations of Community Pharmaceutical Services. A Report for the Department of Health*, Birmingham: School of Pharmacy Aston University and M.E.L. Research.

Jepson, M., Jesson, J., Kendall, H. and Pocock, R. (1991b) *Consumers Talking: A Qualitative Study of High User Groups, Working Paper 4*, Birmingham: School of Pharmacy Aston University and M.E.L Research.

Jesson, J. (1997) 'Pharmacy practice research, ethical issues and local research ethics committees', *International Journal of Pharmacy Practice* 5(1): 54–56.

Jewkes, R., Abrahams, N. and Mvo, Z. (1998) 'Why do nurses abuse patients? Reflections from South African obstetric services', *Social Science & Medicine* 47: 1781–1795.

Johne, A. (1994), 'Listening to the Voice of the Market', *International Marketing Review* 11(1): 47–59.

Johnson, E.M., Scheuing, E. and Gaida, K. (1986) *Profitable Service Marketing*, Homewood, IL: Dow Jones-Irwin.

Jones, J. and Hunter, D. (1995) 'Consensus methods for medical and health services research', *British Medical Journal* 311(5): 376–380.

Juran, J.M. (1989), *Juran on Leadership for Quality: An Executive Handbook*, New York: The Free Press.

Justice, J. and Jang, R. (1990) 'Tapping employee insights with the nominal group technique', *American Pharmacology* NS30: 43–45.

Kavanagh, D. and Seldon, A. (1991) *The Thatcher Effect: A Decade of Change*, Oxford: Oxford University Press.

Khan, U. (1998) 'Up and ATAM', *Health Service Journal*, 30 April: 32–33.

Kimberley, J. (1997) 'Developing a tool for evaluating quality assurance in a social care environment', unpublished MBA Dissertation, Birmingham: Aston University.

Kimmel, A.J. (1996) *Ethical Issues in Behavioural Research*, Oxford: Blackwell.

Kingman-Brundage, J. (1989) 'The ABC's of service system blueprinting', in M.J. Bitner and L.A. Crosby (eds) *Designing a Winning Service Strategy*, Chicago: American Marketing Association.

King's Fund Forum (1987) 'Consensus and controversy in medicine. Screening for fetal and genetic abnormality'. Programme and Abstracts. The 4th in a series of Consensus Development Conferences, London: King's Fund College.

Kitzinger, J. (1994) 'The methodology of focus groups: the importance of interactions between research participants', *Sociology of Health and Illness* 16: 103–121.

Kitzinger, J. (1996) 'Introducing focus groups', in N. Mays and C. Pope (eds) *Qualitative Research in Health Care*, London: BMJ Publishing Group.

Korda, M. (1997) *Man to Man: Surviving Prostate Cancer*, New York: Little Brown.

Kotler, P. and Andreasen, A.R. (1996) *Strategic Marketing for Nonprofit Organisations* (5th edition), Englewood Cliffs, NJ: Prentice Hall.

Kotler, P. and Clarke, R.N. (1987) *Marketing for Health Care Organisations*, Englewood Cliffs, NJ: Prentice-Hall.

Labour Research Department (1996) *The Prospective Impact of Community Care Charging*, London: LRD Research Report.

Labovitz, S. (1970) 'The assignment of number to rank order categories', *American Sociological Review* 35: 515–524.

Laing, W. (1998) *Laing's Healthcare Market Review 1998–1999* (annual edition), London: Laing and Buisson.

Lavrakas, P. (1992) 'Attitudes towards and experiences of sexual harassment in the workplace', paper given at the Midwest Association for the Public Opinion Research Conference, Chicago.

Lavrakas, P. (1993) *Telephone Survey Methods, Sampling, Selection and Supervision* (2nd edition), London: Sage.

Le Grand, J. (1990) *Quasi-markets and Social Policy*, Bristol: School for Advanced Urban Studies.

Le Grand, J. (1993) *Quasi-markets and Community Care*, Bristol: School for Advanced Urban Studies.

Le Grand, J., Mays, N. and Mulligan, J. (1998) *Learning from the NHS Internal Market*, London: Kings Fund.

Lloyd, P. (1998) 'Off message', *Health Service Journal* 7 May: 26–29.

Lomas, J. (1991) 'Words without action? The production, dissemination and impact of consensus recommendations', *Annual Review of Public Health* 12: 41–65.

London, L. and Bachmann, O.M. (1997) 'Paediatric utilisation at a teaching hospital and a community health centre. Predictors of level of care used by children from Khayelitsha, Cape Town', *South African Medical Journal* 87: 31–36.

Luck, M. (1991) *A Manual of Market Research for Health Promotion*, Birmingham: West Midlands Health Authority.

Luck, M., Lawrence, B., Pocock, R. and Reilly, K. (1988) *Consumer and Market Research in Health Care*, London: Chapman and Hall.

Luck, M., Jesson, J. and Taylor, J. (1991) *Women and HIV*, Birmingham: Health Promotion Unit, West Birmingham District Health Authority.

Luck, M., Jesson, J., Zamir, T. and Channa, R. (1992) *Coping with Childhood Respiratory Ailments*, Birmingham: Aston University Business School and Birmingham FHSA.

Mann, T. (1996) 'Clinical Audit in the NHS', *Using Clinical Audit in the NHS: A Position Statement*, Leeds: NHS Executive.

Marshall, C. and Rossman, G. (1989) *Designing Qualitative Research*, London: Sage.

Martin, C.R. Jr (1994) 'The congruence of new product and new service development', in Management of Services: A Multidisciplinary Approach, paper presented at the 3rd International Seminar in Service Management, Aix-en-Provence, France.

Martin, C.R. Jr and Horne, D.A. (1992) 'Restructuring toward a service orientation: the strategic challenges', *International Journal of Service Industry Management* 3: 25–38.

Martin, C.R. Jr and Horne, D.A. (1995) 'Level of success inputs for service innovations in the same firm', *International Journal of Service Industry Management* 6(4), 40–56.

Mattingly, C. and Garro, L. (1994) 'Narrative representations of illness and healing', *Social Science and Medicine* 38(6): 771–774.

McCarthy, E.J. (1978) *Basic Marketing: Managerial Approach*, Homewood, IL: Irwin.

McFadyen, J. and Farrington, A. (1997) 'User and carer participation in the NHS', *British Journal of Health Care Management* 3(5): 260–264.

McGlynn, E.A., Kosecoff, J. and Brook, R.H. (1990) 'Format and conduct of consensus development conferences', *International Journal of Technology Assessment in Health Care*, 6: 450–469.

McIntyre, D., Bloom, G., Doherty, J. and Brijlal, P. (1995) *Health Expenditure and Finance in South Africa*, Durban: Health Systems Trust and World Bank.

McKenna, R. (1991) 'Marketing – ein neues Paradigma setzt sich durch', *Harvard Manager* 3: 27–34.

McNulty, T. Whittington, R., Whipp, R. and Kitchener, M. (1994) 'Implementing marketing in NHS hospitals', *Public Money & Management* 14(3): 51–57.

McQuarrie, E. (1996) *The Market Research Toolbox*, London: Sage.

Meyer, A. and Bluemelhuber, C. (1998) 'Dienstleistungs innovation', in A. Meyer (ed.) *Handbuch Dienstleistungs-Marketing*, 1, Stuttgart: Schaefer-Poeschel Verlag, 807–826.

Millward, A., Tricker, M. and Green, J. (1995) *An Evaluation of the JIGSO Initiative. Report for the Countryside Commission*, Birmingham: Alison Millward Associates.

Mobily, P.R., Herr, K.A. and Kelly, L.S. (1993) 'Cognitive behavioural techniques to reduce pain: a validation study', *International Journal of Nursing Studies* 30: 537–548.

Mohamed, H. and Bachmann, M.O. (1998) 'Block appointments in an overloaded South African health centre: Quantitative and qualitative evaluation', *International Journal of Health Care Quality Assurance* 11: 123–126.

Morris, J. and Lindow, V. (1993) 'Community care support force', *User Participation in Community Care Services*, Leeds: NHS Management Executive.

Moscovice, I., Armstrong, P. and Shortell, S. (1988) 'Health services research for decision makers: the use of the Delphi technique to determine health priorities', *Journal of Health Politics, Policy and Law* 2: 388–410.

Muir Gray, J.A. (1998) *Evidence-based health care: How to Make Health Policy and Management Decisions*, Edinburgh: Churchill Livingstone.

Newcastle Inner City Forum and CHC (1983) *Women's Health and Health Service in Newcastle upon Tyne*, Newcastle: Newcastle Inner City Forum and CHC.

NHS CRD (1997) 'Screening for prostate cancer', *Effectiveness Matters* 2(2): 1–7. (http://www.york.ac.uk/inst/crd/prostate.htm).

NHS Executive (1995) *High Security Psychiatric Services; Changes in Funding and Organisation. NHSE2898*, Leeds: National Health Service Executive.

NHS Management Executive (1990) *Contracts for Health Services: Operating Contracts, Executive Letter EL[90] MB/24*, London: NHS Management Executive.

NHS Management Executive (1992) *Purchasing for Health: the Views of Local People, Executive Letter EL(92)1*, London: NHS Management Executive.

Nie, N.H., Hull, C.H., Jenkins, J.G., Steinbrenner, K. and Bent, D.H. (1975) *Statistical Package for the Social Sciences*, New York: McGraw-Hill.

Noble, I., Moon, N. and McVey, D. (1998) 'Bringing it all back home ... using RDD telephone methods for a large scale social policy and opinion research in the UK', *Journal of Market Research* 40(2): 93–120.

Norman, R. (1991) *Service Management*, Englewood Cliffs, NJ: Prentice Hall.

Oakley, A. (1981) 'Interviewing women: a contradiction in terms', in H. Roberts (ed.) *Doing Feminist Research*, London: Routledge and Kegan Paul.

OECD (1988) *Ageing Populations*, Paris: Organization for Economic Cooperation and Development.

OECD (1995) *New Directions in Health Care Policy*, Paris: Organization for Economic Cooperation and Development.

Office of National Statistics (1995) *General Household Survey 1995*, London: HMSO.

OPCS (1990) *Standard Occupational Classification*, London: HMSO.

Oranga, H.M. and Nordberg, E. (1993) 'The Delphi panel method for generating information', *Health Policy and Planning* 8: 405–412.

Parasuraman, A., Zeithaml, V.A. and Berry, L. (1986) *SERVQUAL: a multiple-item scale for measuring customer perceptions of service quality*, Report No. 86–108, Marketing Science Institute, Cambridge: MA.

Parasuraman, A., Zeithaml, V.A. and Berry, L. (1988) 'SERVQUAL: a multiple-item scale for measuring consumer perceptions of service quality', *Journal of Retailing* 64: 12–37.

Paton, C., Birch, K., Hunt, K., Jordan, K. and Durose, J. (1997) 'Counting the costs', *Health Service Journal*, 21 August: 24–27.

Patton, S. (1999) 'I want to tell you a story', *Health Service Journal* 25 February: 22–24.

Payne, M. and Ballantyne, D. (1993) *Relationship Marketing*, Oxford: Butterworth-Heinemann.

Pearce, G. and Platten, N. (1998) 'Achieving personal data protection in the European Union', *Journal of Common Market Studies* 36(4): 529–547.

Pearse, I. and Crocker, L. (1943) *The Peckham Experiment*, London: George Allen and Unwin.

Phillips, C., Palfrey, C. and Thomas, P. (1994) *Evaluating Health and Social Care*, Basingstoke: Macmillan.

Pill, J. (1971) 'The Delphi method: substance, context, a critique and an annotated bibliography', *Socio-Economic Planning Science* 5: 57–71.

Pollitt, C. (1990) *Managerialism and the Public Sector*, Oxford: Basil Blackwell.

Propper, C. and Eastwood, A. (1989) 'The reasons for non-corporate health insurance purchase in the UK', *Discussion Paper 52*, Centre for Health Economics, York: University of York.

Propper, C. and Maynard, A. (1989) 'The market for private health insurance and the demand for the private health insurance', *Discussion Paper 53*, Centre for Health Economics, York: University of York.

Purdon, S. and Thomas, R. (1995) *The Feasibility of a Telephone Survey of Health Related Behaviour and Attitudes. Report to Health Education Authority*, London: Social and Community Planning Research.

Reed, J. (Chairman) (1992) *Review of Health and Social Services for Mentally Disordered Offenders and Others Requiring Similar Services. Final Summary Report*, CM2088, London: HMSO.

Reed, J. (Chair) (1994) *Report of the Working Group on High Security and Related Psychiatric Provision*, London: Department of Health.

Reinert, A. (1988) *Wege aus der politischen Apathie?*, Frankfurt a. M: Peter Lang.

Riessman, C.K. (1993) *Narrative Analysis*, London: Sage.

Robrecht, L. (1995) 'Grounded theory: evolving methods', *Qualitative Health Research* 5(2): 169–177.

Robson, C. (1995) *Real World Research*, Oxford: Blackwell.

Rowe, G., Wright, G. and Bolger, F. (1991) 'Delphi: a re-evaluation of research and theory', *Technological Forecasting and Social Change* 39: 235–251.

Ryan, J. (ed.) (1995) *Sinews of the Heart*, Nottingham: Five Leaves Publications.

Saltman, R. and von Otter, C. (1995) *Implementing Planned Markets in Health Care*, Buckingham: Open University Press.

Saltman, R., Figueras, J. and Sakellarides, C. (1998) *Critical Challenges for Health Care Reform in Europe*, Buckingham: Open University Press.

Sapsford, R. and Jupp, V. (eds) (1996) *Data Collection and Analysis*, London: Sage Publications and Open University.

Scheuing, E. and Johnson, E. (1989) 'A proposed model for new service development', *The Journal of Services Marketing* 3(2): 25–34.

Seidel, J. and Kelle, U. (1995) 'Different functions in the analysis of textual data', in U. Kelle (ed.) *Computer Aided Qualitative Analysis*, London: Sage.

Sheaff, R. (1991) *Marketing for Health Services*, Buckingham: Open University Press.

Shostack, G. (1982) 'How to design a service', *European Journal of Marketing* 16(1): 49–63.

Shostack, G. (1987) 'Service positioning through structural change', *Journal of Marketing* 51: 34–43.

Smith, D.H. (1987) 'Stories, values and patient care decisions', paper presented to the University of South Florida, Tampa, Communicating with Patients.

Smith, R. (1997) 'Informed consent: the intricacies', *BMJ* 314: 1059–1060.

Social Exclusion Unit (1999) *Teenage Pregnancy*, CM 4342, London: The Stationery Office.

Social Science and Medicine (1998) 'Narrative representations of illness and healing', [Special Issue], 38(6).

Soderberg, L.G. and O'Halloran, J.D. (1992) ' "Heroic" engineering takes more than heroes', *McKinsey Quarterly* 1: 3–23.

Stauss, B. and Weinlich, B. (1997) 'Process-oriented measurement of service quality applying the sequential incident technique', *European Journal of Marketing* 31(1): 33–55.

Stevens, S.S. (1946) 'On the theory of scales of measurement', *Science* 103: 677–680.

Stewart, R. (1998) 'More art than science?', *Health Services Journal* 26 March: 28–29.

Stocking, B. (1985) 'First consensus development conference in the UK: on coronary artery bypass grafting. Views of audience, panel and speakers', *British Medical Journal* 291: 713–716.

Stocking, B., Jennet, B. and Spiby, J. (1991) 'Criteria for change', *The History and Impact of Consensus Development Conferences in the UK*, London: King's Fund Centre.

Swift, B. (1996) 'Preparing numerical data', in R. Sapsford and V. Judd (eds) *Data Collection and Analysis*, London: Sage Publications and Open University.

Syedain, H. (1994) 'Technology finds a voice', *Marketing* November 17, XIV.

Sykes, W. and Hoinville, G. (1985) *Telephone Interviewing in a Survey of Social Attitudes: A Comparison with Face-to-face Procedures*, London: SCPR.

Tabrizi, B. and Walleigh, R. (1997) 'Defining next-generation products: an inside look', *Harvard Business Review* 75: 116–124.

Thomas, R. (1991) Characteristics of households with and without telephones, *Joint Centre for Survey Methods Newsletter* 11(3), London: Department of Employment.

Thompson, C.J. (1997) 'Interpreting consumers: a hermeneutical framework for deriving marketing insights from the texts of consumers consumption stories', *Journal of Marketing Research* 34(4): 438–455.

Thompson, G. (1991) *Markets, Hierarchies and Networks: The Co-ordination of Social Life*, London: Sage.

Thornton, P. (1988) 'Creating a break: a home care relief scheme for elderly people and their supporters', *Age Concern Institute of Gerontology – Research Report No. 3*, York: Social Policy Research Unit.

Tolson, J. (1995) 'Getting ill', in J. Ryan (ed.) *Sinews of the Heart*, Nottingham: Five Leaves Publications.

Townsend, C., Pearn, M. Mottram, R. and Sidey, E. (1991) *Managers Working for Patients. Bureaucracy to Enterprise*, Bristol: NHS Training Directorate.

Tricker, M. (1994) *Community Identity in Derbyshire*, unpublished report for North Derbyshire District Council.

Urban, G.L. and von Hippel, E. (1988), 'Lead user analyses for the development of new industrial products, *Management Science* 34(5): 569–582.

Vang, J. (1986) 'The consensus development conference and the European experience', *International Journal of Technology Assessment in Health Care* 2(1): 65–76.

von Hippel, E. (1978) 'Successful industrial products from customer ideas', *Journal of Marketing* 42: 39–49.

von Hippel, E. (1986) 'Lead users: a source of novel product concepts', *Management Science* 32(7): 791–805.

von Hippel, E. (1988) *The Sources of Innovation*, Oxford: Oxford University Press.

Walbridge, S.W. and Delene, L.M. (1993) 'Measuring physician attitudes of service quality', *Journal of Health Care Marketing* Winter: 6–15.

Wallace, D. (1996) 'Experiential learning and critical thinking in nursing', *Nursing Standard* 10(31): 43–47.

Walsh, K. (1989) *Marketing in Local Government*, London: Longman.

Walton, M. (1989) *The Deming Management Method*, London: Mercury Books.

Ware, J., Snow, K., Kosinski, M. and Gandek, B. (1993) *SF-36 Health Survey: Manual and Interpretation Guide*, Boston: The Health Institute, New England Medical Center.

Westaway, M.S. and Wolmarans, L. (1993) 'Acceptability of the tuberculosis service: scale development', *International Journal of Epidemiology* 22: 543–547.

WHO (1985) *Targets for Health for All*, Copenhagen: World Health Organization.

Willets, D. and Goldsmith, M. (1988) *A Mixed Economy in Health Care*, London: Centre for Policy Studies.

Wistow, G., Knapp, M., Hardy, B., Forder, J., Kendall, J. and Manning, R. (1996) *Social Care Markets. Progress and Prospects*, Buckingham: Open University.

Worcester, R. (1995) 'British public opinion', in *Attitude Research in the Public Sector*, Esher: IMAC Research.

www.bfi-tirol.or.at (1999) 'Wir über uns'.

www.bmag.gv.at (1999) 'The Hospital Reform in Austria'.

www.sozver.at (1999) 'Gesundheitswesen in Österreich'.

www.vhs.at (1999) 'Struktur der Volkshochschulen'.

www.wifi.at (1999) 'WIFI – Internet Magazin'.

Yates, J. (1995) *Private Eye, Heart and Hip*, London: Churchill Livingstone.

Young, K. (1991) 'Consumer-centred approaches in the public/voluntary/personal services', *Public Money and Management* Summer: 33–39.

Youssef, F.N., Nel, D. and Bovaird, T. (1996) 'Health care in NHS hospitals', *International Journal of Health Care Quality Assurance*, January: 15–28.

Zaltman, G., Duncan, R. and Holbeck, J. (1973) *Innovations and Organizations*, New York: John Wiley.

Zeithaml, V.A. and Bitner, M.J. (1996) *Services Marketing*, New York: The McGraw-Hill Companies.

Index